Talk for Writing in the Early Ye

Talk for Writing in the Early Years

How to teach story and rhyme, involving families
2–5 years

Pie Corbett and Julia Strong

McGraw Hill

Open University Press

Open University Press
McGraw Hill Education
8th Floor
338 Euston Road
London
NW1 3BH

email: enquiries@openup.co.uk
world wide web: www.openup.co.uk

and Two Penn Plaza, New York, NY 10121-2289, USA

First published 2016

A catalogue record of this book is available from the British Library

ISBN-13: 978-0-3352-5021-9
ISBN-10: 0-3352-5021-1
eISBN: 978-0-3352-5022-6

Library of Congress Cataloging-in-Publication Data
CIP data applied for

Typesetting and e-book compilations by Transforma Pvt. Ltd., Chennai, India

Praise for this book

"Jam-packed full of ideas, activities and suggestions to develop your current practice both for teachers new to Talk for Writing and more experienced. As I was reading, I was jotting down all of the ideas that I was excited to develop within our EYFS and school. Pie explains the benefits of embedding storytelling clearly and with passion. I loved the thread of high expectations for all of our children whilst also recognising that 'everyone succeeds in their own unique ways'. Reading real-life examples which included the child's voice and finding out more about the research that supports the methods deepened my understanding and appreciation of using Talk for Writing within the classroom. I felt like I was having a personal 'masterclass' from Pie himself as he shared his genius storytelling skills and I was metaphorically tucking his suggestions up my sleeves ready to use in the classroom."

Claire Underwood. *Nursery Teacher and Assistant Headteacher at Eastfield Academy in Northampton, UK*

"Packed full of sound advice and helpful guidance, this comprehensive book addresses the importance of talk at the centre of language and literacy development. Corbett and Strong take a strongly principled approach in their guidance, making reference to research and good Early Years practice, as well as highlighting the importance, amongst other things, of parental involvement, time and a literate environment in supporting children's writing.

All of this theory is underpinned by a wealth of practical activities, ideas and resources that will support teachers' confidence in teaching this subject area and children's progress as story tellers and writers."

Rose White, *Senior Lecturer, University of East London, Cass school of Education and Communities, UK*

"Pie Corbett and Julia Strong's engaging book starts from the premise that stories are of "magical benefit and wonder" and so they should be the entitlement of every child. We are led through a structured and easily accessible approach that allows children to build up a "living library of poems and stories" and become writers themselves, by hearing and using story language and developing a deep understanding of story architecture.

The book offers a wealth of practical ideas and resources to get people started and the multi-sensory approach helps to build up the confidence of practitioners and parents to become interactive storytellers alongside their young children."

Julie Cigman, Early Years consultant, trainer and writer

"Pie Corbett and Julia Strong have done it again! A fun, practical, down-to-earth guide to teaching stories and rhymes to young children and their families. Each well-researched chapter breaks the Talk for Writing process down into clear steps and provides a bank of time-saving resources that teachers can use to create storytelling environments for their youngest learners. The accompanying online resources provide useful clips to demonstrate the activities and methods described in the book. Talk for Writing in the Early Years is a must have for all early years practitioners."

Sarah Collymore, Headteacher, St. George's CE Primary, Battersea, UK

"Pie Corbett and Julia Strong continue on their mission to transform the quality of writing with this new book. Whether you are new to the Talk for Writing process, or whether, like us, you have been developing this work over time, you cannot fail to be inspired by how this book continues to develop your understanding around how good quality texts and meaningful talk support children becoming confident speakers, proficient readers and purposeful writers.

This book brings together Pie and Julia's wealth of experience, alongside research and examples from a range of schools using these techniques successfully on a day-to-day basis, in one easy-to-read book that supports schools to improve their provision. As a Talk for Writing training centre, one of the many questions we are asked is 'Where do we start?'. This book provides examples and advice that can be translated to any school or setting. We will definitely be buying this book for all our Early Years Team to support their continuous professional development."

Ian Clennan, Headteacher, Selby Community Primary School, Yorkshire, UK

"Talk for Writing in the Early Years provides a fantastic bank of resources to support teachers in creating and inspiring the next generation of confident story tellers and writers. By focusing on both how language is acquired and how EY practitioners can support this, as well as highlighting the importance of the role of parents as educators, Pie and Julia share a clear, systematic

approach to developing Talk For Writing with younger children. The book is full of simple to implement, practical and playful activities that both academic research and practising teachers show make a difference in developing children's use of language."
Francesca Beers, Deputy Head of Easton CE Academy, UK

"This is an immensely helpful book about the role of stories and rhymes in the lives of children and their families. It should inspire early years practitioners and schools to establish and nurture talk and stories at the heart of the curriculum. If this seems too challenging, do not despair, because these very experienced authors provide detailed guidance, practical resources, inspirational encouragement and evidential case studies.

Even more exciting, the Talk for Writing project is set in the context of richly varied provision for play and learning in early years settings and successfully involves parents as first educators. It is so heartening to find the significance of stories and the shared writing and reading of Big Books in schools, promoted and explained. I am delighted that in this enjoyable text and the accompanying online resources the real basics of literacy are set out clearly for professionals and parents."
Marian Whitehead, Language and Early Years Consultant, UK

"This wonderful book is a welcome addition to the pioneering Talk for Writing series. The well-known authors of the widely successful Talk for Writing approach have effectively adapted the process for emerging readers and writers. The authors offer practical and insightful ways for younger children to engage with Talk for Writing to support their developing literacy. They carefully and systematically take readers on a journey through the multisensory imitation, innovation and invention stages that underpin Talk for Writing. The book is also packed with practical and imaginative resources for busy practitioners and accompanied by enriching video materials to support practice. The lively and entertaining sentence, spelling and story games are another invaluable resource to stimulate and motivate young children, and the authors provide valuable guidance for practitioners to engage families in the literacy activities. This is an essential Handbook for all early years practitioners."
Dr Janet Rose, Principal Lecturer and Award Leader in Early Years Education, Bath Spa University, UK

Contents

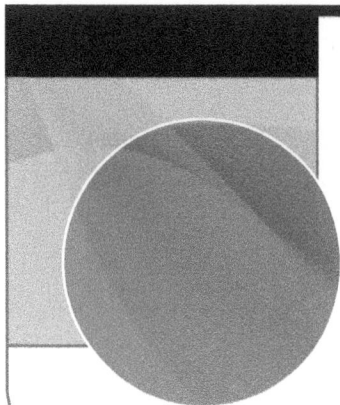

Video Clips

Acknowledgements

This book is dedicated to all the early years practitioners up and down the country whose enthusiasm and hard work in trialling the approach have helped make this book a reality. In particular, we would like to thank the inspiring early years practitioners in St George's, Battersea, and Porter Croft and Lowedges in Sheffield.

In addition, we would like to thank Pam Fell, for enabling our work with reception children and their parents in Sheffield, Jean Gross, formerly the Communication Champion, for her endless inspiration and support, and Neil McClelland, formerly Director of the National Literacy Trust, for his pioneering work in trying to ensure that all the literacy organisations in the country recognise the centrality of early years in a child's literacy development.

Pie Corbett and Julia Strong, July 2015

Guided tour

Icons

Making learning visual is key to the Talk for Writing approach. Icons throughout the text help to guide the reader through the approach as explained here:

	The handout icon indicates where it is useful to refer to a handout.
	The action icon indicates where the key points have been summed up.
	Throughout the imitation to invention process, teachers are encouraged to devise activities that will warm up the words and phrases that are key to linking story text together as well as warming up the vocabulary of the content of the stories. These activities are flagged up by this warming-up-the-words-and-phrases icon.
	Linking the parts of sentences together as well as linking separate sentences together is key to achieving coherent text. This icon flags up where linking text is particularly focused on.
	Central to the Talk for Writing approach is the idea of children internalising short stories or model non-fiction text. This imitating-the-text icon indicates such activities.
	Underlying the Talk for Writing approach is the concept of internalising useful words and phrases. This process is aided by encouraging the children, once they can write, to store these words and phrases for future use like a magpie hoarding shiny objects – hence the magpie icon.

✓	This icon indicates where advice has been gathered from early years Talk for Writing research projects.
▶ VIDEO	The video icon indicates where the video is particularly relevant.

Part 2 of the book consists of two chapters. Chapter 9 outlines research that shows the central role that family plays in a child's education. Chapter 10 shows how the Talk for Writing storytelling approach can be used to engage and then involve families. Throughout, the term 'parent' includes foster parents.

On pages 12–14 there are three handouts that provide an overview of the imitation, innovation and invention process that underpins the Talk for Writing process. The page references on these handouts also provide a useful guide.

Online videos

A wealth of online resources accompany this book:

- There are 33 video clips (together lasting over 2 hours). These include Pie presenting videos and tried and tested approaches at early years conferences as well as clips showing teachers putting Talk for Writing into action in a range of early years settings. This should be invaluable for schools and settings wanting to provide in-service training on the approach. Please be aware that these materials cannot be used for commercial gain.

- Online teaching notes providing advice on how to use the video clips to support staff training.

- 21 early years stories and story maps for you to use and adapt with children.

- Copies of the three handouts on imitation, innovation, and independent application and invention (see pp. 12-14 in this book) to support training sessions.

To access this material online, please follow this URL: www.mheducation.co.uk/professionals/open-university-press/olc/t4w-early-years

Part 1
Developing the Talk for Writing approach

The Talk for Writing process

www.talk4writing.com

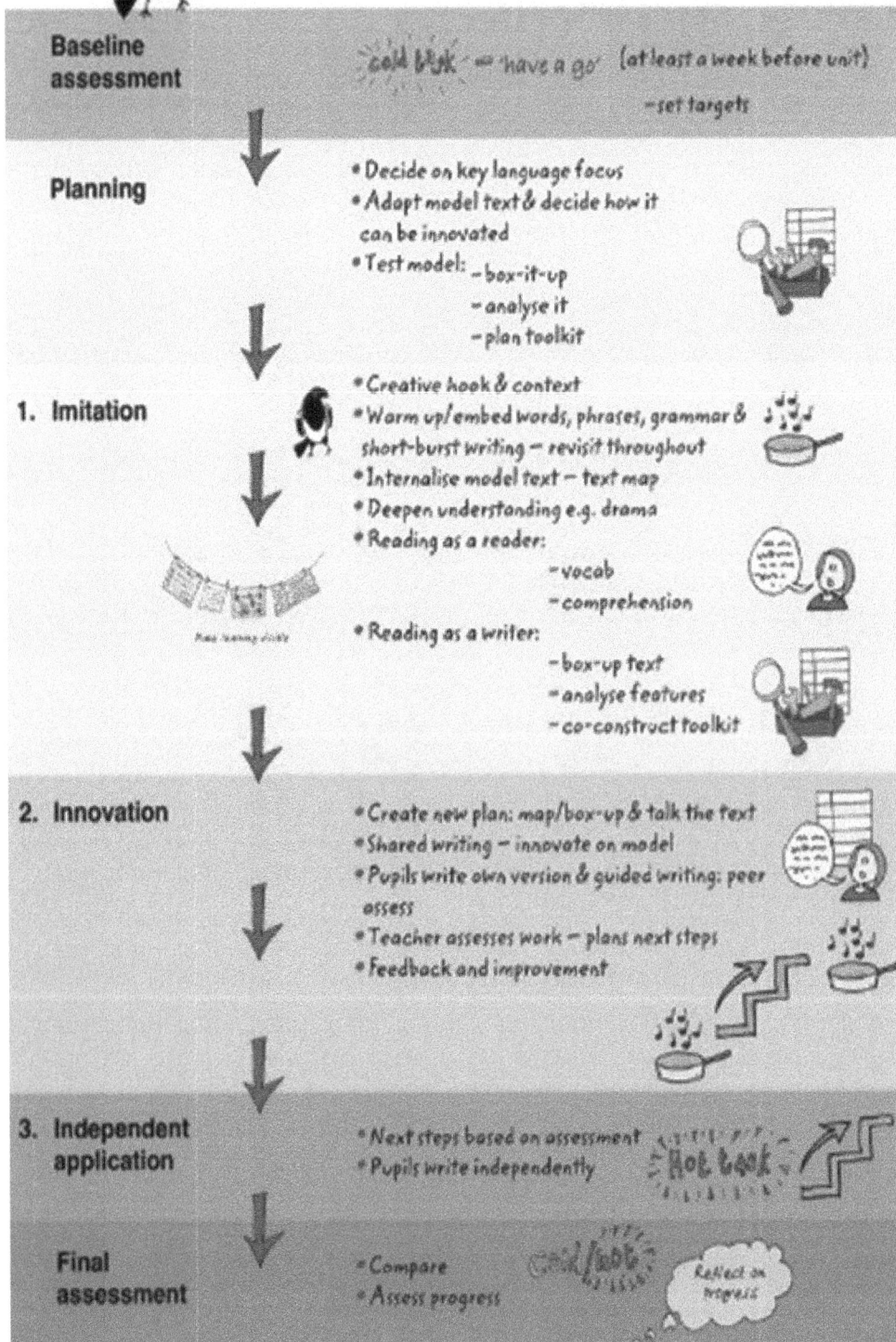

Baseline assessment

cold task → 'have a go' (at least a week before unit)

→ set targets

Planning

- Decide on key language focus
- Adapt model text & decide how it can be innovated
- Test model: – box-it-up
  – analyse it
  – plan toolkit

1. Imitation

- Creative hook & context
- Warm up/embed words, phrases, grammar & short-burst writing → revisit throughout
- Internalise model text → text map
- Deepen understanding e.g. drama
- Reading as a reader:
  – vocab
  – comprehension
- Reading as a writer:
  – box-up text
  – analyse features
  – co-construct toolkit

2. Innovation

- Create new plan: map/box-up & talk the text
- Shared writing – innovate on model
- Pupils write own version & guided writing: peer assess
- Teacher assesses work → plans next steps
- Feedback and improvement

3. Independent application

- Next steps based on assessment
- Pupils write independently

Hot task

Final assessment

- Compare
- Assess progress

Reflect on progress

1

The centrality of story and the origins of Talk for Writing

This book begins sixty years ago. I was one of five boys and for the first six years of my life we lived in an end-of-terrace cottage in a small village. It was a two-up, two-down with an outside toilet and the bath was a tin tub. In the summer, this was filled with water and we splashed around outside. Initially, we were not on mains water, so we staggered across the road to the water pump with huge buckets. My parents were not wealthy but we had riches beyond belief – because we were read to.

Every day, we would settle down in the kitchen at about two in the afternoon and the lady's voice on the radio would ask, 'Are you sitting comfortably, then I'll begin.' *Listen with Mother* provided a daily story. In the winter, I would sit on the kitchen floor with my feet stuck in the bottom oven, warming my toes, sucking my thumb and listening to the radio. Every night, we were read a story. While there were no books in the house, we were taken to the library. It is hard to imagine how thrilled we were to come out clutching a hard-backed book.

Our parents sang nursery rhymes to us and my dad told us stories. Some of these were traditional tales – he used to tell a terrifying version of 'The Hobyahs' but he invented stories also. There was an on-going saga that featured a useless detective called Bracegirdle Bathwater who continuously, battled against his deadly enemy, Moriarty. Around the kitchen table there was an endless sea of talk. Indeed, sometimes it seemed as if everyone was talking at once!

From an early age, I caught a love of reading and poetry from my home. It was a comfort then and remains so now. As I grew up, we had our ups and downs, but story and poetry were a constant. Even now, I find it hard to sleep unless I have settled my mind with a bedtime story. So it was that this book about the role of stories and rhymes, and families and schools in children's lives began so long ago. What I knew instinctively then, that stories are of some magical benefit and wonder, I still believe. The difference is that now I understand so much more about why this might be so and how schools can establish story at the heart of their work with children and parents so that others can have their inner world developed and their language grown.

What is Talk for Writing?

Thirty-two years later, here is my first daughter, Poppy, who was then just three:

> *'Well, Pops was going to collect some berries and some conkers and she was going to collect some fir cones then she met a monkey and then she met a tiger. Then she met her grandma. Then she met the elephant. Then she met the lion. Then she met her father and then she met her mummy. Then she went to Flopsy Mopsy. Then Flopsy Mopsy and Peter Rabbit went outside to collect some berries, fire cones and conkers and while they were walking they saw some coconuts falling to the ground and they collected some and then they went home. Then they played. When it was night the little girl went bed. It was morning time in the early evening so they went to playgroup.'*

Already her stories are full of everyday events such as picking berries in the autumn and the impending visit of her grandma mingled with the current favourite story of Peter Rabbit. She is drawing on her story resources – reading and life. Children cannot create out of nothing. They need both rich experience as well as a language bank inside the mind to draw upon. Where the reading of stories and poems is a regular part of daily life, children are helped to internalise a living library of poems and stories, like templates that can be used for their own imaginative flights of fancy. These children will acquire a store of patterns, rather like building blocks that can be used to imagine and invent stories. For instance, even the earliest stories read to young children involve them in drawing upon their reading as well as their immediate lives.

Teachers may be tempted into thinking that children are unimaginative. The issue is usually not a lack of imagination. Too often it is a lack of the building blocks of narrative. Imagination concerns manipulating what you know to create something new. However, it is not uncommon to find children arriving in school with a meagre diet of stories and rhymes. Indeed, many professionals who work with young children believe that language deprivation is increasing.

The approach in this book is based upon how children learn language – through **imitation, innovation** and **invention** of language. The earliest words that children learn to use are a direct imitation of the language that they often hear. Generally, children pick up on words and phrases that 'work' for them, that get a reaction. These may well be described as

1 VIDEO

The centrality of language development

words that are in some way **'memorable'** and **'meaningful'**. Children tend not to make much of words that they do not understand, as they are just 'sounds' rather than powerful labels that can be used to order and organise the world. The meaning of words gradually grows over time as children hear words and phrases used in different contexts. This helps to refine a child's understanding. At first, every four-legged creature might be called a 'horse'. But gradually, over time, the child begins to build on this concept, distinguishing between horses, cats and dogs.

Of course, the vocabulary that children pick up is generally based upon the words that they often hear, so **repetition** is important to early language development. Early years practitioners can harness this notion of **'memorable, meaningful repetition'** as a basis for language learning. It means that if we want to develop children's vocabulary, phrasing and ability to talk in sentences, then we can set about:

- using specific vocabulary **repetitively** in a range of contexts – for instance, this might include the names of colours, words to help us describe size, or words to link ideas (connectives* – see footnote on page 215);

- ensuring that such vocabulary is made **memorable** by using expression and actions as we speak;

- ensuring that such vocabulary is used in different contexts, accompanied by explanations so that children gradually begin to understand what a word or expression **means.**

Of course, **attentive listening** is also essential to language acquisition, so that the experienced practitioner will need to use language in an interesting, expressive fashion, often dressed up by engaging in a playful or arresting manner to draw children's attention. Not much will be learned from a teacher whose speech is monotone and lacks that element of attractive playfulness. It is important to notice children's language use and where steps forwards are made. It can help to reinforce learning if you **restate** what the child has said. Where an immature utterance is used, you might also **recast** this by repeating exactly what has been said but putting the child's words into Standard English. So, if a child said, 'We goed to the farm,' you might recast this as, 'Yes, we went to the farm.' In this way you are remodelling the standard version. This must not feel as if it is 'correction'. 'Correction' may hinder a child's language development. Finally, a skilful practitioner will also take what children say during their play and repeat it, **extending** by embellishing or explaining further. This helps children to hear how language might be used to develop ideas. It is worth remembering that language grows through **modelling, recasting** and **extending**. It is worth listening carefully to children's speech, as their early utterances will tell you what needs to be modelled.

International research universally highlights the importance of stories as the key mode in which the human mind thinks. Indeed, quite extraordinarily, there is not a single piece of research that does not support the notion that story is crucial to human development. All researchers concur. Stories are essential to cognitive development. They are not just a frivolity to end the day. They are central. Research shows that stories are important because they develop:

- comprehension;
- abstract, critical and logical thought;
- memory and concentration;
- a sense of belonging, confidence and motivation;
- the ability to learn information that is communicated in story form;
- language (listening, speaking, writing and reading);
- composition/writing (not just narrative).

Indeed, neuroscientists and psychologists agree that the mind actually uses story architecture to help us understand the world. Our brains operate as neural story maps, using story as a template to explain and cope with experience. Story is the key method of internal processing used by the mind.

Constant experience of stories helps children **internalise narrative patterns:**

- the story as an experience of memorable, meaningful images;
- the underlying template of a story – the plot pattern;
- the building blocks – characters (with their goals and struggles), settings and events, as well as openings and endings;
- the flow of the sentences – syntax;
- words – especially memorable sensory detail and connectives.

Constant involvement in reading and storytelling also helps children develop the habit of sitting, listening, concentrating and following a line of thought. These are some of the basic prerequisites for early schooling. Furthermore, we should not lose sight of the notion that stories pass on cultural values, allowing readers to revisit and broaden their experience. Simple early stories from the different heritages that are represented in the class can be learned, binding a class together. Traditional tales provide route maps to life so that we can better understand and

2
VIDEO
Why narrative and story reading is so important

explain ourselves to the world and the world to ourselves. Stories can help children make sense of the inexplicable. They may bring comfort or disturbance. A good story stays in the mind forever, making the child's inner world a larger space.

Those who struggle with language may well have not yet built up that storehouse of narrative possibilities. Storytelling has to be a daily routine – it is as important as phonics. Indeed, what is the point of segmentation becoming a skill without a story to write! Finally, this is not to do with ideas of being 'unimaginative' or 'unintelligent'. Narrative is a necessary, 'primary act of mind' according to Barbara Hardy, and natural to all human beings – we are story creators whether we like it or not.

The initial work on Storymaking was carried out at the International Learning and Research Centre, funded by the then DFES through the Innovations Unit, as well as being supported by CFBT. It was co-led by Mary Rose and myself (Pie Corbett). It was an attempt to explore a systematic, cumulative and dynamic approach to language acquisition. Initially, narrative was used as a strategy for learning another language. This was based on work carried out at the University of Rome by Professor Taeschner over ten years. This was then followed by teacher research into the link between storytelling and writing.

Since then, many local authorities and clusters of schools in different countries have explored Talk for Writing, deepening our understanding about language development, for there is still much to be learned. Such projects involve teachers in researching the role of story in child development. Talk for Writing is therefore a shifting and dynamic process about which we are forever developing our understanding and practice. It is less effective when reduced to simplistic class routines without teachers thinking carefully about what is happening and adapting their teaching as they learn.

Many schools have found that daily Talk for Writing can have a dramatic influence on progress in language acquisition and composition/writing. For instance, the initial teacher research focused on children in reception classes. At the start of the year, only 2% of the sample was able to retell a whole story. By the end of the year, 76% retold a whole tale. In a study carried out in Lewisham (reported in *Stories to tell, stories to write*, available from Lewisham Professional Development Centre, Kilmorie Road, London SE23 2SP), 100% of the primary-age pupils tracked made at least average progress in writing and 80% made three or more sublevels progress in one year. By contrast, the same pupils did not make such good progress in reading, with 73% making average progress and only 33% making three sublevels progress. Interestingly, boys made better progress than girls.

It is worth noting that the teachers involved in this project had attended a one-day conference on Talk for Writing, followed by support

3 VIDEO

Why enriching young children's language matters

from their literacy consultants. Complex developments require time, attention and support. The published booklet *Stories to tell, stories to write* provides useful case studies that illuminate the teachers' and children's journeys as story creators. It also highlights the value of Talk for Writing for children who have English as a new language as well as those who struggle.

An overview of Talk for Writing

Talk for Writing involves teachers, children and families engaging with stories and rhymes. For a number of years, it has been a key strategy in many primary schools. A key aspect is to help children to build up a bank of tales, developing their imaginative and linguistic repertoire. The foundation of this work involves early years and KS1 settings establishing the very roots of imaginative play and early language development through stories and rhymes.

Evidence from many research studies looking at early language development highlights the importance of children being read to as well as the role of interactive language and play. Indeed, the answer to the question, 'What helps children do well in school?' is quite simple and is well researched. What matters most is an upbringing that involves supportive relationships within a rich language context, including plenty of family chatter, being read to, as well as storytelling and singing rhymes. This has the most dramatic effect on children's educational chances. Indeed, doing well in school is not a matter of wealth. It has more to do with the quality of children's early experiences of reading, story, rhyme, talk and play.

Talk for Writing builds upon this simple understanding by developing systematic approaches to early language development through story and rhyme:

a. **Rhymes** – establish tried-and-tested approaches to helping children acquire a bank of well-known rhymes. Knowing a bank of rhymes and poems feeds the mind with images, rhythms and language, as well as being a communal chant that involves sharing a pleasurable experience together, listening to each other and working together. Rhymes and songs give pleasure and create little communities where we all know the same rhyme. I can recall years ago, when Poppy was only a few months old, pacing up and down the bedroom with her on my shoulder trying to comfort her. Then out of nowhere, I remembered – sing to her. Nervously, I began to hum and then soothingly sing. Within seconds, she was asleep.

   Knowing rhymes, plus the ability to rhyme, identify rhymes and non-rhymes has been shown to be a key indicator of later success

VIDEO
6

What babies and young children learn from hearing stories

in reading and spelling. It is suggested that this is to do with both training the ear to listen attentively to sounds, thus tuning children into the distinct sounds of the language (an early basis for phonological awareness), and the ability to make analogies between sounds (e.g. this word is 'red', therefore that probably says 'bed'). This ability to recognise similar sound patterns is, of course a great help with early spelling and simple decoding.

b. **Storytelling** – teach children a bank of well-known stories so that over time they begin to internalise the imaginative world as well as the language patterns. These are then used as a basis for creating new stories, drawing on the known patterns as well as reading and children's lives. Finally, the children can make up new stories by calling on the imaginative bank of ideas plus the language patterns.

Both of the above strands – 'storytelling' and 'rhyme' – are underpinned by creating many opportunities for children to 'play at' the stories/rhymes as well as developing a strong sense of themselves as young writers and tellers.

What are imitation, innovation and invention?

Talk for Writing involves three simple phases, often referred to as the three 'Is': **Imitation**, **Innovation** and **Independent application/Invention**: see Talk for Writing process on page 2. This concept was originally developed by me in 2000 and published as a basis for all narrative writing in a flier published by the National Literacy Strategy (© the Department for Education and Families 2001). It has since been developed and explored by thousands of schools across the country. An initial early project, carried out by the International Learning and Research Centre, based 'storymaking' on previous research carried out by Professor Taeschner at the University of Rome. The findings of the project are available in the centre's archives.

Imitation involves the joyful act of learning stories so that the child knows and understands and takes to heart the tales. Very young children love to listen and join in with simple tales. It seems to be a quite natural part of their development to alight upon a favourite tale that they want to hear again and again until, in the end, they know it word for word. This stage is common to all children who are read to or have stories told to them. Familiar tales may be a comfort but their power to build an inner world and develop a linguistic repertoire should not be underestimated.

The teacher or early years practitioner selects a story, rhyme or song that they think the children will enjoy. This is then told to the children, encouraging them to increasingly join in. A story map is used so the children can see what happens in the story. Actions are also used to reinforce the meaning of the story but also to emphasise language patterns, such as 'once upon a time'.

The combination of *hearing, saying, seeing* and *moving* helps children gradually learn the story or rhyme. This is supported in other ways, as it is crucial that the children understand what the words mean. Practitioners may provide toys, costumes, images and different activities so children know what a 'cat' looks like and bake gingerbread!

Once the children have experienced the story and processed it in many ways through playing at the story in role-play areas, the text can then be shared as a picture book or homemade Big Book. This can then act as an early introduction to reading, as the children can now see what the words look like when they are written down – and because they already know what the words will say, they can join in more confidently with reading.

Innovation is the natural step that children take when learning language of taking the patterns that they know and playing with them to create new versions and utterances. Once the children know their story really well, then they can begin to make changes to make the tale their own. The story map can be altered to create a new version of the story. This may involve choosing new characters, changing a setting or objects or events. Extra detail might be added or the nature of a character altered so that the wolf becomes a kind character! Innovation can be quite simple or more complex.

The class story map can be changed so that a new version emerges. Toys can be set out to allow children to make their own choices and create new versions. They may draw new maps and then retell their own versions. These should be shared and celebrated. The class version can be written down using shared writing in front of the children, bit by bit over a number of days. This is then turned into a new Big Book for reading.

Recording of the children's versions can be through their map-making, using digital recorders to capture what a child says or through the child writing or an adult scribing. By the end of the innovation phase, the children will have created their own new version of the story as well as taken part in a group or class version, led by the teacher. It is worth noting that a few nursery and action rhymes lend themselves to simple innovation but in the main it is worth concentrating on stories, as these lend themselves to more creative possibilities.

Invention involves children making up their own stories independently. When they are doing this, they are drawing on their own life experience but also the stories that they have had read to them as well as the oral stories and rhymes that they have been internalising. Young children enjoy playing at stories as a natural and crucial aspect of their growth, exploring their own concerns and interests. Teachers can encourage this by setting out playful situations that invite story invention – toys, costumes and role-play areas are vital to this early work. Adults should intervene to play alongside children, making up stories as well as joining in with their inventions. Indeed, story invention should be a daily part of children's experiences.

Many classes also supplement the informal approach to storymaking by specifically establishing a routine whereby every day one or two children have their story written down by an adult. These are recorded in a special 'our stories' book. Later in the day, the stories are shared aloud and acted out. This sort of work has been written about extensively by Vivian Gussey Palin and explored in England by Make Believe Arts. This aspect is crucial because it means that every so often, each child has the opportunity to tell a story and have it valued. It also provides the teacher with valuable information about a child's linguistic development.

At least once a week, a more formal approach can be taken where children gather as a group or class and the teacher leads them through making a story up. There are many ways in which this can be done, using toys, puppets, map-making or writing. In this way, a reception class might be involved in making up thirty stories over the year. Of course, where this is done as a pleasurable activity, the children naturally want to 'have a go' themselves, so that storymaking becomes an everyday activity with constant creativity.

On the next pages, are three handouts that provide an overview of these three stages. You might want to download them from the online video platform linked to this book, or from www.talk4writing.com/resources and use them to make notes when reading the related chapters or when planning a Talk for Writing unit. The page references indicate where the book provides detailed advice on what the stage might mean as a child progresses through the early years.

The importance of shared writing from the start

By the end of the reception year, some children will be able to write whole stories down. They may be writing the original, an innovation or invention. Given the complex demands on a young child in terms of pencil control, phonics/spelling as well as developing composition, very young children should not be asked to write a story down unless they can easily tell their story. If a tale has been developed orally first, it means that a large chunk of cognitive space has been released so that when they write, the children's attention can be focused upon transcription rather than trying to cope with the demands of composition at the same time as transcription. In other words, the idea of developing composition orally first makes the act of writing easier for an emerging writer.

Imitation Stage for Foundation Years

Key process	Key points	Comments
• **Initial assessment/ observation**	• Find out what the children can do – ask, "Can you tell me a story you know?" and "Can you tell me a new story?" Record and make transcripts as a baseline – repeat termly: Collect written samples/ maps: see pages 48 – 50. From this – plan for groupings, class teaching and individual focus/targets.	
• **Select or adapt a model story text** that will engage the children.	• See pages 46 – 48 and pages 63 – 64 plus the Story Bank in appendix 2 and suggested picture books for retelling in Appendix 3. • Use the baseline to establish what language patterns to focus on, e.g. If the children are at the *'and then'* stage, include alternative simple connectives to develop the children's ability to link ideas, e.g. *once, who, one day, first, next, after that, unfortunately, luckily, so, finally*: pages 50 – 59 plus Appendix 1.	
• **Start with a creative 'hook'** • **Oral learning of model text** – internalising language patterns • **Activities to deepen understanding**	• Introduce the story with a creative hook, e.g. chasing a bear across the playground! • Daily oral retellings of the story (whole class, groups & pairs), see page 45. • Use map and actions: see pages 46 & 70 – 73. • Hand the story over: see pages 66 – 69 • Daily activities to help children understand text, e.g. story play, drama, making porridge, building bridges, being trolls, etc.: see pages 73 – 78.	
Reading as a READER **Reading as a WRITER**	Turn text into a big book and read – discuss vocabulary and comprehension: see page 84 – 85. Look for and discuss the underlying pattern, main scenes and notice simple writing tools such as using a question mark: see pages 85 – 86	
Daily spelling and sentences	Notice and practise spellings of common tricky words and sentence patterns needed to innovate. See pages 79 – 81 and Appendix 1.	

Innovation Stage for Foundation Years

Key process	Key points	Comments
Planning • **Think about when to start innovation** • **Think about how to innovate** • **Introduce innovation in playful ways – modeling how to change the story**	• When to change story: see pages 93 – 94. • How to pitch the innovation – simple substitution, addition, alteration, etc.: see pages 94 – 100. • Play at innovation by providing toys, puppets or story cards and model changing a story with the class, different groups and through independent play.	
• **Draw and retell**	• Start innovation by changing class map with children's ideas and retell new version: see page 100. • Help children change their maps and retell: see pages 101 – 103. • Use props, toys, story cards to help children choose new ideas. • Types of innovation: see pages 103 – 107.	
• **Shared writing** • **Guided writing** • **Individual writing/ recording**	• Use **class shared writing** to write the new version down, bit by bit over a number of days: page 109 – 111 and video 24 showing shared writing in a nursery class. Display shared writing and publish as a Big Book. • Use **guided writing** – in groups, at similar stages: see page 110 and video 28. • Children write or record independently – using audio/film, drawings, words, sentences or whole chunks – bit by bit over a number of days. Nursery children will play, draw and retell – record their new versions – share and celebrate.	
• **Daily spelling and sentence activities**	• Provide spelling cards of common tricky words for those writing, e.g. once, was. • Model phonics in writing, tricky word spelling and careful handwriting. • Orally rehearse sentences, using patterns from the model needed for the innovation, e.g. *'Once upon a time, there was ...'*.	

Independent Application/Invention Stage for Foundation Years

Key process	Key points	Comments
• **Moving from telling to writing**	• Use playful situations to encourage children to revisit and develop known stories independently: page 121 –125. • Ensure there's a listener for the inventions: pages 120 – 121. • Model inventing stories – through play, storytelling, mapping and writing.	
• **After innovating, lead children into developing their own versions more independently**	After Innovation: • Model how to draw and retell another new version. Pages 113 – 120 • Model how to turn new version into writing, as appropriate; use shared/ guided recording/writing. Pages 143 – 145 • Encourage children to increasingly draw on all the stories that they know. • Publish and celebrate inventions.	
• **Establish these 3 core practices:** **a. Daily play at invention** **b. Daily opportunity for several children to have a story recorded and shared** **c. Weekly class or group story**	• Daily opportunities for children to 'play' at inventing stories. Adults model making stories up through play. Pages 136 – 140 • Set up a permanent writing area for children to draw, record or write stories independently. • One or two children daily have their own story recorded and acted out. Pages 140 –142 • Hold a weekly session where a group, or class, invent a story which is mapped or written down and made into a Big Book for future retelling and reading. Alternatively, daily add another section to an ongoing story that stretches over a week. Pages 128 – 135	
• **Daily spelling and sentences**	• Maintain daily spelling and sentence games to secure tricky words and phonics for spelling as well as speaking in Standard English.	

The pictures tell the story of why reception children at St. George's School, Battersea, have such good handwriting

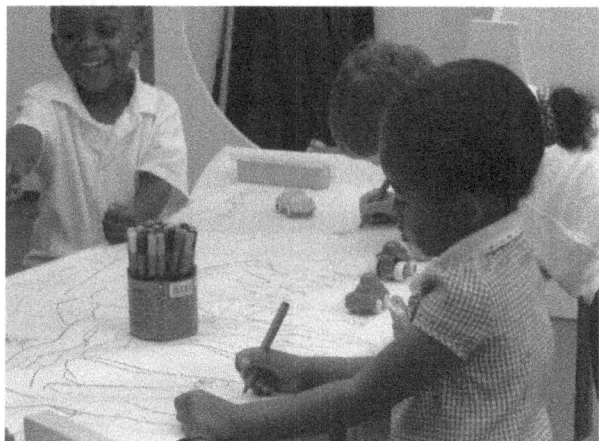

Nursery children learn to hold a pen while enjoying drawing activities.

The nursery teacher models how to write simple short text.

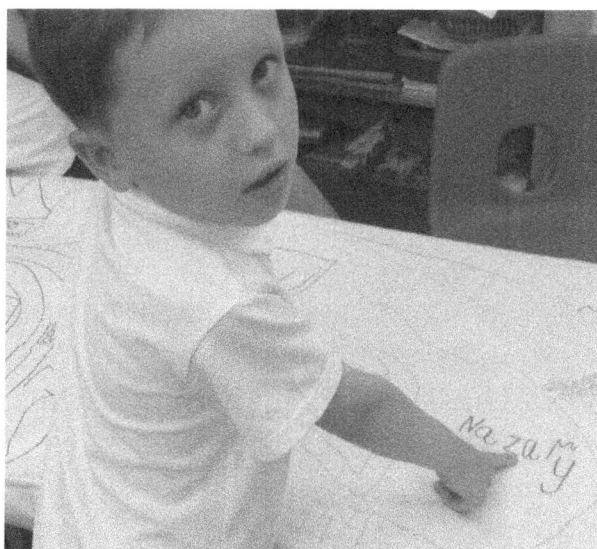

Nursery children can proudly write their name by the end of the school year.

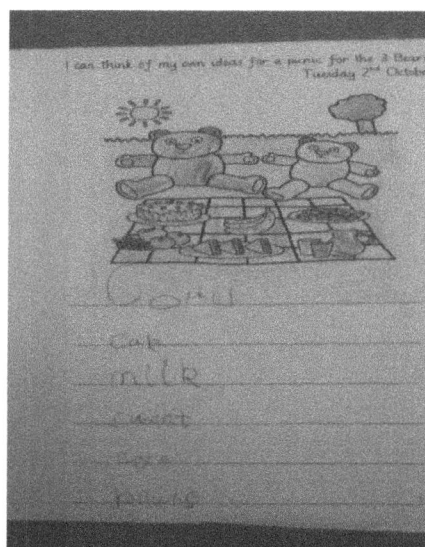

By October of their reception year, the children can write simple lists like this.

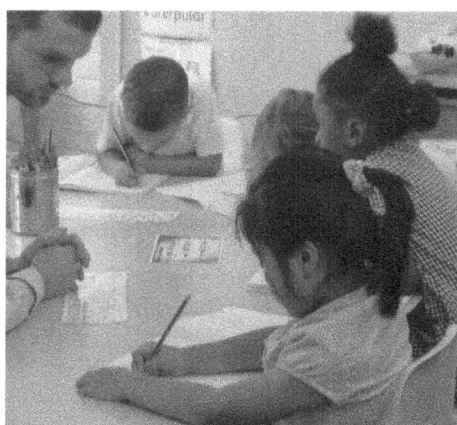

During the reception year, children get guided sessions, learning to write neatly.

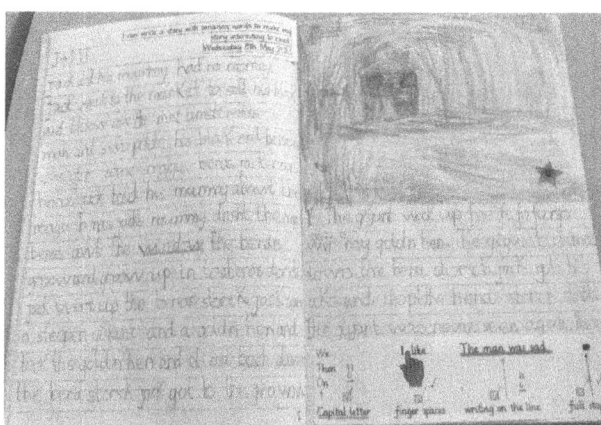

Therefore, six months later, they can write like this. This writing was done by the same child who wrote the list above.

Of course, there will be children who are not yet developmentally ready to write. This may be to do with pencil control or an inability to memorise and use phonic patterns. However, every child should be able to retell and make up stories. Preschool children also enjoy being writers. To encourage very young children to play at writing, they do need to witness adults writing with enthusiasm – stories may be recorded as well as other sorts of writing – reminders, notes, messages, signs, information, etc. By using a flip chart, writing may be modelled with the children joining in and helping (see images on page 15). The transcription will usually be the adult's job, while the children make suggestions for what might be written down. However, older children may enjoy 'sharing the pen' to write letters or even try simple words.

In classrooms where adults writing as well as reading is a common feature, as long as pencils and paper are provided, many children will automatically begin to 'play write' themselves. This may be read back to an adult, turned into a book and celebrated by reading to others. Over time, children's mark-making may take on the form of letter shapes and, as phonics/handwriting are taught, gradually words will emerge. You will notice children picking up that writing moves left to write, top to bottom.

Although not every child will find holding a pencil easy or have a sound grasp of phonics (and 'tricky' words), what should be true is that every child has a repertoire of nursery and action rhymes to chant and stories to tell. Generally speaking, those whose language development starts at a lower base will end the year knowing a bank of stories and will be able to retell the original versions that were learned, innovating with different levels of sophistication. Everyone will be inventing in their own ways. What matters is that everyone succeeds, in their own unique ways.

Shared writing gradually shifts from writing down what we say into the more purposeful crafting of language. The teacher will draw upon the key connectives and language patterns but also push children to select words with care, using powerful words as well as a touch of alliteration, similes and, by seven years of age, the sorts of patterns that a fluent, confident writer will use. In this way, the children are constantly involved in composition at a high level. For instance, at seven years, the children may experiment by beginning sentences with adverbs, e.g. *'Carefully, he crept into the cave'*.

Imitation, innovation and invention from the start

In many countries, the national expectations of young children's composition underestimates what they are capable of in terms of their ability to internalise and create stories. Many teachers are unaware of children's extraordinary ability to learn stories and rhymes. However, by using a multi-sensory approach, teachers soon discover that children have a remarkable ability to learn stories. Furthermore, if you listen to how very young children play with words and adapt what has been said to them, then you know that even those with very limited vocabulary can be helped to move to the innovation stage. Once a child knows a simple story such as The Little Red Hen, it is not too hard to change that to The Little Red Rooster. Once the first story has been learned, then move straight into a class or group innovation. Do not delay.

Furthermore, some teachers believe that children cannot invent new stories. The truth is that a large majority of all children's play and talk hinges around story invention. Of course, a three-year-old's story might just be 'doggie barked' – but what an exciting story that is! Lying behind this two-word story may be a whole story about going to school with Mum and a dog leaping out, barking madly so that they had to run for it! Of course, if you are only three, then the tale will not come out in a fluent, literate manner. So, however fragmentary, we must notice and value the children's inventions. The more you put stories into their heads, the more their inventions will develop. The more we build children's imaginative world and linguistic bank, the more they will be able to use their imagination, think in the abstract and use talk to make their way in the world.

Key points learned from teacher research projects

Initially, the most important ingredient in developing this work is the headteacher's genuine and active support. It is so easy for a 'good idea' to become lost among a host of other 'good ideas'. The teacher needs to have permission to focus on establishing both storytelling and rhyme in the class. This key aspect is linked directly to the teacher's own belief in the importance of the concept and its potential as a vital ingredient in the children's development. Without a passionate commitment from the teacher, the idea will founder. The third essential ingredient is the quality of the relationships between the teacher, teaching assistants and other adults involved.

Many settings and schools across the country in areas of economic and language deprivation have found that the approaches described have had a powerful impact upon children's language development. For instance, evidence from the old 'communication, language and literacy' section of the Foundation Profile in one Sheffield school showed that by the end of the first year of school, 75% of children involved were at or above national related expectations. This contrasted with the previous years' intakes where, on average, only 30% of the children had made similar progress. As one teacher reported, *'It has allowed them to get the common language of story.'*

Aladdin's Cave: The 'Talk for Writing and Learning' classroom

Over the last ten years, more and more specialists working in the area of early childhood have reported a steady decline in children's ability to communicate. At first, I thought that this was just a function of getting older and beginning to think that, years ago, everything was rosier. However, early years specialists, speech therapists and teachers all make similar comments. Language deprivation is a major issue in our schools. The hardest hit are children from poor backgrounds who experience a difference in millions of words that they hear before coming to school.

Our big challenge in nurseries and schools is how to increase and deepen vocabulary, help children acquire a range of sentence structures, and broaden children's spoken repertoire to include everyday chatter as well as more formal patterns, so they can easily adapt how they talk for a range of audiences and purposes. In other words – being able to talk more like a book as well as having the language needed to think.

We believe that Talk for Writing as a whole-school approach and philosophy addresses this issue. So, what makes an effective Talk for Writing classroom where talk flourishes? What does the research suggest? What can we draw from common sense and our observations in many schools? What actually works? The rest of this chapter relates what we know from research on the Talk for Writing classroom. Rather than burden the reader with research references, I have suggested four books at the end that contain research references to the salient points that are being made.

Motivating Aladdin

Before focusing on the key elements that research suggests should be in an early years setting, it's worth considering what we can learn from research about what is going to motivate a small child to learn and what might intimidate them. An excellent way of doing this is to look at the research of Carol Dweck, Professor of Psychology at Stanford University, on 'The effect of praise on mindset' and 'Teaching a growth mindset'. Type those phrases into Google and you will be able to access two very useful clips on YouTube that talk you through the research. These could be useful to discuss at staff meetings.

These clips make us think about the climate that supports progress through encouraging self-improvement and the climate that inhibits progress through encouraging fear of failure.

In the research, they had two groups: one group they praised for ability ('Oh, you're really good at that!'); the other group they praised for effort and strategy ('Ooh, you really tried hard at that!').

Over time, they found that the ones that get praised for effort and strategy are the ones who are more likely to succeed and make more progress. These children have a growth mindset. The ones that get praised for ability, being good at something, are the ones that are more likely to become frail and are less likely to take risks, less likely to go for the harder problem, in case they fail. These children have a fixed mindset.

This is blindingly obvious but completely contrary to what I'm increasingly seeing in primary schools, which is all about labelling children and creating fixed mindsets. At Key Stage 1, I've seen ladders on the wall for reading, writing and maths, so that everyone can clearly see who's on the bottom of the ladder and who's at the top. This is a severe form of labelling.

This labelling of ability contradicts everything that we know from the international research on the topic. We should be praising effort and strategy – 'Well done! I like the way you used your spelling card. That was a really good idea and it really helped you.' If children try hard, use helpful learning strategies, have useful feedback and teaching and practise, practise, practise, they can improve. All of us can improve.

This can-do attitude should underpin the learning culture in every classroom and nowhere is this more important than in the early years. It is at the heart of formative assessment and creates a growth mindset: it is this that will motivate children to try hard and to self-improve. If you get that atmosphere, then you will see progress. If you continually ascribe 'levels' to children, it demotivates those at the bottom of the ladder and influences those at the top not to take risks.

If you create an atmosphere that labels children, that fixes their idea of what they can achieve, you create the wrong sort of learning culture, you sap the will to try and Aladdin will learn to fail.

Aladdin's Cave: The story classroom

Ideally, there should be plenty of space. This not only avoids a sense of feeling hemmed in but also allows one to create interesting spaces for different forms of learning. There will be a place for small-world play, an inviting reading corner, a storytelling castle, a writing area, a space for maths, a construction place for building, easels and materials for model-making. Such areas will be clearly defined and labelled, using words and symbols. The use of a program such as 'communicate in print' can be very handy, as the main words have small drawings that help a child to understand.

One key outcome of the research is the idea of quieter areas. These might take the form of a cubby-hole, a tent, a play house or a special side area. Whatever is provided, quiet spaces are important, especially where adults and children can easily hear each other and proper conversations may take place as well as hard work and serious play! Even in the general classroom space, noise levels should be calm so that children can hear themselves think and everyone can hear what others are saying. If language and learning are to flourish, then a quiet atmosphere is crucial. How can anyone create a sense of story with a hullabaloo going on in the background? Outside, there may also be a little hut, a beach shelter tent or a willow den for quieter play.

Learning to listen and tuning the ear into the rhythms of language is vital. Songs, rhymes and joining in with stories is all part of learning to listen, distinguishing sounds as well as joining in together. In storytelling, it is very common to have one child booming out a story or song without listening to the pace of everyone else, almost as if they were trapped in a world on their own. There should be a range of simple percussive instruments (including some homemade shakers) as well as chime bars. Tambourines, shakers and rain-makers are all handy for stilling a class as well as introducing story time. Simple beats and tunes can be put to rhymes and used to enhance stories.

Many early years settings like to pin up the curriculum. This has always struck me as a waste of space. Parents do not read it and, if they did, would probably not be able to make any use of the information. There is often also a board of teacherly notes. All of this could be taken away and space given to displaying children's work – art, writing, printing, models, drawings as well as story maps, story pictures and story writing. Children's work needs to be labelled, including their name, and well presented. Displays should be changed so that everyone has work celebrated with their name attached over time. Draw the children's attention to these as well as their parents. There should a well-displayed story map of the current story that is big and bold somewhere in the classroom, preferably where the teacher draws the class together. Alongside this, there will be photos of the children showing the main actions for key connectives such as *first*, *next*, *so*, *but* and *because*. These will be added to during the year as more are learned. There will also be flipcharts for writing as well as handy displays to remind children of spellings and sentence patterns, and useful banks of characters and settings.

There will also be 'learning displays' where children are invited to take part. There may be questions or directions or things to think about or interactive stories. These displays may require children to do something or provide feedback. Where there are displays about different stories, relevant books may be displayed or made available for reading. In some nurseries, space is found for story maps and transcriptions of children's stories for parents to read. In other settings, film clips of children telling stories are played in the reception foyer.

To help children tell stories there may be cards, toys, pots of ideas, masks or puppets to choose from together with instructions asking the children to use them to make up a story or re-enact a story. Resources also need to be labelled (with words and pictures) and well organised so children and adults can easily find them and put them away. Of course, the play equipment needs to be tidied so that children know where everything is and can fetch what they need independently. Sound mats and spelling cards for different stories should also be available.

There must be a book area that is inviting and used by the children and adults. This should have a range of good books, including many that are familiar. This should include class stories that have been learned and made up. It is worth remembering that with these stories the children will be more likely to be able to read, as they know what the words will say! The main text that is being learned will be available and there may be other versions as well.

As well as a book area, there should also be a writing space or table. This might be included in the role-play area but there should be a specific space with paper, pencils, mini whiteboards and maps, as well as envelopes and a post box! Small booklets for making mini books are also essential. Include materials for practising handwriting as well as spelling cards and sound mats.

The next point seems obvious but good lighting, preferably natural, is also important. I find strip lighting makes me feel ill and there must be other people and many children who find the same! The colours chosen for backing paper and displays should be attractive with a balance between more muted colours as well as some vibrant and jolly images. Years ago, I remember a headteacher warning me to tone down displays in case I 'over-excited their visual imaginations'!

Great classrooms have a wonderful selection of robust toys, often balancing natural with man-made materials. There should be small-world objects and toys, animals, jigsaws, collections of objects such as shells or buttons, castles, boats, sand trays, water play equipment, tracing activities, threading, tweezers to pick up items, playdough and Plasticine-type materials, model-making, Lego, percussive instruments, chime bars, and so on. For story, there will be costumes, hats, relevant toys, puppets and masks. Tabards are handy in different colours – these are simple rectangular cloths with a space for the head and can be used to become anything that you wish! Hats are also handy for helping children adopt a role.

Thought has to be given to what is being learned through each activity. This can be signalled on a card or by using a 'talking tin' to remind children or the adult what to do and what is being learned. Take the simple activity of using playdough, for example:

At home	At school
Having fun rolling the dough around	• Adult modelling the words 'squash', 'squeeze', 'stretch' • Making the dough into lengths • Adult modelling 'long, longer, longest'

Ideally, the room should not feel cramped or squashed. If children bump into each other all the time, this may lead to frustration. Outside, there will be a good space for using larger construction toys as well as mini vehicles. There may be a special role-play area with relevant equipment and even costumes such as a road that I saw being constructed leading to the giant's castle! Little tents may be used to create 'talking tents' and objects or toys placed within to lure children into imaginative play.

Over the years, much has been said about the importance of role-play areas. Ideally, these change to suit the story that is being told or the topic being studied. So a giant's castle ('*Jack and the Beanstalk*') may turn into a farmyard ('*Little Red Hen*') or even a bakery ('*Gingerbread Man*'). In the area, there may be activities to promote reading, writing and maths as well as costumes, puppets and toys such as a mini kitchen. The more children 'play at' the story, re-enacting and exploring the events, the more likely they are to understand the story and develop their vocabulary.

Role-play areas that invite children to play in different ways, drawing on different vocabulary and forms of speech, are an important part of language development. So, too, are story corners and spaces, small-world play and the constant re-enactment and development of stories. Make sure that you ring the changes, as this will invite different ways to talk. I'll never forget the small boy who approached me while I was crouched in the class café with a clipboard. He glanced at me, with a towel over his arm, rather like a miniature waiter and said, '*Cappucino, Sir?*'

- Create specific role-play areas for playing at the current story as well as a space for retelling old stories and inventing new tales, e.g. a storytelling castle.
- Create quiet areas where stories may be invented and told.
- Celebrate children's story maps and writing as well as film clips of retelling.
- Create interactive story displays so children can add to stories, change them or create new ones.
- Have an inviting book area that includes the texts of stories that have been learned as well as class stories.
- Have a specific place for guided writing and story-making, led by an adult with spelling cards, sound and handwriting mats available.
- Display the story map and photos of children showing key actions.
- Set up play situations for writing.
- Have a space where children's invented stories can be shared in the round and acted out.
- Keep the classroom calm and have spaces where children can concentrate, be heard and hear each other as they work on developing their stories.
- Provide banks of characters, settings and words so that children can make choices when creating.
- Provide story mats and boxes as well as writing and recording equipment, such as blank story maps and cloth story mats.
- Use the outdoor space to encourage story play.
- Provide toys and objects, costumes, hats, small-world toys for children to use for their story play.
- Provide percussive instruments and chime bars for children to use when developing stories and chanting rhymes.

What happens in Aladdin's Cave?

I am often haunted by what I see because it matters so much. If a child has a good start in a nursery or reception class, this can influence what happens for the rest of their lives. We know from the EPPE study that one of the most important influences on future success in education is the relationship between a key worker and a child [Sylva, K., Melhuish, E., Sammons, P., Siraj-Blatchford, I. and Taggart, B. (2004) *The Effective Provision of Pre-School: Education (EPPE) Project: Findings from Pre-school to end of Key Stage 1*. London: Department for Education and

Skills]. Small children need to form positive, warm relationships with an adult who is there for them, will love them regardless and makes the child feel accepted, noticed and encouraged. Small children need positive relationships with adults who are warm, enthusiastic and respect what children bring and build upon it. They need stimulation, consistency and aspiration. This also applies, of course, to parents. You can go a long way if you take the time to praise mums: '*You do such a good job with Jimmy reading to him.*' Being a mum is not always easy. Mums also need encouragement – all of them!

Years ago, some early years teachers used to let the others play while hearing children read one to one. If there were thirty children in the class, this would basically take almost the whole day! Obviously, there has to be a balance between whole-class songs, rhymes, stories, phonics and discussions alongside small-group work with an adult. Gradually, over time, children's ability to sustain interest and attention strengthens. Effective classrooms have clear routines and systems, with smooth, calm transitions so that everyone knows the signals for stilling and moving. Places on the carpet are clear, so there is no opportunity for an argument to arise about who sits where! There will be class and daily group work on common areas such as phonics for spelling and reading, guided reading and writing, as well as handwriting. There will be daily maths activities such as counting or sorting.

Shared reading is important, using either a picture book or more usually a Big Book. This is a chance for everyone to become familiar with the basics of handling books and turning pages, as well as a chance for book discussion. The model text in Talk for Writing is turned into a Big Book and then read with the children. This aids fluency as well as forming a bridge into writing, as the children see what the words and sentences look like when written down. It is also an opportunity for oral comprehension, discussion about word meanings (it is good for children to say '*what does that word mean*') and word choices, as well as innovating on sentence patterns. Many classes have the same book over a week, varying the focus each day:

- *Monday*: **read through** – predicting on each page what will happen next. Discuss initial reactions, links to own lives as well as preferences, likes and dislikes.

- *Tuesday*: **words** – re-read and notice word choices. Discuss difficult vocabulary. Use Post-its to cover words and try synonyms to see how they influence meaning.

- *Wednesday*: **sentences** – read through and look at the sentences. Innovate and change some sentences by swapping words over. Look at punctuation.

- *Thursday*: **characters and settings** – re-read and discuss the characters. Talk about motives (why) and feelings (how). Talk about the setting.

- *Friday*: **big picture reading** – re-read and talk about how the book makes us feel. Why is it special? Which is the most important picture? What was it about? What would a character learn? How did the character change?

There will also be planned activities that involve discussions as well as working in groups with an adult. This will involve some modelling of language, playing or creating together, as well as general discussion, questions and comments. Research emphasises the importance for such discussions to be based upon what very young children are interested in as much as our own intentions. The cunning teacher makes good use of children's interests and comments, building on what is said and taking discussions into new lines of thought. We can also lure them into new directions that seem fruitful. Turn-taking and listening are vital, as they encourage further explanation on the part of children. These planned discussions occur around many different tasks involving art work, maths and, of course, activities related to stories. Retelling, map-making and writing sessions are key to the whole process.

While we must ensure that the children have regular and planned opportunities to talk with adults, they should also be involved in purposeful discussions with other children. Much discussion will occur during play but the whole business of paired talk in groups as well as on the carpet is important. Train the children how to turn and face a partner, talk and then swivel back to face the teacher, ready to share ideas. In all of this work, it is important to have noticed children who are reluctant to join in and ensure that they do not miss out on discussions with adults and their peers. They may need one-to-one attention and the use of a toy or some other focus to take the spotlight off the child. What must not happen is that a year slides by and a child has missed out on developing their talk through interaction with either adults or other children.

How to talk in Aladdin's Cave

It is very easy to stop children from talking, and this usually happens when we become too 'teacherly'. In the main, most small children will settle down with some toys or an activity such as making sand castles and chatter soon begins. However, this source of conversation will grind to a halt if an adult looms into view with the direct purpose of questioning the children. Firing questions that seem like a test is off-putting for anyone but, at the age of four, it soon stops the talk and the play shrivels. Children's eyes flicker left and right, seeking an escape route! Sometimes, the questions are ones for which we already know the answer: *'What colour is it?'* The child stares thinking, *'Surely she knows it is red – she taught us that!'*

- Plan guided sessions for story learning, map-making, retelling, and inventing as well as teaching writing.
- Plan shared writing sessions to teach everyone at once.
- Establish daily reading as a class and in guided groups with one-to-one where needed.
- Plan for a daily storytelling session and 'rhyme of the week'.
- Plan for a weekly story invention session or do a bit each day.
- Plan for several children a day to tell their own story and then share these with the class, re-enacting the tales.
- Plan for daily, specific opportunities for children to work and talk with an adult in a group session.
- Plan for regular activities where children play, work and talk with their peers.
- Observe carefully to ensure that every child is included and provided for – pick up on quiet children who do not join in with storytelling or learning rhymes, and provide small group work or one-to-one to build confidence.

None of us really like closed questions. Either you know the answer or you do not … and then you feel silly. In his marvellous book about reading *Tell Me* (Stroud: Thimble Press, 1993), Aidan Chambers explores the whole business of developing the children's reading through Socratic discussions. The teacher acts as an interested listener and orchestrates the discussion but the children do most of the talking and thinking. His main technique hinges around inviting extended thinking through asking children to *'tell me'* what they think. He starts simply with likes and dislikes. Open-ended questions are bread and butter to most teachers and combined with *'tell me'* seem to invite extended explanations and thinking. *'Tell me how the pirate captured the shark'* is not a question – it is an invitation, especially if the words are spoken with relish! Key question words will hinge around *'what, how, where, why, when'*. Of course, the whole business of standing up and telling a well-known story is a great confidence giver!

The skill with small children is to gently slide into the play, to play alongside and become one of their group. Conversation soon begins and the adult can pick up on what the children are talking about. Sometimes this is to do with the activity and the teacher can suggest new avenues of thought or introduce a challenge: *'What would happen if we made it taller?*', or suggest '*Let's build it higher*'. More formal group work with older children will be more directed but it is still important to have trust between children and adults so that children are happy to comment and raise questions as they work.

To develop talk in the classroom, there are a few key ideas to hold in mind. Jean Gross talks about 'surprises' that trigger talk. I still recall the story a teacher told me of the head who arranged for a camel to visit the school at Christmas time. She wanted to remind the teachers about the importance of first-hand experience and enriching children's lives. That head now leads one of the great Talk for Writing training centres in the country (Penn Wood Primary) where visitors can see what it all looks like in action. You don't, perhaps, have to go to the lengths of fetching camels but each story should be accompanied by a museum of relevant objects, sound effects, music, song, costumes or puppets to help generate language and deepen understanding.

Talk also arises from activities that encourage children to raise questions. Discussing stories is vital as a pathway to understanding. In their story work, children should also be involved in activities that involve collaboration, instructing, explaining and giving their ideas, as well as talking through their work and what they have been doing.

It seems obvious to suggest that we use children's names and look at children as we speak to them. Many children find holding eye contact hard and we need to reassure them, drawing them in. Even though my knees now have arthritis and creak, I still find myself preferring to get down to their level. Towering five feet above them acts as a barrier.

If I were in charge of education (and no, I don't want that job – really!), I would make sure that every early years teacher used sign language such as Makaton. Gestures and specific actions are useful to emphasise meanings and especially helpful for those new to the English language. Backing up ideas with hand movements to show differences in size when looking at the wonderful picture book 'Titch', helps to show children what the words mean. Of course, Talk for Writing has gestures at its heart as a way of making language features memorable and meaningful. The ones that work most effectively suggest the meaning, such as holding up one finger for '*first*'. Fascinating research has shown that parents from well-off families tend to use more gestures when speaking, as do their children. These children made the greatest gains in vocabulary from 14 to 54 months and the study concluded that the use of gesture to support talk in the first 14 months helps to explain the differences in vocabulary that children have when they come to school [Rowe, M.L. and Goldin-Meadow, S. (2009) Differences in early gesture explain SES disparities in child vocabulary size at school entry, *Science*, 323 (5916): 951–3].

Many schools have been using pictures and symbols to reinforce meaning. Visual timetables are common and approaches such as 'communicate in print' are most helpful in underpinning the meanings of words. If children are to understand vocabulary, then the more we can use an action or mime accompanied by some sort of visual prop (images or toys or real objects), the more likely they are to understand and retain the vocabulary. Bags of 'props' for teaching should be part of the basic early years teaching tools. In Talk for Writing, maps and toys are essential to capture language as well as create new ideas. We use them for stories but maps can just as easily be used for solving maths problems or to capture what happened when we went to the park.

When teachers talk with children, clarity is essential as well as a reasonable pace so that children have time to internalise what is being said and think. Time is needed for a response to be shaped and turns taken. Gabbling away too quickly will not help. Many teachers naturally use the old technique of an oral cloze procedure by leaving gaps in sentences, rhymes, songs and stories for children to fill in the key word or idea. This isolates a key word or idea and draws attention to it ('*so they turned the corner and there on the path stood … a wolf!*'). This technique also means that extended talk can become interactive and it is a great technique when telling a story, as it allows the children to listen to some parts, join in at other points and fill in the gaps as the tale jogs along.

No one likes to talk with someone and then find that what they have said has not been picked up on. Such behaviour is considered rude in adult life and yet, strangely, it seems fine not to recognise what a child has just said! Of course, you cannot pick up on everything but paying attention to what children say and confirming that we have noticed is important. It doesn't mean that we have to stop and hold a massive conversation, as sometimes a simple '*Yes, I saw the pigeons too*' may suffice. Effective teachers enjoy what children say and respond encouragingly. The child 'serves' and the teacher 'returns', a form of to and fro that encourages children to chatter. Following a young child's line of play and thought is more likely to have a positive effect on language development, than being over-directive and stifling children's lines of thinking.

There is much to be said for talking about '*what we have done*'. Many classrooms keep photos and film clips, recording the year. Children love looking back at themselves from the giddy heights of the summer term to see what they were like on entry to school. In this sense, stories of our home and school life are a great resource for language development. In the same way, good 'learning journey' books also give great pleasure as children can see how they have moved from mark-making to writing. Recordings of children's storytelling will also show them – and their parents – how far they have developed and make a useful addition to our observations and assessments. The oral story is just as important as evidence as the written version.

Talk for Writing schools teach children a 'rhyme a week' so that they gradually build up hundreds of rhymes and poems. A 'literature spine' identifies about a dozen key picture books that will be read and re-read until the class has them by heart (see the Scholastic Reading Spine for an example http://shop.scholastic.co.uk/piecorbett). These key books are supplemented by other titles, including non-fiction books. Added to this are the stories that lie at the heart of Talk for Writing that are retold and learned, then read and explored and used as a basis for creating new stories. All of this work feeds both the imagination and a child's linguistic competency.

A key aspect for early years providers to consider is the importance of minimising background noise. Noisy classrooms mean that children cannot think let alone hear clearly what is being said. Noise limits learning. Providing quiet spaces and making sure that guided reading and writing happens in a calm and quiet environment will pay dividends.

Much has been written about the need to repeat what children say, as this shows that we have heard and noticed the child, and are showing interest. It may also be a chance to tweak the sentence or extend the idea a touch, demonstrating language development – often known as 'recasting' (*'We goed to the playground'* = *'We went to the playground'*) and 'extending' (*'It was bear'* = *'It was a big, brown bear'*). 'Extending' allows us to add description, build in another idea or develop and explain. Of course, the additions need to be minimal, as responding with too long an extension will provide too much of a linguistic leap. Along these lines, it is also important to comment on what children are doing – *'I love Andy's map with the pirates on it'* – as well as using open-ended prompts and questions to show interest: 'Oohhh, *tell me what happens next in the story.*' This shows that we have noticed and value the child's work as well as turning their activity into language. Talk for Writing is underpinned by children imitating texts orally by learning them and then retelling and extending them.

We have to work hard on developing vocabulary. Children need to be vacuuming up many new words in the early years and for that reason new and surprising experiences are essential, as they demand talk and we need words to talk about what is happening. A large amount of vocabulary comes from reading, especially when that reading is repetitive. Stories have to be worked with to help children understand what the words mean. A key aspect of vocabulary growth is ensuring that we model new language in a range of contexts, especially where the words are linked to the experience. Talking 'just above' the children's vocabulary and 'just beyond' their linguistic competency provides a constant model of how to extend talk. There is a real skill in noticing how children speak and pitching just above. Furthermore, as you move through the year, it is worth revisiting key language features from previous stories but also be aware of adding to the next story. This is not a matter of length but of richness and density of vocabulary as well as gradual complexity in sentence range and structure.

Children need to hear plenty of talk and a rich range of vocabulary and different word types. Talking down to children merely traps them with what they already have. As Jean Gross suggests, '*Chatty parents tend to have chatty children.*' I remember one parents' evening finding myself bemoaning the fact that the teachers had found one of my children irritating because he chatted so much. But of course he would – it's how I earn my living! Talking got me here.

When children are playing or carrying out some sort of procedure such as sorting shapes, it is helpful to provide a running commentary by turning the event into words. This can be especially useful for daily routines so that they have been labelled and spoken through a number of times. This is not just a matter of telling children what to do but more about providing them with the words that they will need when talking about their work. For instance, I was recently working with Year One children and we had just completed reading the Big Book of our class oral story. The children were talking about how the different characters had been feeling at different points in the story. I paused them and we practised how we could talk about the characters. We tried, '*I think xxx felt yyy because ...*' I modelled this a few times and then we tried saying the sentence together. Immediately, the children began using the stem when replying to my questions. It is essential to talk through routines, as it helps some children remember what to do and what is expected. This helps children feel secure.

Teachers should provide children with choices and ask them to explain their chosen ideas. This happens in many ways in the class but is especially important when innovating and inventing stories. Banks of characters and settings should be generated or provided so children can begin to choose for themselves. Writing is about making choices. Deepen understanding through presenting choices that involve contrasts. This can be useful when working on performing a story. *Which parts should be quick? Where should we go slow? Where could we leave a dramatic pause? Is there a part of the story that should be loud or soft ... or even spoken in a whisper?*

The importance of teachers and other adults being good listeners cannot be emphasised enough. However, we should also encourage children to develop as good listeners. Notice when they are concentrating hard and listening well. Notice when they respond to what has been said. Praise and label this behaviour: '*I loved it when you smiled at the funny part in the story. I could tell that you were listening really hard.*'

- Use specific gestures to emphasise key story language features and support meaning both in story time as well as other classroom activities.
- Ensure actions are agreed between staff and consistently used.
- Use map-making for stories as well as for recording other activities and events.
- Use 'communicate in print', or something similar, to support children when reading.
- When talking with children, speak clearly, without rushing, pausing for thinking time.
- Clearly enunciate stories and rhymes so that children retell with clarity and expression.
- Purposefully teach children the sentence stems and patterns that they need – model these and have children say them together and use them.
- Be aware of modelling vocabulary and sentence patterns just ahead of the children's competency, building these into everyday activities as well as making sure each story consolidates but also enriches and extends.
- Use repetition that is memorable and meaningful to help children's vocabulary develop.
- Teach vocabulary in context of experience and encourage children to make use of new words.
- Comment on what children are doing, extend what they say and recast where there are immature utterances.
- Encourage children to talk and extend their stories by showing genuine interest, using open questions and 'tell me'.
- Engage children in making choices when changing and creating stories, offering contrasting and surprising ideas.
- Teach good story listening and turn-taking as well as children talking in a bold, clear voice.

Research and Aladdin's Cave

There are four very useful resources for anyone interested in what research tells us about language development and especially story. Without wishing to flood you with hundreds of references, I'll suggest four useful starting points for students, researchers and others interested in digging deeper. The above chapter is based on what the research studies that informed the books below have told us.

- **Time to Talk** by Jean Gross (London: Routledge, 2013). This is an essential read for all primary school teachers and early years practitioners. Jean Gross was the government's communications champion and spent her time gathering evidence of 'what works'. The book is rich with ideas and examples as well as providing very clear commentary that draws together key research into the issues that we have with talk and how to support language development. A marvellous book that should be influencing practice. Jean provides useful references to research studies, papers and books.

- **Better Communication Research Programme** (Communication Trust, 2012: www.thecommunicationtrust.org.uk/projects/better-communication-research-project/). This project arose from the work of the 2008 Bercow Report and focused on children with speech, language and communication needs. The three-year research programme produced seventeen reports, published by the Department for Education in 2012. I find the 'communication supporting classroom observation tool' to be a very useful checklist and it is clearly linked to sixty-two research papers. Every early years practitioner should be familiar with this schedule. While the title is off-putting, the document is handy.

- **Story Proof: The Science Behind the Startling Power of Story** by Kendall Haven (Westport, CT: Libraries Unlimited, 2007). In researching the book, the author reviewed over 350 research studies from fifteen separate fields of science and discovered that every single one was positive about the benefits of story. This is an uplifting read and the author provides nineteen pages of references!

- **The Meaning Makers: Children Learning Language and Using Language to Learn** by Gordon Wells (Portsmouth, NH: Heinemann, 1986). This book is based on the research project that tracked children's language development over their primary years and its impact on learning. It basically showed that story was a key influence on educational success. Although it was written years ago, it makes an invigorating read and establishes the importance of narrative in terms of educational success. It was this book that made me realise that there was more to story than I had assumed.

Telling your first story

Figure 1. Story map for *The Little Red Hen*.

Early years teachers are familiar with the business of reading to children. Many have acquired the skill of reading upside down so that the children can see the images in a picture book. A 'Big Book' placed on an easel is essential for book-sharing sessions. Whether these sessions are with a class, group or informally snuggling up for a quick read with several children, much is being learned. Most importantly, our passion for books and the way in which we make the story experience magical will begin to develop a lifetime's passion for reading. Armed with our own love of story and a good book, little can go wrong.

A skilled teacher, through the simple act of reading to children, will be able to familiarise the children with many early aspects of reading – loving the story, imagining and discussing what happens, commenting, talking about favourite parts of a story or aspects that we don't care for. Raising questions, thinking about what happened, what might have happened, what will happen next – all of this is part of early appreciation and deepening understanding. When children who have not been read to at home arrive in school or a nursery and their main experience of reading has been phonics, books may make little sense to them. A child's rich experience of being read to, learning and telling stories and rhymes will all help the early development of becoming a reader.

Children will also pick up incidentally terms like 'cover', 'page', 'title', 'author' and begin to notice that words always stay the same, as well as start to understand the notion of a letter, a word, a sentence and that pictures can be explored. The reader moves from left to right, turning a page at a time. Punctuation may well be commented on and noticed, especially through reading with expression. As children are taught phonics and tricky words, they will begin to be able to increasingly join in with decoding. All of this is essential to teaching early reading.

However, on every project that I have run, the majority of early years teachers have never told a story without the support of a book. Some find this idea nerve-wracking and believe that they will not be able to accomplish it. Do not fear – I have yet to meet an early years teacher who could not become a classroom storyteller. It is worth remembering two things.

1. This is not about you being a storyteller – it is about getting the children to be storytellers.

2. Teachers already have all the skills of a storyteller – the ability to scan a group, use their eyes to draw a child in, vary their voice for effect; in fact, the only thing you may lack is knowing a story to tell.

Early nerves will stem from a lack of confidence. Once you get going, you will be adding another strategy to your repertoire as a teacher. Many teachers find they love storytelling and it becomes a daily part of the pleasurable task of working with children.

Preparation

I am going to imagine that you have never **told** a story before with the children joining in. The first thing to do is find a story that you will enjoy telling and you think the children will enjoy. Look at the story bank in Appendix 2 and select a story. I would suggest that you start with one of these stories because I have told them many times and I know that they will work. A simple one to cut your teeth on would be that tried-and-tested favourite, '*The Little Red Hen*'.

Look at the chapter 3 video clip *Learning the model text orally* to see me helping a conference of teachers learn how to help a class internalise this story.

5 VIDEO

Learning the model text orally – *The Little Red Hen*

The Little Red Hen

Once upon a time,
there was a little red hen
who lived on a farm.

Early one morning,
she woke up
and went outside.

There she found some corn.

'Who will help me plant the corn?' said the little red hen.

'Not I,' said the bull.
'Not I,' said the cat.
'Not I,' said the rat.
'Oh very well, I'll do it myself,' said the little red hen –
and so she did!

'Who will help me water the corn?' said the little red hen.

'Not I,' said the bull.
'Not I,' said the cat.
'Not I,' said the rat.
'Oh very well, I'll do it myself,' said the little red hen –
and so she did!

'Who will help me cut the corn?' said the little red hen.

'Not I,' said the bull.
'Not I,' said the cat.
'Not I,' said the rat.
'Oh very well, I'll do it myself,' said the little red hen –
and so she did!

'Who will help me carry the corn to the mill?' said the little red hen.

'Not I,' said the bull.
'Not I,' said the cat.
'Not I,' said the rat.
'Oh very well, I'll do it myself,' said the little red hen –
and so she did!

'Who will help me grind the corn?' said the little red hen.

'Not I,' said the bull.
'Not I,' said the cat.
'Not I,' said the rat.
'Oh very well, I'll do it myself,' said the little red hen –
and so she did!

'Who will help me knead the bread?' said the little red hen.

'Not I,' said the bull.
'Not I,' said the cat.
'Not I,' said the rat.
'Oh very well, I'll do it myself,' said the little red hen –
and so she did!

'Who will help me bake the bread?' said the little red hen.

'Not I,' said the bull.
'Not I,' said the cat.
'Not I,' said the rat.
'Oh very well, I'll do it myself,' said the little red hen –
and so she did!

'Who will help me eat the bread?, said the little red hen.

'I will,' said the bull.
'I will,' said the cat.
'I will,' said the rat.
'Oh no you won't,' said the little red hen, 'I'll eat it myself' –
and so she did!

Retelling © Pie Corbett 2010

Learning the story is based on visualising the tale so you can 'see' it in your mind, and 'rehearsing' so that you have gone over it enough times to feel confident – these things assist in 'memorising' the story. Most early stories are sufficiently patterned for you to be able to know a version word for word. Stories for older children may well be told in a slightly different way each time, especially as you grow in confidence.

It helps if you write the words out yourself. The simple act of writing will begin to put the words into your mind. Many teachers find this process helpful because they can also adapt the story in any way that they feel necessary. They might want to simplify a tale or to build in some new feature, such as adding in adjectives or extra descriptive sentences or setting the tale locally. Once you have decided on the text, draw a story map. Keep this simple and clear. DO NOT use an icon for every word, as this will make the map too complex and cluttered. You need just enough to remind you of what happens next. If you are going to use my map, then draw it for yourself. Again, the act of drawing the map will help to fix the pattern. If, when telling the story, you find a section where you keep stumbling, then just add in an extra drawing to help you – or even a word. When you have fixed the map, draw a big bold version on a piece of paper the size of a flipchart. This can be your 'best one'.

Now try and learn the words. Part of the skill here is to try and see the story in your head. DO NOT get rid of the map. Learn the story as you look at the map. Tackle it in sections. Begin with the first three lines:

Once upon a time, there was a little red hen who lived on a farm.
Early one morning she woke up and went outside.
There she found some corn.

Just keep saying these three sentences until you have them fixed. This is the hardest bit. The rest is easy, as the pattern is the same for each section.

'Who will help me plant the corn?' said the little red hen.
'Not I,' said the bull.
'Not I,' said the cat.
'Not I,' said the rat.
'Oh very well, I'll do it myself,' said the little red hen –
and so she did!

I chose a bull, cat and rat because they move down in size and because cat rhymes with rat and cats chase rats. Try building any mnemonic into stories that will help you.

When learning stories, make sure that you know the opening really well, as a shaky start can undermine confidence. With a story such as 'The Little Red Hen', the opening needs fixing, the middle section is repetitive and then be quite certain of the ending or the effect of the story may be lost.

Keep retelling until you can retell the story with confidence. You will discover over time that the better you know the story, the easier it is to teach. Ideally, when you are teaching the story, you will want to know it so well that it is on 'automatic'. This means that your attention will be focused not on trying to recall what happens next but on what the children are doing!

I find 'going over' the story just before sleep helps. This may sound bonkers but it actually does help as the mind continues working as you sleep. I lie in bed, close my eyes and retell the story in my head. What else helps to fix it – I take the dog for a walk and declaim it aloud. I have stood in front of hotel mirrors retelling tales. I retell in the car – until, in the end, it is mine.

Another tip is to record the story onto a CD or iPlayer, so that you can listen to the tale in the car or as you go jogging! When recording your voice, do this in sections. Say a sentence and then leave a similar space. Then record the next sentence and leave a similar space, and so on. In this way, you can listen to your voice saying the first sentence, and then in the space, repeat the line. I find that this method is essential for me when learning a more complex tale.

The other key aspect that you will need to think about will be the actions. If look on YouTube (https://www.youtube.com/watch?v=WOeSoTz22jg), you can see me performing this story with a small class of four- to five-year-olds in a country school. You can copy my actions or invent your own. Again, you DO NOT need an action for every word. Just use enough actions to support the basic meaning. Rehearse telling the story with the map and actions until you have it fixed. All you need now is a class to teach!

Without wishing to labour the point, it is important to keep the focus on 'telling the story' with expression. Don't clutter it up with a complicated map or too many actions. You may well find it easier to learn a story standing up so that you can use expression and pretend that you are telling it with the class.

The first telling

Settle the children onto the carpet. I like to get myself into a corner or at least into a space where there is a backdrop and not a window behind me. That way there will be no distractions. Pull the children in close and settle them down. Make sure every face can see yours. Explain that you are going to tell them a story. Look round the group, drawing everyone's attention with your eyes – and begin.

It can help to:

- pin your map up behind the children, if you feel nervous, so you can glance over their heads for a reminder if need be;

- ask an assistant or another adult to stand behind the children with the text to prompt if need be;

- have a mini map or the text beside you.

I usually explain that there are parts in the story they join in with and encourage that as I am telling the tale. As you are telling the story, do not rush. Use your eyes to scan the group. Look into the children's eyes for longer than you might usually do – they are not seeing you, as they will be 'seeing' the story. Trust the story to hold their attention. Savour the words. Give rhythm to the repeated elements. As they start to join in, signal for them to continue, perhaps saying, *'so she said … who will …'*. Do not worry if they just sit and listen, staring at you. This is good, as they are imagining the tale.

I find that often I lean slightly forwards when telling a story to younger children. We lean into the tale. I try not to move too much, as that can be distracting. In the same way, having glove puppets whirling around can also become a distraction. Usually, the simple triangle between teller, story and listener is all that is required.

Good retelling hangs around 'varying' your voice in relation to the meaning:

- **Vary the speed** – which sections need to be pacy and where should you slow down? Where would a dramatic pause be helpful?

- **Vary the volume** – are there any places where the words would benefit from being spoken loud – or soft – and where might a dramatic whisper help?

- **Vary expression** – use your voice to express the meaning.

- **Vary voices and sound effects** – young children can be held by a story where the characters have different voices and sound effects are used. Though be wary of too much larking around, as you can get lost with which voice goes with which character!

This first retelling is just for the pleasure of the story. You may feel that it would be worth retelling straight away. Or come back to it later.

Talking about the story

Most stories will benefit from immediate discussion. In *Tell Me* (Stroud: Thimble Press, 1993), Aidan Chambers suggests a simple way into talking about stories or rhymes. Ask the class what they enjoyed. Then move on to anything they didn't like. Did they notice any patterns? Was there anything we are not sure about? Our views, ideas and questions can be listed and discussed. Many schools use 'philosophy for children' and the children are used to raising questions that can then be discussed. Of course, some stories appear to have little to talk about, although even something as simple as *'The Little Red Hen'* has its puzzles. Why did she ask them if they wanted to eat the bread when she had no intention of giving them any? Or, did she only decide not to give them any when they didn't suggest that she should eat the bread? At its simplest level, why didn't she share? Why didn't they help? What happens if we behave like that? Should she forgive them? These questions might be developed through discussion or through hot seating the hen and the other animals! Keep such discussions light and easy. Children will also lob into the melting pot their own experiences. This is good because they are making hooks between their own lives and the life of the story.

Joining in

On the second retelling, ask the children to help you and join in. Once you have retold it, tell the children that you are going to draw a story map to help everyone remember what happens in the story. Retell the tale with the children helping you and draw a fresh map in front of the children. **This is crucial**. The children must see how to draw a story map. In fact, the more you start to use the process of mapping as a general way of recording the better. You can map any story – trips to the park, any class events, maths problems … the possibilities are endless. The map is an early and powerful form of writing/recording. It means that everyone can start recording ideas without the need for spelling. The more you model mapping, the more children will want to map ideas and stories themselves.

Keep retelling

Once you have told the story several times, you can relax because if you forget a bit, the children can help you out. I often tell children that because I am SO old, I'll need their help to remember the story. Don't confine the retelling to 'literacy' but retell it a number of times across each day. You could begin or end sessions with a song and a retelling. In this way, you might have retold the story a dozen times by the Wednesday and the children will be becoming increasingly confident.

This will be made even more powerful if you set up a story corner with a map or floor mat plus toys from the story. This means that the children can play at retelling the story. Make sure that this is modelled by an adult and that you intervene during such play to play at the story with the children. Another early activity is for everyone to draw their own map. This is essential, as it is the beginnings of early recording, learning that marks on the page can represent something that is fixed and it always says the same thing. There is no harm in providing laminated maps for children to use in play and the children should also be allowed to take these maps home.

Handing the story over

It is tempting to dominate the retelling. On the very first project, I observed a number of teachers leading the class in retelling and I noticed that they were booming the tale out loud and this seemed to rob the children of the chance to take on board the tale for themselves. Gradually withdraw from the retelling so that the children take on more and more, becoming increasingly independent and able to tell the tale on their own. Their focus should shift from looking at you to looking at the map so that they can retell the tale without you. I tend to say something like, 'If I stop saying, you keep going'. You can keep the actions going and mouth the tale. Maybe just use actions before getting to the stage where they can tell the story to you. Then they are ready to retell in groups before moving to pairs. Listen in to group and paired retellings. Have them perform. If they revert to 'and then', then you know that they need to return to whole-class retelling as the pattern is insufficiently internalised.

Deepening understanding

Of course, you can teach any child to retell a story or poem. Once you know how to do this, you will be surprised by the children's extraordinary ability to learn language in this way. They can learn far more than we ever imagined. However, that does not mean that they understand what they are saying. I remember inspecting a school in London and the reading was very impressive in Year 2 … until I asked a question. What the children were doing was actually very confident decoding but they didn't understand what they were reading.

In the same way, children can chant a story but that does not mean that they understand what they are saying – and they will not internalise the vocabulary and sentence patterns unless they understand. So, it is worth thinking through which words, phrases and parts of a story will need some extra support so they understand what they are saying. This may mean using puppets, objects, toys, images, film clips or 'acting out'. Dramatising the story is important because it allows children to experience and process the tale in a physical way. They move to what is happening and this helps them to internalise the patterns. Saying the word 'cat' is one thing. But seeing a photo of it and then getting down on all fours and prowling around meowing is far more powerful!

With a story such as 'The Little Red Hen', you may need to show them a toy or photo of the animals, the corn/wheat, grinding this into flour. Of course you'll want to make some bread! Use drama to stand around shaking your heads in role as the animals. Trudge wearily along with the sack on your backs. Hot seat the animals to find out what they were thinking … you are only limited by your own imagination and, of course, the children will have their own ideas as well.

Once they can retell the story happily as a class, then try story groups and eventually story partners. When they are really happy with retelling the tale, turn it into a Big Book for reading.

Innovating to make a new version

When the children know the story really well, make some simple changes to create a new version. Do this with the children. You could use Post-it notes or alter the class map by crossing out and redrawing. Just make a few simple changes such as the names of the creatures and this will give you a new version.

Then lead the children through thinking about the changes that they could make. At first, keep this very limited and simple so that everyone can succeed. They will need to draw new maps with their own ideas. You may need a bank of different animal cards at hand for them to choose from.

Retell the new class version and the children should retell their new version to their story partner. If they are able to write, then you can move through the writing by staging it. By this I mean do a new bit each day, so that the children's stories gradually grow bit by bit. This is helped if you produce simple booklets for their stories with a space on each page for an illustration. Provide spelling cards to help those who might struggle.

In any class, some children will just change their map and retell. Others will produce a booklet with drawings and labels. Others may write sentences. The key is that everyone will succeed, in their own way, by having created a new story.

Building your repertoire

The first story that you tell and get the children to join in with will be the greatest challenge. Do start with a simple one, as that will give both you and the children confidence. It can help to work towards an assembly presentation of your story, as this provides a drive and purpose. You'll have parents coming in to tell you that their child retold the story at home. Sometimes, you will find a very quiet child has done this.

Over the first year of storytelling, you will gradually add more stories to your repertoire. In this way, you will have added another teaching technique to your bag of tricks and it is something that will enrich the lives of the children you teach.

4 Imitation: Creating a bank of story ideas

(This chapter is supported by the Imitation overview – see page 12)

Participation in communal storytelling

Imitation involves children in learning and retelling stories, poems or non-fiction texts. At first, very young children will enjoy listening to the teacher telling a story and often join in with the repetitive, rhythmic and dramatic lines. These early **participation** stories tune the children into joining in with a well-loved tale. Children that have been read to at home will have already achieved this level of 'participation'. However, many children will need coaxing into the routine of sharing and joining in with a story whether it is being told or read aloud.

Those who have only ever watched the television have to learn a new form of concentration when being told a story. The teacher may be quite still when telling the story so that there are no moving images or colours to hold the child's attention, no sudden noises or different voices. No slapstick. The children have to acquire the habit of staring at the teacher and beginning to imagine for themselves what is happening.

Instantly, there may be problems because we cannot imagine what we do not know. For this reason, many teachers introduce vocabulary and concepts to children *before* the story is told. This is especially common where there are children who have English as a new language but nearly all children benefit from some form of 'tuning in' to vocabulary and events. This may be done before the story is initially told. Alternatively, the story can be supported by a limited number of props – toys, images and actions to support meaning.

Most teachers know a range of action stories and rhymes that involve some form of participation on the part of the children – this might involve chanting part of a rhyme or a repetitive section of a story, such as *'Who's that going trip trap over my bridge?'*. Many picture books for very young children include such opportunities for the child to increasingly 'join in' with the story. My own children were all introduced to reading through '*Where's Spot?*'. These sorts of books invite the child into taking part in the reading – by joining in with a repetitive or memorable phrase, by physically interacting with the book, but also through participating imaginatively during the reading.

Big books are especially useful when reading with children, as the pictures are sufficiently large for a whole group to see. Smaller groups can snuggle in with a picture book. This should be a regular activity during the day in any nursery or early years setting. Each area should be provided with favourite books that can be dipped into by adults or by the children themselves. The business of enjoying a well-loved, shared tale is an important part of early language development. Children learn to settle down, concentrate and gradually join in. Where possible, quiet areas should be provided where children enjoy a story away from the distraction of background noise.

VIDEO
6

What do babies and young children learn from being read to?

- Provide boxes of books.
- Make sure that all the children are read to daily, on as many occasions as possible.
- Limit the books to a few favourites that are repeated often and encourage the children to join in.
- Introduce new books now and again.

Through Talk for Writing, we have learned that staying with a story is crucial to language development. Constant repetition of a story helps to build vocabulary as well as lay down sentence patterns. Research carried out at the University of Sussex has demonstrated that repetition is a key element in acquiring new vocabulary. Repeating favourite stories had the strongest impact on language acquisition [Horst, J.S., Parsons, K.L. and Bryan, N.M. (2011) 'Get the story straight: contextual repetition promotes word learning from storybooks', *Frontiers in Psychology*, 2: 17].

Repetition is also needed to build the imaginative world and can be especially powerful if learning the story involves play, props, puppets, model-making, painting or mask-making, so that the children really engage with a story rather than see it as a passing acquaintance. Of course, constant imagining also develops abstract thought, so children become used to thinking about what is not in front of them. They become used to holding and following an idea and following. It is not surprising that children who have plenty of stories in their lives are often the ones who develop abstract thinking across the curriculum. They internalise language and develop concentration as well as the ability to imagine and follow lines of thought. These ideas were further explored by Gordon Wells in his research and can be found written about in an excellent book on the importance of story in achievement, entitled *The Meaning Makers* (Bristol: Multilingual Matters, 2009, second edition).

A careful selection of rhythmic early stories should gently encourage nursery and reception age children to join in with stories, developing this early phase of 'participation'. You will find that children naturally join in with the parts that are musical, memorable or repetitive. Experiment by 'singing' a line and you will find that they are more likely to join in with that section.

The aim is to move from **participation** to the children gradually joining in with the whole story so that they tell it alongside the teacher **communally**. This means that everyone says all of the words together. For this to happen, the telling of a story has to shift the children from passive listening to active participation. Once children are familiar with this routine, they will join in quite naturally without any encouragement from the teacher. At first, children may require encouragement to increasingly join in until they know every word. It is worth making this explicit by inviting them to say the words together. As children start to learn the story, the teacher should gradually withdraw from saying the words so that increasingly the children become more and more independent.

> • The first concern is to encourage children to begin participating in the story. This may be through them saying the words or joining in with the actions.

Parents who read to their children at home will be familiar with this stage. Around the age of two to three years, children alight on favourites that they want to hear again and again. Gradually, they internalise the story until they know it word for word. Beware any parent who tries to short-change their child by trimming the text! Children's ability to learn stories in this way stretches beyond anything that we could possibly imagine. The human capacity of almost every child for auditory learning is very impressive.

In the original teacher research project, the first story that we taught reception children in their first term as four-year-olds was '*Little Daisy*'. This they learned quite easily, so the following year I added more to the story and it became '*Little Jack*'. They learned that quite easily too, so the following year I added even more and the story became '*Little Charlie*'. They learned that one easily as well. I realised that it was adults who determined what was to be learned and too often we underestimate what small children can achieve.

To help the children remember the events, a story map is created and displayed. This uses simple drawings to depict the key events, with arrows showing the plot's movement from one scene to another. As the stories are told, the teacher uses actions to emphasise the meaning of the story as well as the key language features, such as story phrases (e.g. *'Once upon a time'*). Some children find it helpful to see props so that they know what the words mean, while others find using toys helpful so that they see the story happening as the words are spoken.

The combined use of maps, actions and repetition – the group or class saying the tale together – provides a supportive, multi-sensory approach that is highly successful and has been refined by many teachers. The stories need to be repeated, memorably and meaningfully, and these conditions help the children to internalise the story and add the language patterns to their linguistic repertoire.

- Use a simple story map to help children retell.
- Use a few actions to make the retelling interactive.
- Gradually withdraw from telling, so the children increasingly take on more and more of the story themselves.

Very often teachers ask, 'How long does it take?' Of course, this is impossible to answer. In a nursery, three-year-olds might well spend three or four weeks, if not longer, working with a story such as *'The Three Bears'*. On the other hand, *'The Little Red Hen'* might take five-year-olds a week to learn if the story is told several times a day. It is worth noting that the story has to be 'over-learned' so that the patterns become deeply embedded in the children's long-term memory. Storytelling is one of those things that can start the day, bookend breaks and lunchtimes, and be used to send everyone home feeling cheerful. In this way, a new tale can be retold perhaps six times a day so that by Wednesday, everyone is becoming pretty familiar and confident with the tale.

- To learn a story easily, keep retelling it a number of times everyday.

Choosing stories for retelling

When choosing which tale to use, it is worth remembering that stories are experiences. They can be frightening or touch upon a child's very real concerns. Teachers should be careful about the choice of tale and how they handle the children's discussions. This does not mean that the stories should be sanitised to the extent that they lose their bite. Many of the earliest stories that children learn are simple journey stories about a character going out into the world, often facing and overcoming danger, such as 'The Three Billy Goats Gruff', 'The Three Bears' and 'Little Red Riding Hood'. Developmentally, such tales are appropriate for this younger age group who are stepping out into the world beyond home. Traditional tales are essential and many picture books work well, such as 'Owl Babies'. However, some picture books may need rewriting, especially if, like 'Rosie's Walk', most of the story is in the pictures. Some picture books, such as 'Can't You Sleep Little Bear' lend themselves to retelling but perhaps in a slightly simpler version, rewritten by the teacher. Eventually, a comparison may be made with the full, written version.

Personally, I would suggest that teachers new to Talk for Writing start with a simple story. Select one of the traditional tales from the story bank on pages 216–245. These stories have been road-tested by many teachers and work well. Remember that the story you choose will be repeated many times, so it is best to select one that appeals to you as well as the children. Choose a simple story for your first one so that this gives you and the children confidence. The more stories that you work with, the more you and the class will grow in confidence. Indeed, the following year, you will be able to pitch in straight away with a more demanding story.

> • Start with simple journey stories that have plenty of repetition and rhythm.
> • Select from the story bank appendix on pages 216–245 or use a favourite picture book. You may need to rewrite the picture book.

As you become more experienced at working with stories, you will be able to think more about what sorts of stories the class needs. For instance, one teacher noticed that the boys were not engaging with literacy activities but were obsessed by the castle, knights and dragons when playing. She then took 'Little Charlie' and altered it to include knights, castles and dragons. It had the desired effect! Other teachers write their own stories and often use these to address issues in the class. One teacher was concerned with several children who were often not included in play activities by the others. She invented a story about a duckling that was left out by the other ducklings and how sad he felt. Some of the other farm animals were kind and the story's refrain was, 'Don't worry little duckling, you can join our game'. So, the idea is to select the right story for the group of children, bearing in mind that stories can be adapted in many ways.

A useful tip for teachers of younger children is to make good use of 'sound effects' to add to the story, for example 'the creaking' of a door.

Making animal noises is a simple but very popular way of holding children's attention and encouraging them to join in. It is worth thinking about the children, too, because anyone with English as a new language will begin by joining in with the actions and the noises as well. Many of these actions and sounds are universal, such as the *'meow'* of a cat. Some of these sounds can cunningly tie into basic phonics, such as *'shhhh'* when a character is being quiet or *'ssss'* for a snake.

> • Choose stories that will appeal to a particular class or group and make the tales fun by using sound effects for simple participation.

Use assessment to build in language patterns

Creating or shaping the chosen tale is easier if, before starting, you have assessed what the children already do. To carry out such an assessment, it is helpful to use a simple digital recorder. There are two basic questions: *'Can you tell me a story that you know?'* (imitation) and *'Can you make up a new story and tell it to me?'* (innovation or invention). This is best done within a few weeks of entry to your setting/school or class, once the children feel settled. Turn the recordings into transcripts and tuck them away, dated, as your initial assessment. This is an oral form of the cold task that gives you the baseline of what the children can achieve at the beginning of the year or the start of a unit. Repeat the process at the end of each term (the hot task) so that, by the end of the year, you have tracked their progress. This can be supplemented through other observations and sampling. It is very useful to teach children to use a dictaphone, so that they can make their own recordings and these may be housed in a special story folder for each child on a class computer.

Of course, some children may say more when not faced with a microphone – however, taking all the evidence to hand, you will be able to see what they can do when faced with the invitation to retell or make up a tale. In many settings, the children are silent or can only stammer a few words. Those who have been read to stand out as they fluently chatter away, retelling from the favourite stories that they have learned at home. Many children have no clue about stories; some explain that they have no books at home and have not been read any stories. A typical response came from one boy:

Teacher: *Can you tell me a story you know?*
Boy: *Um, this is the story of - they went to buy stuff. And that's the end - it's only that.*

7
VIDEO
Baseline
questions

8
VIDEO
Assessing
progress
using
baseline as a
yardstick

Teacher: *Can you make up a story for me?*
Boy: *A fishy story um, um. Ummmm, I don't know really.*

Within several weeks of starting Talk for Writing, most children are retelling a story. At the end of the year, one reception child was asked by the teacher to retell a story. There was a long silence and then he said, *'The trouble is – I know so many that I don't know which one to tell!'*

If we look at one child's transcripts across three months, the growth can be seen. This is typical of what you will find. It is almost as if the ability to tell stories is dormant and the teacher has awoken the child's potential.

Child A (3 years)
Teacher: *Can you tell me a story you know?*
Child A: *I don't even know any.*

Teacher: *Can you make up a story for me?*
Child A: *I don't know what to make up … a chicken … a chicken met a dinosaur and then the dinosaur was eating the chicken and then the duck met the chicken and the chicken ran away from the duck and also and then there came a rhinocerous and the rhino fighted and someone else came and there was a rhino and the rhinocerous had a fight and that's the end.*

Three months later:
Teacher: *Can you make up a new story for me?*
Child A: *Once upon a time there was a giant who lived in a castle with a princess. Then a wicked mother came and locked her in the tower and then a knight came and saved the princess. Then the wicked mother came and got angry with the knight. The prince got locked up in the cellar and the knight came and rescued him because the knight is very brave and they don't care about the wicked mother. Then came a monster. Then the monster locked (this is the funny bit) the wicked mother up instead of the princess. They have really gooey hands and if you get angry with them, they use their hands on you and they've got germs on and the taste very yucky. That's the end of the story.*

In the next example, the child's experience of stories is limited to film or video.

Teacher: *Can you tell me a story you know?*
Child: *Um, I know one called Cinderella. Cinderella's stepmother's wicked. She's horrible and I've got the video of it. I've got two videos of it. I have. Can't remember the story.*

Teacher: *Can you make up a story for me?*
Child: *Don't know any, don't know.*

The point about this transcript is that the film doesn't care if the child is listening or joining in. Anyway, films do not 'tell' stories – they show them happening, so the language needed to retell the story is not there. On one occasion, I was in a small village school and asked a little boy who was four if he could tell me a story. He launched in with –

Once upon a time there was Steven Gerrard. He went to a hotel ...

At that point, he grinned and the story ground to a halt. He was calling on what he knew but what he knew was not all that helpful. Beside him was a small girl. She launched in immediately and I kept having to slow her down as she made the story up so quickly. It began like this:

Once upon a time there was a girl named Masie. One day they were having a party in space with some aliens and a star fell down. The little girl named Masie found the star and it said to her, 'Help me get back into the night sky,' in its sweet little voice ...

The story progressed and I filled several pages in my notebook. Later on, I found the book that her story was loosely based upon, 'Laura's Star'. She too was drawing on what she knew. The difference was that what she knew was a whole story and that meant that she could create something new. She had a bank of story ideas and the language she needed to express her story.

- Near the beginning of the year and at key points during the year, make recordings and keep dated transcripts of children's storytelling asking, 'Can you tell me a story you know?' and 'Can you make up a new story and tell it to me?' These 'cold' and 'hot' tasks will help you track progress.
- Decide how often to make these assessments and then use them to decide which story and language patterns are needed for language development.

How do you know what language patterns to include? As I have already said, it is crucial to begin by writing out a good version of the story that you are going to teach. Now build in any relevant patterns that have arisen from your assessments and will fit the retelling without spoiling it. Remember that this should include adding extra detail, for instance by using adjectives or adverbs to tell the reader how characters feel or how something happens. Do not be afraid of using new language or building in exquisite turns of phrase. However, make sure that your early stories are not too long. Anything over 350 words that is not repetitive will be too long. Pitch the language about a 'level' above where the children are linguistically so that they are constantly hearing and speaking more mature language patterns.

Build into the stories language patterns that will help the children's development. Consider:
- **word choices** – use powerful language (*crept* not *went*)
- **special effects** – use alliteration and similes
- **sentence patterns** – use simple, compound and complex sentences
- (**connectives*** – see footnote on page 215); – use linking words to gain fluency within and between sentences
- **turns of phrase** – use typical story phrases such as '*in a distant land there lived ...*'.

Looking at the transcripts gives the teacher an idea of what needs to be built into the stories. This is not a precise science but, over time, you will begin to notice key aspects such as the use of detail or a lack of sentences or connectives to link ideas. Be aware of the need to revisit patterns, building the same structures into stories and revisiting them in other class activities where possible. The idea is to build a bank of patterns and ideas, constantly revisiting but also adding new patterns so that the learning is cumulative.

Initially, you may find that the transcripts suggest that children have very little idea of story patterns. Do not be downhearted: it probably means that they have yet to experience the sort of teaching that is needed. It DOES NOT mean that they will not be able to learn a story. Never underestimate the children's power for learning. My suggestion is that you should start with something simple that will capture the children's attention, maybe '*Mr Wiggle and Mr Waggle*'. That usually works well as a first story as it is lively, funny and uses actions and sound effects, which children love! You can see a film clip of me showing teachers how to tell this lovely story on Video clip 13.

Once you have been working on this for about six weeks or so, you will have noticed all sorts of things. Very quickly, you will hear the children re-using the story language in their play and everyday conversation, especially if you set up specific play areas that go with the

13
VIDEO

The importance of storytelling – *Mr Wiggle and Mr Waggle*

story. There was the famous occasion in Lewisham of the five-year-old boy who was new to the country. The class had been working on 'The Little Red Hen'. Something had gone wrong in the class and the teacher asked the boy if he was responsible. 'Not I,' he replied!

When you get to the third or fourth story, you will notice that the children have settled well to the routine – they now know how to listen and join in. Gradually, you build in more and more detail and language patterns so that the first story you start with at the beginning of the year is quite simple and the final one will be more challenging. In this way, you build in progression. For real evidence of learning language, keep listening in to the children's talk. Write down and share their invented stories. Which language features are reappearing? What have they added to their personal story repertoire?

- Listen into children's play and notice those patterns that have been internalised and are being reused.
- Use this information to plan what needs revisiting and what to build into the next story.

Building in the story and language patterns

There are two aspects to consider here:

1. **Small language patterns** – building vocabulary, story language and sentences.

2. **Big story patterns** – building a bank of story ideas, e.g. characters, settings, dilemmas.

To help children's language development, select story language features and patterns that will add to their linguistic repertoire. For instance, not much can happen without, 'Once upon a time'. As you build up the bank of stories, revisit and repeat the key language patterns so that the children experience the words in a range of contexts. Gradually, add in more detail and increase the language bank so that the stories have built into them key sentence patterns and narrative language features that are repeated from tale to tale without spoiling the story. Do remember that you are dealing with a story and it has its own integrity as an imaginative experience. We have come across teachers working with stories packed with so many connectives that the story has lost its power!

This focus and repetition helps the children to begin to internalise the language patterns that can then be drawn upon when children wish to make a story of their own. So, a story might begin with, **'Once upon a time, there was a Little Red Hen who lived on a farm.'**

This is a very handy pattern because it introduces us straight away, without any fuss, to the main character, where they live or the story is set. Such a handy sentence pattern may then reappear in several stories, for example, **'Once upon a time, there was a little old lady who baked a gingerbread man.'** Eventually, the underlying syntactical pattern becomes part of the child's linguistic repertoire and may then be drawn upon, re-emerging to create new story starts, such as: **'Once upon a time, there was a little boy called Gary who lived in Bristol'**.

However, the ability to internalise language patterns and then reuse them, often known as 'generative grammar', only functions when the child understands what the vocabulary and sentence means. Therefore, exploring and processing a story in many different ways is crucial to build understanding and aid language development. Language will only flourish in a meaningful context. This is why the stories have to be accompanied by play, painting, model-making, drama, and so on. Otherwise, the story – or song – might just as well be sounds coming out of our mouths.

Teachers build into the stories that the children learn common story phrasing, so that the children gradually build up a bank of patterns that will help them retell a tale. Openings are traditionally formed and therefore can be often recycled, for example:

> **In a distant land,**
> **Many years ago,**
> **Once upon a time**
> **In a land far, far away,**
> **Once, when the world was young, there lived ...**
> **Long, long ago,**
> **A long time ago,**
> **This is the story of**
> **There once lived**
> **Once, not twice, but once upon a time,**

Of course, everything will eventually end **'happily ever after'** and the threat **'was never, ever seen again'**. The final words of the tale often break a common rule in that a sentence is used that starts with **'and'**: **'And so they made their way home.'** The use of 'and' to start a sentence is a signal to the listener that the end of the tale has been reached and the story is to be wrapped up:

> **And so it was that they lived happily ever after.**
> **And they made their way home**
> **And that is the end of my story.**

But that is another story for another day.
The next day they had a great feast/I wish you had been there!

There are even little chants that children enjoy saying at the end of a tale:

Four-leaf clover/my story is over.
Snip snap snout/my story is out.
Step on a nail, the nail bends and that is how my story ends.
The bridge was mended – and the story ended.
My story is done/run rabbit run.
If you don't believe me/then go see for yourself.
Bee bow bendit/my story has ended.
That was fun/the story is done.

Make sure that your stories are not devoid of new and vibrant language. Children love to learn new words and should be developing their vocabulary at a great rate in the first few years of schooling. Do not patronise them with dull and pedestrian language. Give them powerful stuff! For instance, it is much more fun to have a weary farmer **trudging** rather than **walking** along. Choose verbs with care, as they can suggest so much about a character.

Use adverbs to explain how someone felt or acted – **slowly, quickly, bravely, calmly, sadly** … Build description by using well-chosen adjectives for description, for example, **'The ogre's hands were knobbly and covered in red warts.'** A touch of alliteration can also be fun to use and a good teacher will be aware of encouraging such simple language play, for example **'The snake slithered silently and slowly'**. Finally, little children should also have stories that include both sorts of similes – 'like' and 'as'. Make these up with the children or use traditional similes, for example **'He was as tall as a house and had hands like plates with fingers like bananas'**.

Surprisingly perhaps, prepositions are important. For instance, story sentences may start with prepositions to show the reader or listener where something is found, for example:

Across the road was a house …
Under the table, he saw …
On the ceiling was …
On the other side of the valley …
In the distance …
Far below …
To one side …

- Build in common openings and endings.
- Use well-chosen verbs and adverbs as well as adjectives to build descriptions.
- Use alliteration and similes as well as prepositions.
- Do not dumb down the language.

There is one other language pattern that is crucial. When telling a story, you will inevitably need to use connectives. Connectives are linking words that allow us to link words and parts of sentences, as well as making links between sentences. They are crucial to language development, as they help children link ideas together so that they can talk or write in a more extended manner – arguing, reasoning, justifying, organising, explaining, narrating and recounting. Connectives help us think and communicate (for a separate account about connectives, see Appendix 1 on pages 198–215).

In the English language, the first connective to appear is 'and'. At this stage, somewhere around the age of three, there is an explosion in the amount that children say as soon as they discover how the word 'and' is used to say more and more and more and even more by chaining events and statements together!

For storytelling, we will need time/temporal connectives, including **first, next, later on, after that, finally**. These help to organise a story by sequencing the events in order of what happened. We may also need causal connectives to explain things, such as **because, to** and **so.** Children will need more than 'and' to make links in sentences and should soon acquire **and, and then, so, as, but, after, before.** In their fourth and fifth years, they should also be using **what, when, where, while, who, that, which** and **why,** even if these are not used in a standard form. Ideally, a setting or school would choose a set of core connectives that are used in stories that children learn, to help change stories and invent new ones. These words and phrases become a child's story architecture that provides the structural building blocks needed to create a rounded, whole tale.

If you think about the basic 'story mountain' pattern, you will see how different connectives, including adverbs, may be used to structure a simple story:

Phrases that connect

Story structure	Language	Reason
Opening	*Once upon a time … who …*	Introduce a character in a setting, e.g. *Once upon a time, there was a girl who lived in a forest.* Or introduce an emotion or problem, e.g. *Once upon a time, there was a girl who felt lonely/became lost, etc.*
Build up	*One morning/day/afternoon/ evening/night.* Vary this by using *early/late* and then add in the weather, e.g. *One frosty/sunny/ rainy morning …* Various events happen: *so … first … next … when … while … as soon as … later on … after that …*	The story gets going – the character does something, e.g. *One night, she went for a walk …*
Dilemma	*Unluckily … unfortunately … suddenly …*	A dilemma is introduced – something goes wrong
Resolution	*Luckily … fortunately … so …* Various events happen: *first … next … when … while … as soon as … later on … after that …*	The problem is resolved
Ending	*Finally … eventually … in the end … at long last … happily ever after …*	The story ends – usually with everyone living happily ever after, making their way home, with good fortune!

It is worth having the connectives and other story language up on display. This is really there to remind the adults to use the language in a range of contexts. To learn language, children need to hear the words repeated in a range of different contexts **at least** six times. So, the more that the teacher repeats the vocabulary, the more likely the children are to pick up on it and add it to their repertoire. Display the connectives with the relevant actions and the words written underneath, as illustrated on the next page by Outwood's Edge Primary School, Loughborough, and Montgomery Primary Academy, Birmingham. (Also see page 72 and Appendix 1 on pages 203–205, 212–215 for a range of connective games.)

In the early years, teachers should be modelling spoken language and using sentences constantly. It is worth remembering that not every child comes from a home where adults speak in fluent sentences. In terms of becoming an articulate speaker and fluent writer, one of the biggest challenges is to acquire sentence patterns. These have to be modelled by the adults working with the children. When we are speaking

Figure 2. Display of connectives with actions and words by Outwood's Edge Primary School, Loughborough (Part 1) and Montgomery Primary Academy, Birmingham (Part 2).

with children in an educational setting, it is not a matter of using any old 'chit chat'. It is important to encourage children to increasingly respond in sentences. This will require modelling and asking children to join in: 'Let's say that together.' For instance, in the film you will see Matt Custance asking the children if they have a pencil and a child responds, 'Yes.' He then gets them all to chant, 'Yes I have.' Interestingly, you can see on their faces how much they love the simple routine, which is rather like a little song that they might sing before they start writing.

- Model key sentences in everyday learning and repeat them with the children.
- Make sure to model using more conjunctions than **and: and, then, and then, but, so, or, until, because, as, when, what, that, which, where, where, while, who** …

When telling or reading to children, draw their attention to well-turned phrases and effective use of language. Repeat these with children joining in and 'bank them' for future use. Many early years teachers use a magpie board to encourage children to use such phrases. One of the most handy early patterns is to use a 'run' (the technical term for a repeated phrase), for example **'walked and he walked and he walked …'**. A run adds rhythm but also gives the teller a space in which to think about what happens next. So, **'She ran and she ran and she ran'** or **'She slept and she slept and**

28
VIDEO

Guided writing: the importance of teaching basic writing skills systematically

she slept' adds rhythmic flow and comes as a relief because the teller 'knows that bit'.

Structure	Connectives	Purpose
Opening	*Once upon a time, there was a ____ who lived ____*	Introduce a main character in a setting
Build up	*One day/morning/night + first, next, later on, so, but, or, until*	The main character is doing something
Dilemma	*Unfortunately*	A problem occurs
Resolution	*Luckily + first, next, later on, so, but, or, until*	It gets sorted out
Ending	*Finally + happily ever after*	The story draws to a conclusion

If a teacher in Year 1 was taking on Talk for Writing, the same patterns would be repeated but a few more connectives would be added in to broaden the options, for example, **because, as, as soon as, when, while, which, that, where**.

> - Identify a bank of about twelve connectives and display these with photos of the children doing actions for each connective. Make sure these are sensibly built into the stories and used in everyday class activities as well. Suggested actions for the key connectives can be downloaded from www.talk4writing.co.uk/resources.
> - Make sure you pay attention to developing children's use of the **small language patterns** – words, phrases and sentences.

The main pattern you will see is the basic story mountain pattern (opening – build up – dilemma – resolution – ending). This is reflected in the progression of children's own invented stories. There is a simple story progression that works in this way:

- Usually, children grab hold of openings that introduce a character, often in a setting.

- The next stage is that an incident or a series of incidents occur, although not always related.

- Gradually, these may become linked so that one thing leads to another.

- A key moment is when a dilemma is added in – often heralded by your chosen 'dilemma word', such as **unfortunately, suddenly, at that moment ...**

- A harder part of the process is to then resolve the problem. A word such as **so** or **luckily** can be helpful.

- The final and most difficult aspect is to round a story off, showing what has been learned. An early start to this is to use **'happily ever after'**.

Do not worry if the children's early storytelling is rambling or fragmentary. You can only start from where they are. Over time, it will mature and develop, especially if you have a strong programme of Talk for Writing accompanied by daily sharing of books. Of course, to help a child develop storytelling or any aspect of talk, you have to be a good listener, otherwise why would a child bother?

The bigger pattern for story involves both the overall structure of narrative plus the building blocks such as having a bank of possible characters to draw upon. Of course, teachers will be aware of the power of three. There are three brothers, the youngest always being down-trodden but eventually winning through where the older ones fail. There will be three mountains to cross, three rivers to bridge and three trials to test a heroine. In the same way, early stories may well be cumulative. So in '*The Enormous Turnip*', one person pulls another, while in '*The Gingerbread Man*', everyone joins the queue to chase the naughty man down the lane.

Here are the most common story patterns. The more these are repeated and made obvious, the more the children will internalise a few basic patterns that will help their own story inventions:

- **Cumulative** – these build up bit by bit, e.g. **'There was an old woman who swallowed a fly.'** These work well for little children, as they are based around a repetitive pattern.

- **Problem/resolution** – these stories start okay and then something goes wrong that needs sorting out. These are very good for young children, as they hinge around one single problem.

- **Warnings** – these begin with a character being warned NOT to do something or go somewhere; of course, the character disobeys and then everything goes wrong! '*Little Red Riding Hood*' was warned not to stray from the path: she did, though, and look what happened!

- **Journeys** – most stories for small children involve journeying from one place to another and often back home again. This provides a simple structure. All you then need is something going wrong on the way.

- **Wishing** – these hinge around someone doing something good and being granted a wish or two or even three. However, the wish is wasted or someone becomes greedy and misuses the wish.

- **Lost and found** – something precious is lost and then found again.

- **Beating a monster** – many early tales involve a character having to face a monster of some sort, and usually winning through cunning or being helped by someone to whom the main character was kind.

- **Character change** – these stories usually begin with a character down on their luck before good fortune helps them out, e.g. '*Cinderella*'.

- Begin to build up a few common big story patterns.
- Make these obvious and re-use them so that children begin to become familiar with such patterns and can use them to make up their own stories.
- At first, stick to journey and cumulative tales.

Common characters should be collected for further use. There will be a bunch of 'good' characters such as princesses, princes, kings and queens (who may also be thoroughly bad) as well as Jack and Mary. Kind animals should be listed as well as characters that behave badly – giants, trolls, wolves, snakes, goblins and foxes all tend to get bad press in stories. As well as good and bad characters, some are tricky and clever – especially spiders, cunning foxes and Jack is pretty clever as well!

Poster A

Character bank

king, queen, princess, prince, farmer, mother, father, grandfather, grandmother, beggar, wise old woman, brothers, sisters, servants, hero, heroine, giant, ogre, woodcutter, thief, gnome, dwarf, dragon, unicorn, eagle, fox, wolf, snake, lion, tiger, ants, bees, spider, cat, dog, hare, rabbit

It is also worth being aware of the power of giving a character a 'feeling' or attribute. A simple bank of these can be handy, as they begin to give depth to a character and will also determine how they behave:

Feelings bank

Poster A

angry, happy, sad, lonely, kind, generous, jealous, cruel, mean, stupid, clever, brave, bold, lazy, lying, selfish, helpful, sad, friendly, boastful, greedy

It is also handy to have a settings bank to hand that includes forests, lakes, rivers, bridges, towers, marketplaces, fireplaces (where there are cinders to sleep upon), castles, roads to travel down, and so on.

Settings bank

Poster A

mountains, lakes, ponds, ocean, sea, river, stream, swamp, hills, valley, forest, woods, hedge, fence, tower, cottage, castle, market, farm, kitchen, doors, corridors, windows, gates, bridges, cave, path, road, alley

Another repeated feature consists of various special objects – magic lamps, spinning wheels, needles, a comb (that will become a hedge of thorns), a mirror (that will turn into an impassable lake), magical fruit, a tree, a ring of invisibility, a cloak, etc. Of course, if you can bring the object into the classroom, then that will make the whole story much more interesting and is guaranteed to capture the children's imagination. Special objects are often magical.

Magical objects bank

Poster A

ring, shoe, crown, cloak, gown, cup, ball, spinning wheel, needle, lamp, lantern, beans or seeds, whistle, stones, apple, peach, candle, sack, bag, purse, flute, pipe, carpet, box, cage

One problem for young storytellers and storymakers is to think of a problem – a dilemma – for their main character. Again, there is a small bank of possibilities worth knowing about.

Poster A

Story dilemmas bank

- A character is warned not to do something but does it
- A character has a flaw, e.g. is greedy, silly, hungry, jealous
- A dream comes true
- A character is chased
- A character gets lost
- The way is blocked
- A wish comes true
- Someone is sent on a journey
- A monster or threat appears
- A character is turned into something else
- Something precious is lost or stolen
- A name is forgotten
- A wish goes wrong
- You want something but are stopped from getting it
- Someone is trapped
- The main character really wants something and sets off to get it

- Collect problems from oral stories as well as picture books and everyday life.
- Keep an ongoing bank of characters, settings, animals, objects and dilemmas. These will be useful when inventing and innovating on stories. They are the children's bank of possibilities.

Imitation: Helping the children become storytellers

(This chapter is supported by the Imitation overview – see page 12)

Capturing interest with a creative hook

Before learning the story itself, many teachers introduce the tale with some sort of creative 'hook'. The hook is a way of engaging the children, introducing the story as well as maintaining interest over time. To give you a flavour of what we mean by a hook, here are a few ideas for hooking the children in and introducing a story:

- The adults learn and act the story out for the children – in full costume.

- Objects from the story are found.

- Use a 'story box' from which each day a new 'clue' from the story appears.

- Footprints appear in the classroom.

- A character from the story appears in costume and talks about what has been going on.

Acting the story out from start to end can be very helpful for some children, as it places the whole text in their imagination.

- Before learning the story orally, use a creative hook to introduce the children to the tale. This should at least involve a dramatic retelling of the text.

11 VIDEO

Captain Kim

10 VIDEO

Getting to know the story really well

Starting a story session

Most early years settings have a fixed routine for story and rhyme time. Of course, this should be supplemented informally at other times in the day – during play, just before lunch, last thing before the children go home. The stories and rhymes are there **to be learned** and they are there **for our pleasure**. Many teachers have a drawstring bag, into which for each story they pop a fluffy toy. This can then be used in 'choosing time'. A child picks out a toy and then the class retells the respective story or rhyme. In this way, the bank of stories and rhymes is kept alive by constant revisiting.

Story sessions might begin by singing a rhyme or using a musical instrument to tune children into 'listening'. I saw the storyteller Ben Haggarty use a Tibetan bell that he rang. We all strained to hear the moment when the bell's echo ended. Once we were silent and listening hard – he began, softly, to tell a story. I have used a rain stick and asked the children to listen for the final rain seed to fall. Simple drumbeats can be used or clapping hands with the children repeating the pattern. Of course, some stories have obvious rhymes that go with them: **'When Goldilocks came to the house of three bears'** makes an obvious accompaniment to a retelling of *'The Three Bears'*.

Some classes have a 'story carpet' that is unrolled rather like a flying carpet to whisk the class away to storyland. Others have story music that is always played and children come from all corners of the class, settle down and quieten, ready for the story. These sorts of routines are important, as they provide a comforting routine that signals a shift in activity. The message needs to be, **'Settle down, listen – a story is about to begin.'** Storytellers often use a simple chant to begin a story session. Like a signal to settle, a session may start:

Shhhh – listen!
Shhhh – listen!
A story comes.
A story goes.
Shhhh – listen!
Shhhh – listen!

It is important to think about the size of the group for storytime. Four- and five-year-olds should be able to sit as a class. However, in a nursery or other pre-school settings, thought will need to be given to the make-up and size of the group, especially if the story is to be acted out. A cast of thirty might lead to problems when chasing bears!

It is worth having a special place where storytime occurs. This could be in a corner or some quiet area. A special mat may be provided. One teacher I remember visiting had a very fetching lampshade in the shape of a star; another used a crescent moon shade (both, I think, from Ikea). They had created special areas using drapes so that their sessions felt special. Many teachers talk about the need to spend some time settling the children. Every child needs to be able to see the teacher. They should not be too close together but it is helpful if you can pull them in close so that an atmosphere can be created and you can use the story to 'hold' the children's attention.

Here are several pieces of advice from early years practitioners in Banbury:

- *'Make sure you smile at the children – as this will hold attention.'*

- *'Familiarise yourself with the story so that you can retell it with confidence, as this will make it easier to teach. If you are struggling to remember the words, then you may lose the thread and their attention may wander. Time spent retelling pays off.'*

- *'Trust in the power of the story – it will hold their attention.'*

- *'Retell your story with expression, as this helps to hold attention, engage the imagination and makes the language more memorable. Vary the speed, volume and expression, including dramatic pauses. The children's retelling will reflect your telling.'*

- *'As a group, tell the story together and act it out. Set up props in a special area for acting out.'*

- *'Retell and act a story out inside and don't forget to take the story outside as well.'*

- *'Use "call and response" to help children learn. You say a line and they repeat it.'*

A communal story involves the children increasingly joining in until they have learned the whole story. There is a small bank of ideal stories that have a strong repetitive pattern that make a good starting point. 'The Enormous Turnip', 'The Gingerbread Man', 'The Three Billy Goats Gruff' and 'Chicken Licken' are all sufficiently repetitive and memorable to help you make a confident start (see the Story Bank in Appendix 2 for versions of these stories).

Remember, this is not a memory test, nor is it to be confused with 'learning by rote'. If anything, it is learning by heart – knowing a story so well that its pattern is embedded forever. This approach mimics a stage that all children who are read to at home, or who have stories told to them, pass through. At an early age, maybe two to three years, children alight upon a story and demand it relentlessly – often driving their poor parent to distraction! And they learn it word for word – getting cross if the adult tries to miss any parts out! This universal stage seems to suggest that acquiring narrative patterns is an essential aspect of human growth.

Learning a story communally is somewhat similar to small children learning *'The Farmer's in his Den'* or an adult singing a popular song. There are a few key conditions that need to be fulfilled, as the embedding of a story in a meaningful manner involves multi-sensory teaching:

- Plan plenty of retelling – so the children hear and say the story (auditory learning).

- Use actions to support retelling (kinaesthetic learning).

- Use a story map (visual learning).

- Make the story memorable, meaningful (ensuring children understand the story).

- Establish a simple, familiar routine for storytelling.

Shan Holland with her nursery class at Whitley Park Primary, Reading

Handing the story over

As the children increasingly join in with a story, the teacher gradually withdraws until the children can tell the story on their own. My own method is to keep telling the story with the children but start 'mouthing' silently the words. Then I just retell with actions until, in the end, they can do it alone. If the pace slows or they miss a beat, then just leap back in.

You will notice that some children do not join in at all. Try sitting them up front beside you or sit them next to another adult. Some of these children are waiting until they feel comfortable with joining in. You may notice that after a while their hands start to move and gradually, with some encouragement, they join in. Others may need to follow up the class session in a small group or on a one-to-one basis. Some children find it hard to look at the map and at the teacher at the same time.

Some children may need to work with the story in a more concrete way. It can help to have a small box, such as a hat box, and pop in toys that go with the story. A 'story floor mat' that has the key story pathway sewn or Velcroed on may then be used. Some children just need to hold the toys to help them retell. It is worth watching carefully

and thinking about what helps this child retell a story. In the picture above, reception children at Nether Edge Primary, Sheffield are using a puppet theatre to re-enact '*The Three Billy Goats Gruff*'.

The children begin by listening to the story and gradually are encouraged to join in until they can communally say the whole tale. As this is happening, the teacher gradually withdraws from dominating the storytelling until the class can say it on their own. It is important to remember it is a 'handing-over process'. This is the transition from dependence towards independence, through which the children increasingly internalise the vocabulary and language patterns that the teacher specifically set out to teach.

Stories may then be told in circles together or passed round the circle. Only remove the supportive scaffolding of the teacher's presence when the story is in the children's long-term working memory. The idea is to embed the story as a living image in their minds, not by rote learning of words (which would soon fade).

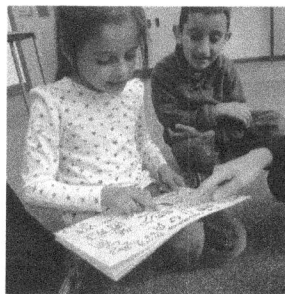

Finally, children sit in pairs facing each other to retell the story like a mirror or by taking turns in a supportive manner. They should use their maps to help them, as it is not a memory test. Telling from the maps is an early form of reading. As Megan, aged four said, '*I'll go and get a story map. I can't read properly but I can only read those two (pointing at two maps).*' In the picture above, a reception child from Nether Edge Primary in Sheffield is 'reading' the story on her own using a story map to help her tell the tale.

13 VIDEO

The importance of storytelling – *Mr Wiggle and Mr Waggle*

15
VIDEO
Internalising
the text

Remember – the stories have to be 'over-learned' in order for the children's linguistic competency to be developed. It is unwise to move on until the children have the pattern in their long-term working memories so that the story can be accessed automatically, and the children will then be able to innovate and play with the ideas and patterns.

Once the class is happy with retelling the story together, move on to group retellings. Think carefully about the makeup of the groups so that you mix the more confident and the less confident in a supportive manner. These groups may need their own story map. They stand in a horseshoe shape facing the map and retell. Again, an adult can work with the group but the aim is for the group to become increasingly independent in telling. Groups can then perform for each other or children in other classes.

As the children become more confident and independent in retelling as a group, you may then wish to move to children retelling in pairs. To do this, they sit down facing each other with their own maps in front of them. It is key that they face each other so that they gain a sense of audience and get used to looking in each other's eyes. You will need to model this with another adult or a child. They can retell standing, sitting on chairs or seated on the carpet. First of all, work on children being able to retell in a pair confidently, facing each other like mirrors. Then you can develop this work. Try retelling:

- as a pair, saying the story at the same time;

- word by word, bouncing it back and forth;

- chunk by chunk (sentence by sentence);

- silently, miming the story;

- using 'babble gabble', where the children try to race through as fast as possible;

- in pairs, like a mirror;

- passing it round the circle, perhaps handing on a story microphone, conch or stone (remember that anyone can choose to pass it on without speaking if they go blank!);

- forming two lines that face each other and playing story tennis – word for word, back and forth;

- in a line, passing it up and down.

Work with the children to develop retelling with expression. Vary the pace, volume and expression. Say sentences aloud or softly and get them to copy you. Model saying sentences in different ways and ask the children to choose which would fit the story best. Should it be spoken loud, soft, in a whisper, fast, slow or with expression? Work with the class map and discuss which bits need to be spoken in which ways. All of this helps to reinforce the meaning of the story and will also reveal the punctuation! In many schools, children are constantly encouraged to speak up with a 'clear voice'. Make something of this, as it helps shyer children – it's a bit like acting.

In the end, you will get to a stage where individuals or pairs come to the front to retell the story to everyone. Make this special by using a story cloak, story hat or story chair. Those on the carpet can help the chosen teller by whispering the story as it is spoken aloud. Of course, class stories should really be taken to an assembly to share with everyone.

Talk for Writing schools have the advantage that everyone is engaged in the same endeavour. This means that skills are gradually and cumulatively revisited and developed, which ultimately leads to faster progress and higher standards.

Of course, it helps if the children hear the language structures being used by their teacher and other adults in different contexts. Imagine a teacher revisiting language structures from the story wherever they may fit: '*First, I want you all over here. Next, we will have our milk break. After that, you can choose.*' Our proposition is that children's language growth will be even more powerful if they experience key language structures repetitively in school – and ideally also at home (see Chapter 10).

While we are interested in children's language development, none of this will be obvious to the children. They will be happily joining in with stories, adapting different tales and creating their own as a natural part of their school and home life. Like much early learning, it happens without the child realising that it is occurring.

Some classes use digital cameras and recorders to help the children capture their stories, providing an easy way for listening back to what has been said and improving. Films can be played to other classes or used in assembly. Some schools play films of children retelling stories in the foyer. Once stories are well known, then children retell individually to other children, possibly in other classes. In this way, the scaffolding is gradually removed from class, to group to pairs to individuals retelling tales.

- Retell the story as a class and gradually withdraw until they can tell it pretty much on their own.
- Then move to groups and eventually pairs.

14
VIDEO

Children in Neath, Port Talbot, presenting stories

How to make story maps effective

It is advisable to have practised the map at home – trying to make one up on the spur of the moment will not work. You do not need an icon for every word – just enough to jog the memory. It is better to have a sparse map as you can always add in an extra icon if the class find learning a section difficult.

The teacher should draw a clear, bold story map that uses arrows or dotted lines to show the sequence of events rather like a pathway through the tale. With young children, the map should consist of drawings. Older pupils may add extra words that need reinforcement.

Draw the map in front of the class after the first telling with the children making suggestions. A typical story map from the nursery class at St. George's, Battersea, is shown above, in this case for 'The Three Little Pigs'. The reason for drawing the map in front of the children is so that they see how it is done – then they can begin drawing their own maps. Large maps can be stored away and hung in front of the children as needed. The children should initially copy the map before later attempting to draw their own. It is worth noting that what may look like a few random squiggles to an adult may be perfectly 'readable' to a child as their map.

Another key point is to use your own drawing skills – NOT clip art or images cut from magazines, and keep your drawings as simple as possible so the children feel they can do it too. It is the processing and reproducing that really helps the child to internalise the story and this will be weakened if you use images drawn by others.

The children should then draw their own maps. This is important because it helps them retell and process the story, turning the words into images. This process helps anyone recall the story more easily. Once children know how to map, the technique can be used for capturing almost anything – maths problems, history, religious stories, a trip to the shops, science experiments and concepts, instructions, ideas – anything can be mapped.

As I have mentioned, it is crucial that storytelling does not become a 'memory test'. Therefore, the children should use their own maps, and some may also find it helpful to have small models or toys to move around as they retell a tale. Teachers should avoid 'correcting' children in case an element of 'fear' about 'getting it right' creeps in.

Often, story maps are drawn onto large sheets of card or on rolls of tough lining paper so the story moves from left to right. Some useful ways of making sessions visual include:

- a map;

- arrows on the map to show the story's direction;

- wallpaper maps or large sheets of card, sugar paper or flipchart paper;

- only having icons for key events;

- keeping the map simple, bold and clear;

- using a map to support retelling – not to make it more complex;

- drawing the map – do not use clip art or photos, as the hand/brain connection is key and it also may undermine children's confidence in their own mark-making;

- using a washing line or coat hangers to hang up maps;

- using colour to make different words or sections of a story stand out;

- repeating common phrases or words, e.g. always use a pair of open hands to represent '*Once upon a time,*'.

When drawing the map, it may need to be done over several sessions or even days if the children become restless. So children understand some of the ideas or animals or objects or events in a story, use images and photos, toys, masks, mime, real objects and props. It is always worth thinking about your story and what might need explaining or further support so the children understand the vocabulary.

Some children need extra support and teachers may use pictures, photos or objects to show what words mean. While these can become cumbersome and clutter up a story, they may be essential for helping understanding of vocabulary, especially where children have English as a new language or have limited experience.

Create large wall maps using the children's own paintings and drawings. Older children can also write captions and labels for different sections of a story, identifying key events. Some teachers also produce a clean, small version of the class map. These can be laminated and will

17 VIDEO
Using a roll of wallpaper as a text map

18 VIDEO
Reception teacher Katie Hanson explaining the impact of the approach on children learning English as an additional language

be sturdy enough for constant use; the one pictured on page 70 above, from St. George's in Battersea, are available A4 size for the children to use and stored in big folders in the classroom. These could be taken home by the children to share with their parents. If they are laminated, they may also be used for simple innovations.

Playground maps bring storytelling into playtime. These are large maps painted onto the playground. There are paths across the maps as well as a cottage, a castle, a tower, bridges, swamps, forests – and these can be used for children to retell stories or invent new ones.

Very young children in nursery and reception classes also benefit from using three-dimensional maps. Such maps can be created easily using sheets or cloth on the floor together with toys. This is important, as some children need the concrete experience of holding the toys and moving them along the map as they tell the story. The whole mapping process – including the use of models, toys, puppets and images – is intended to build visual memory so the children do not just hear the story but also 'see' the story.

- Draw a big class story map.
- Children should draw their own maps.
- Provide durable mini versions of the class map. Use floor maps to make them three-dimensional.

How to make the actions effective

The stories are told with accompanying actions. These fall into two categories. The first are actions that 'show' an event, such as 'running down a road'. These actions can be invented by the children, which has the added bonus of helping them gain a sense of ownership over the process. The other type of action relates to supporting the language patterns that you want the children to learn. In the main, these will be the transferable patterns that can be used again and again. These key connectives are spoken clearly with a simple accompanying action. For instance, for 'once upon a time' you open your hands like a book opening. These actions have to be consistent from class to class to avoid confusion. Not every connective will have an action but schools may identify key language features they wish to emphasise in relation to children's language development (see page 57 for how to use pictures to support the actions for the key connectives).

The acquisition of such language features should be built gradually into the stories so that they are repeated and cumulatively acquired. Emphasise the connectives as you say them so that they are more likely to stick in the child's memory. Teachers have noticed that children rapidly learn a range of connectives and begin to use these in other contexts. This is further supported if teachers and assistants use the target language features in other contexts with the accompanying actions. This purposeful repetition of key vocabulary, connectives and sentence patterns is an important part of Talk for Writing and many adults who work in the classroom will need to see the teacher modelling how to do this and have their attention drawn to how this might be done.

Another key aspect of helping children understand the stories and inhabit the world of the tale is through drama. Acting and miming stories as well as playing with soft toys, felt boards, story mats and models helps children to relive and manipulate the story, making it both memorable and meaningful. One interesting story activity is based on 'Kim's Game'. This involves having a story with, say, ten key objects or toys or images. These are held up as the story is told so each item goes with a sentence. You could then try removing the map, allowing the children to select the items, put them in order and use them for retelling.

Some children benefit from having a long map on the ground and 'walking the story steps', telling it as they walk alongside the map. This idea can be taken further by stamping out 'full stops' to emphasise punctuation. The Storytelling Schools movement also uses 'stepping' to emphasise key parts of a story – a step being taken for each new scene or key event.

- Underpin key language features with set actions. Establish a common, cumulative bank across a school.

Playing at the story

It is crucial to set up opportunities to 'play at' the story – this might involve retelling in the sand tray, dressing up, playing with models, enacting a story in the playground, 'hot seating' characters, and so on. The more children revisit, explore and process a story, inhabiting the story world through model-making, drama, painting and playful exploration, the more likely they are to understand what the story means. Some activities will be formally planned by the teacher, whereas others will be more of an invitation to informally 'play at' the story.

One nursery teacher made the observation that until she started storytelling, many of her children found it hard to play together. However, she noticed that as they all came to know the same story, it helped them to play cooperatively 'at the story'. Without a shared imaginative world, children may find it hard to play together. They have to be able to enter each other's imaginative world. It is crucial, too, that adults play with and alongside the children, modelling how to play, modelling language in a natural and easy manner, and opening up the possibilities. This does not mean interrogating children with a barrage of teacherly questions or instructing them by taking over the play. It means waiting and then gradually participating in the play, alongside the children, and offering suggestions or modelling ideas but being ready to encourage the children to make their own suggestions.

Teachers often report hearing the children using vocabulary, phrases and sentences from stories independently in their own play and talk. Make a note of this – and think about aspects not yet being used. Their errors and gaps tell you what to model and emphasise next. The assessment leads into the teaching.

Make sure that toys and costumes and a role-play area are made available so that children can role-play the story. Ensure that imaginative play and re-enactment is for everyone and not just a few children who seem drawn to this sort of activity. Drama is, of course, a natural way for children to engage with a story, for they are 'playing at' the story, exploring its nuances. This sort of play helps children revisit the sequence of events as well as recycling the language patterns in an easy and natural manner. It is also a great way of leading into innovation because children will quite naturally want to embellish and change stories, especially if an adult is there to open up the possibilities of what might happen. It is worth considering a good balance (say, fifty/fifty) between activities that the teacher decides upon and sets up alongside the children's own choices – research does suggest that most learning occurs when children pursue their own interests and leads. The cunning teacher sets out opportunities and then seizes on children's growing interests, intervening to push learning forwards, opening up possibilities. Ideas for playing with a story at the imitation stage include:

- **Free role-play** – provide a play area such as a bears' cave or Grandma's cottage complete with dressing up clothes and objects from the story to act as a simple invitation to 'play at' the story.

- **Puppet theatre** – change the puppet theatre to suit the story using finger or stick puppets (or felt boards).

- **Story maps** – provide paper and card to make maps of different sizes, colours and shapes. Provide blank, laminated maps that have the basic story path mapped onto it.

- **Story toys** – collect toys and objects that go with each story. Set these out for children to use when re-enacting.

- **Retell the story and imagine** – the teacher retells the story with children acting it out freely in an open space. Every so often, settle everyone down. Get them to look around as if they were still in the story – what can they see, what can they hear, what are they thinking.

- **Small world** – use kitty trays or shoe boxes to create tiny story worlds, complete with toys and objects from the story.

- **Art** – provide materials for drawing, painting scenes, making models that are based on the story.

- **Video story boxes** – Ken Holmes introduced me to the simple idea of taking an old video case and turning it into a mini story world. The child designs a cover and you can pop into the box, for example, 'dolls house sized' items from the story, a zigzag version, the story map, lollipop stick puppets. These mini story boxes are very popular with children.

- **Gesture** – children decide on a gesture to go with a section of the story. Stand in a circle and take it in turns to make a gesture perhaps with a word or phrase that sums up that part of the story. Everyone copies the gestures in turn like 'Simon Says'.

- **Favourite lines** – go round a group/circle with everyone saying their favourite line or word.

- **What they said** – draw characters from the story; use large speech bubbles to recall different things the character said. Also add labels about the character, using the children's ideas. This can also be shown as a new map that includes how the main character feels or thinks at different points of a story.

- **Dressing up clothes** – build a bank of clothes/props for each story for role-play and performing.

- **Freeze frame** – children form a tableau at a key moment. Children can say aloud what they are thinking or feeling or wondering.

- **Hot seating** – a child or adult is interviewed while in role as a character. Years ago, I saw the Little Red Hen on the hot seat; the reception children were all in role as farmyard animals, asking questions about her behaviour.

- **I can see** – pause at a key moment. Each child is in role – what can they see, hear, feel – what are they thinking, feeling, hoping, regretting? This game helps children become part of the story.

- **Gossip** – a character from the story gossips with someone who is not in the story about what is happening. Do not underestimate how skilled some children are at gossiping!

- **Phone a friend** – sit children back to back in role as a character; a child phones a friend to talk about what is going on. It can help to have plastic mobile phones!

- **Writing-in-role** – this could be a message, letter, diary entry, advice note, police report, etc. Children talk and then write in role. Of course, very young children can have an adult scribe their ideas while 'sharing the pen' so that they write the letters or words that they feel confident with.

- **Story boxes or museums** – collect images, photos, texts, toys, objects, clothes, etc., related to the story and display in a box or along a shelf rather like a museum. Label some of the items.

- **Mime** – mime a scene from a story. Can the others guess which scene? Mime what might happen next. Retell the story round a circle. Keep pausing at points where a character moves and the children have to mime, e.g. looking round the farmyard, saying good morning, putting the gingerbread man in the oven.

- **Role-play** – this could be re-enacting a scene or role-playing the next scene – or a scene that must have happened but is not in the story.

- **Act the story** – this works well when the teacher narrates the story as the children act it out in a large space such as a hall.

- **Objects or costumes** – tell the tale of the character, or place an object from a story in the centre of the group to then decide what should happen.

- **Cut up stories** – literally cut up a story into sections or pictures and the children have to re-sequence them and use this to retell their story.

- **The missing link** – a sequence of images from a story with a key section missing. Children draw and tell the missing section.

- **Cloze procedure** – choose a section that you want to focus on, e.g. characterisation. Omit key words for the children to complete. This can be done orally with the teacher telling the story but leaving spaces for key words or phrases.

- **Retell and sketch** – you read a section or tell it – the children have to listen carefully and draw or paint or make models of the scene. Follow this with the next suggestion.

- **Listen and retell** – now read the same section aloud and the children have to then retell, recalling as much as possible.

- **First thoughts** – after hearing a story, everyone thinks of a word that captures their feelings or that seems to sum up a key theme in the story. Then, on the count of three, all say their word aloud. Collect and discuss.

- **Best lines** – everyone selects their favourite line and says it aloud.

- **Create a text** – use shared writing to invent a text that might go with the story, e.g. a postcard arrives for Jack; a sorry letter arrives from Goldilocks.

- **Wondering** – take each character in turn and generate questions that we would like to ask the character.

- **Pause a story** – and write messages, advising a character or warning them. Draw a map for a character on a journey. Provide the old lady with a gingerbread recipe. Populate stories with texts, clothes, objects and toys.

- **Create a shoebox of story mementos** – items from a story, e.g. a slipper, a kitchen rag, a torn fragment from a dress, an invitation.

- **Be a character** – sit in a circle. Children stand up and move round the circle, moving like a character at a certain point in the story. So they might move through the forest as Little Red Riding Hood.

- **Gifts** – sit in a circle. Each child then moves into the circle and mimes giving a pretend gift to a character. This might be something that the character will need such as a bowl for the Little Red Hen to mix up the dough.

- **Settings** – sit in a circle that is a 'space' in the story such as Grandma's cottage. Children mime putting objects into the room, e.g. a cat, a chair, a teacup.

- **Reaction** – children mime reacting like a character, e.g. shivering when it is cold.

- **Describe it** – the teacher mimes a key object or creature or person from the story. The children all then say a word to describe it. A long list is made. Try this for similes so the fox is quick as a …? Or, her coat was as a red as …?

- **Sound effects** – retell a story and the children put in 'sound effects' and 'noises' to go with the story, such as animal sounds to accompany the gingerbread man.

- **Percussion stories** – use drums or body percussion (claps, stamps and taps) to add energy and rhythm to certain parts of a story.

- **Songs** – sing any rhythmic or patterned part of a story so that it sounds rather like a chorus.

- **Story objects** – collect objects that go with a story such as Jack's magic beans. The children can handle the beans as they retell the story.

- **Story shell** – the shell is able to hear your story! Children tell their story to their own story shell. Or put their shell to their ear and hear the story that the shell is telling. You can buy little baskets of shells at most seaside resorts.

- **What if/supposing** – pause the story at a key moment and then discuss what might have happened if the character had behaved differently: *'What if they had not chased the gingerbread man?'* Use new ideas to retell new versions.

- **Change** – in this game, the children become a character or animal in the story and move round in role. At a given signal, such as a drumbeat, everyone freezes. The teacher then calls out 'change' and the children become a different character. This works best when you have a story with lots of characters or animals such as *'The Gingerbread Man'*.

- **Talk to me** – in this game the teacher or another adult or a child becomes a character from the story. This can be enhanced by dressing up, putting on a hat or just using a mask. The character enters and sits down. The rest of the class then can ask questions of or 'have a chat' with the character. What would they say to the troll?

- Set up play situations so the children can re-enact the story, alter the story and explore and deepen their understanding of the story.

Word and sentence work

The writing of very young children will be what they say. A child's ability to tell a story with expression is an important step as a young writer. The oral retellings should be noted because they are great evidence of impact. You should notice growing confidence, children being able to make up longer stories, a growing vocabulary, the use of a broader range of connectives beyond 'and', the appearance of story phrasing from other tales and standard sentences appearing. Their stories will also begin to grow in shape so that they become increasingly built around a sense of beginning, middle and end.

The children's progress is also revealed through the story maps. These may appear random at first. After a while, you will notice the story sequence being captured as the children gain more control. This is also supported by the evidence gathered from samples of work of pencil control and handwriting. If children are interested in writing, they will naturally copy adults and begin to make marks on the page. The picture above shows a nursery child at Outwoods Primary, Loughborough, impressively drawing a character while in role as a cat! As soon as a child shows interest in drawing or mark-making, the teacher should sensitively help them to hold a pencil as illustrated on the video. Time has to be spent on gross and fine motor skills work. Begin with blank sheets of paper and then move on to trying to get letters to sit on a clear, red line (the colour helps the child to see the line). Gradually move to two lines until, by the end of the reception, most children can write in 'handwriting books' that have four lines, helping the child with ascenders, descenders and the main body of the letters. The teacher will need to spend time each day modelling letters, words and sentences using flipchart paper that has lines. It is worth being fussy and showing children how to write with care. The truth is that many nursery children can hold a pencil comfortably and begin to gain good control. Some will take longer.

Related to all of this will be the children's ability to use phonics for spelling. Every phonics session should include spelling and the gradual introduction of tricky words. Some of these tricky words can be help-fully built into the stories. It is worth having a very strong phonics pro-gramme so that the children's writing can be liberated. For this reason, we recommend schools use the Sounds Write.

Pay attention to the spellings and sentences that children will need when they come to write. It is worth making a more obvious link between

26
VIDEO

Nursery teacher Julia Whitehorn helping children enjoy phonics for spelling and early writing at Warren Farm School, Birmingham daily phonics and the act of writing the story down. Spend time repeating, innovating and saying sentences aloud. All of this can be engaging and fun – but it is also purposeful because we need to be able to spell and do sentences in order to write our story. Early on, you will be using group or shared writing to model the act of writing, with the children offering ideas. Gradually, however, children will increasingly wish to write words and sentences to go with each story. By the end of the reception year, many children will be able to write chunks of stories. Often all of them can, especially if the teacher stages the writing bit by bit so that each day another part of the story is drawn and written.

- **Spelling** – identify key words that the children will need if they are going to be moving into writing. These will be the generic words required for a new version. These can be practised in daily phonic/ spelling sessions and provided on spelling cards to ensure that common spellings are spelled accurately and this becomes a habit. It is worth having a spelling card for each story. For instance, almost every story benefits from spelling 'once' correctly rather than 'wuns'. Spelling lists could be differentiated according to spelling confidence.

- **Sentences** – identify the places where you can make a change to the story. Orally rehearse innovating on these sentences to prepare the children for the next stage of the process when they will be creating new versions of the known tale. For instance, if the story opens with

Once upon a time, there was a Little Red Hen who lived on a farm.

this could be changed many times by thinking of different animals and where they might live. Make sure that the children say 'whole sentences' and do not just give single words as suggestions. For example:

Once upon a time, there was a tiger who lived by the sea.
Once upon a time, there was a cat who lived in a forest.
Once upon a time, there was a mouse who lived in a big city.

- **Dictation** – older pupils will also benefit from simple dictation as preparation for writing. The sentences should be from the story and include key spellings that they will need when they come to write.

- Work on handwriting. Relate some spelling and sentence work directly to the story as a preparation for writing.
- Model spoken sentences and say them aloud with the children joining in.
- Provide spelling cards for each story.

Understanding the story

Understanding the story is crucial because otherwise the process of storytelling becomes a form of hollow chanting and will neither build the child's imagination, nor develop abstract thought, let alone help them develop their language. Teachers need to think about which aspects of a story might need further reinforcement – perhaps through showing pictures, using puppets or acting out a key scene. This will help those children for whom English is a new language or who may have limited experience. Gingerbread will have to be baked, porridge cooked and a bear's cave built!

Building meaning is crucial to the children's language development because if the children do not understand what the sentences mean, 'generative grammar' cannot operate. 'Generative grammar' is the amazing facility that the young brain possesses to take a familiar language pattern and use it as a basis for creating new utterances. The most obvious example of this occurs when children say, *'I goed home'* rather than *'I went home'*. In this case, the brain has worked out that the underlying pattern for the past tense usually has an -ed ending such as *'I jumped'* and has applied it to the verb 'to go'. Of course, the English language is not as regular as others and the past tense of 'go' is 'went'. Nonetheless, it shows that the child's brain is using what speech therapists call 'generative grammar' to work out an underlying pattern and use it as a basis for further utterances.

If the children do not understand what the sentences mean, then their linguistic competence will not be influenced. This is important because in order for the children's language to develop, they need to understand what the sentences mean. 'Generative grammar' will not function without meaning. In other words, as long as the child knows what a sentence pattern means, if it has been firmly embedded through memorable and meaningful repetition, the child will be able to generate an endless variety of similar sentences using the same underlying syntactical pattern:

> **Unfortunately, there was a troll living under the bridge.**
> **Unfortunately, there was a giant living in the forest.**

It is important that the children understand the meaning of the sentences and stories. Discussion about feelings, events, motives, goals, struggles and how characters change is important. Of course, stories may also be made meaningful in other ways – baking gingerbread men, wearing a red cloak and cooking porridge are all activities that will reinforce what the stories mean.

Memory is assisted by repetition but also by 'perceived relevance' – if the child thinks it is worth recalling, then the memory is more likely to pay attention! A classroom where a storymaking culture is valued is more likely to contain children building up a bank of well-known tales. The child has to believe that learning stories is something worth attending to and concentrating upon over time. Luckily, it is fun!

The density of sensory detail also assists memory. Many teachers have noted that children almost always retain quirky expressions and details. Build in good description to the stories and avoid stories that are lacking in rich language. Indeed, memory is assisted greatly by the use of visual images, so bring stories alive and process them in many ways. Generally speaking, the more you do with a story – the more it is reprocessed in the mind in different ways, the more memorable it becomes.

Furthermore, visualisation alongside emotion provides a most powerful strategy for mental associations. Enjoyment is central – seeing the story, acting it out, mapping it, drawing and model-making it – all of this builds the imaginative memory of the tale. This means that playing at stories and drama is a powerful tool for learning. We also tend to recall things which are associated with strong feelings – being able to retell stories makes us all feel good about ourselves; we get a positive reaction from others, especially adults; stories make us laugh or feel sad or scary. They are powerful experiences!

The process of Talk for Writing is built around success – the gradual removal of the scaffolding only when success is guaranteed. Young children should not be placed in situations where failure is likely! In this way, children associate Talk for Writing and story with happiness and something they are successful at.

- Ensure children understand the story by discussing vocabulary, using objects and images, drama and other activities to assist comprehension.
- Assist memory by repetition, making the stories relevant to the children, good use of sensory detail, processing the tale in many ways, making sure children enjoy storytime, visualising the tale and moving to the story.

The whole routine of storytelling with young children can be enhanced through imaginative props:

- **Storytelling castle** – a specific area in the class where children can tell and retell stories. Try adding toys, story maps and costumes. One class erected a cardboard castle, while another used a tent.

- **Storyteller's hat** – a fancy hat for telling.

- **Storyteller's chair** – dress up the chair with tin foil, add drapes or repaint an old chair. Some schools have story chairs in every class and some have a giant story chair in the playground.

- **Storytelling chest** – find or build a special story chest for your story props. This can be set out as an activity.

- **Storyteller's cloak** – have several cloaks complete with velvet and shimmering stars!

- **Magic carpet** – I first saw this in a Wiltshire reception class – a special carpet for the children to take a flight into a story world.

- **Story music** – to establish atmosphere, try using the same piece of music or a story song to settle everyone into a story mood.

- **Story lights** – a star shape or crescent moon.

- **Story box or bag** – use this for puppets or secret objects or characters. These could be used to make up new a new story. One class I visited had a fluffy toy for each story they had learned. The teacher let a child choose which story they would retell at the end of each day.

It is worth noting that initially children very much imitate the rhythm and sound of the teacher. If their storytelling is dull, you know where that came from! Remember when telling a story to use your eyes to hold the children's attention. Vary your voice in volume, pace and expression in relation to meaning. Pause and emphasise any feature you want the children to internalise.

- Make storytelling memorable, special and meaningful.
- Tell stories with expression and work on children's retellings so that they retell with expression and meaning.

Reading as a reader

A key means to deepening understanding of the original story involves 'reading as a reader'. Once the children are familiar with the story, it is turned into a Big Book for shared reading. Children need to see what the words look like when written down and see how the words are spelled, the sentences constructed and punctuated. Of course, if you are using a picture book, then this will be read instead. Try using Big Books where possible because it makes reading easier with large groups, as everyone can see!

16
VIDEO

How to help children retell, read and understand a story

The wonderful thing about this stage of the process is that because all the children know the story word for word, it means that they can all read the text. The Big Book may now be read again and again, gaining fluency and confidence. You may wish to reread the story just for fun and fluency. However, you could also plan to reread the Big Book and shift the focus each day:

- Read through and ask for **general comments** – discuss preferences, responses, own experiences in relation to the text.

- **Prediction** – discuss what might have happened before the story and what might happen next.

- **Questions** – encourage the children to begin to raise questions.

- **Feelings** – discuss how characters might feel, why and where the text gives clues.

- **Structure** – look at how the story is structured and what it seems to 'be about'. Match the written text to the story map.

- **Patterns** – identify repeating patterns and try innovating on these.

- **Discuss word choice** – try changing words in sentences to see how, by doing so, it alters the meaning. Use Post-its to make this more fun. Make the words obvious by isolating them. Teach children to 'look' carefully at the words as they read them. Draw on phonic knowledge and skill, as relevant. Focus on tricky words in context.

- **Discuss adding in** detail and experimentation.

- Discuss **sentences** and try changing them, innovating in simple ways or being playful. Again, isolate the sentences and make them obvious. Say them aloud in a clear voice with children listening and then copying them.

- Look for the different **punctuation** and see how it helps the reader.

- **Attention** – teach children to read carefully, paying attention by looking at the words as they are being read aloud.

The reading phase of Talk for Writing is where the children begin to see the link from the oral, imaginative experience of a story and begin to build a bridge towards writing. When children move into writing, it is helpful if they can see the text in the Big Book as well as the class version that has been developed through shared writing.

Well-loved stories that the class can retell should ultimately be written down and illustrated. Some teachers not only produce their own homemade Big Book versions of stories but also create wall stories or mini booklets for independent reading. One option is to do this in front of the children as part of the process. These have proved very popular, especially where the children have illustrated the pages and made the booklets their own.

Have your map to one side, retell the story sentence by sentence and gradually write down the tale as it unfolds. Of course, as you are writing down what the children say, no creativity is involved. However, you are modelling handwriting, spelling and punctuation, showing how to turn the words they say into writing. You could do several sentences each day, with children helping sound out words or remind you of how to spell tricky words. Keep this lively and fun. Turn the shared writing into the Big Book of the story for reading.

Most children's early retellings can be recorded with a handheld dictaphone such as an 'easispeak', which is simple to use, holds up to four hours of dialogue and can be downloaded with ease onto a computer. It is also worth devoting time to jotting down children's stories in a class storybook, as this provides further evidence of their development and can be shared with the class. You will also want to capture early attempts at writing and story mapping.

- Turn the story into a Big Book.
- Use for rereading to develop fluency and comprehension as well as word and sentence work.

Reading as a writer

'Reading as a writer' is the bridge into writing. This involves raiding our reading to improve writing or oral composition. We can be purposefully on the lookout for good words, special sentences and story ideas all the time! For instance, introduce the children to other versions of the story that you have been learning. Differences can be noticed, discussed and gathered for potential use when the class comes to innovate. Reading other versions broadens the children's frame of reference, extending the range of possibilities that can stem from the same basic story idea.

Daily reading of Big Books as well as a rich diet of quality picture books continues alongside storytelling. Ideas and language can also be drawn from books to add to the general store of language and possibilities. This habit of 'reading as a writer' and drawing on one's reading as a resource for composition is a powerful habit that should be encouraged. The teacher can model it, by explicitly suggesting where a told story might be enriched by something from a different picture book or one of the previous oral tales.

For instance, when creating a story about a baby fox, one class drew upon their recent reading of '*Owl Babies*' to add in a terrible problem. The baby fox woke up to discover that his mother was not there! The rest of the story was about the baby searching for his mum who, of course, appeared at the end of the story to reassure the baby (and the children). Stories for very young children should be comforting.

I remember telling a story that featured some children going into the forest for a walk and meeting a wolf. A four-year-old piped up, '*Yes, but it was a baby wolf*'. The same child, on another occasion, reassured herself when her character was in a dangerous situation, walking alone in a forest, by saying, '*but she had an axe*'. The simplest of motifs become symbols of safety and comfort. All of us need the axe metaphor to protect us through life. The point here is that this child was building up a bank of possibilities that could enrich storytelling. This is what has become known in many schools as the fine tradition of being a 'story magpie'.

- Read other versions of stories.
- Draw attention to underlying patterns; gather vocabulary and ideas.
- Be story magpies.

Building and maintaining the story bank

The simple idea of Talk for Writing is to build up a bank of well-known tales from nursery through to Year 2 at Key Stage 1. It might well be possible during a year to enjoy and learn anything from six to ten stories, possibly building up a bank of about twenty to thirty stories over the four years. This is in addition to the picture books, class and family stories, as well as the stories of the children's own lives. This 'story bank' provides a powerful imaginative and linguistic repertoire for children to draw upon when creating their own worlds. Known tales can be told to other classes, performed in assemblies or filmed. Many children do not experience a rich and cumulative language experience at home. This has to happen in school. It needs to be planned for and be insistent, systematic and rigorous. Decide which stories (from the bank and picture books) will be used in each year so that you avoid duplication and can also build up resources as you go along.

See Appendix 3 for a suggested list of picture books ideal for retelling.

Moving from one tale to another may mean that by the end of the year the first tale will have slipped away – it is important, therefore, that the process is cumulative, meaning that every so often old favourites are

revisited and retold. In this way, a genuine bank of patterns becomes part of the children's repertoire that may then be drawn upon in their speech, their play and their own storytelling. Of course, they will also draw upon their own experiences, television, reading and whatever is uppermost in their minds. Cumulative and multi-sensory learning demands sensitive, intelligent and creative teaching that constantly reacts to children's needs and expects every child to succeed.

A 'story sack' containing a soft toy to represent each story learned is a useful resource. Children are invited to dip into this and select an old favourite for retelling. Try to keep the bank of tales alive.

- Build up a cumulative story bank.

Creating a storytelling environment

Small children enjoy direct teaching when it engages their interest in storytelling and rhymes. Storytelling, chanting rhymes and singing are all crowd pleasers and a great place to begin to feel part of the class 'company', learning how to learn with others. Storytelling benefits from the teacher setting up opportunities for children to 'play' at the story in a range of contexts as well as children creating their own opportunities for story play. There will be obvious opportunities for cross-curricular work such as the baking of bread when learning *The Little Red Hen*. However, other more informal activities may invite the children to revisit and explore their understanding of the story as well as reusing the story language. For instance, how about setting up a Bear's Cottage complete with differently sized furniture and porridge bowls!

Other simple ideas involve providing clothes and objects from a story for children to use. Felt boards and characters can be handy. Some classes use large floor mats with a story world drawn upon it. The sand tray may be dampened and a story map drawn. A few figures may then be used for retellings and innovations. Models and figures for each story should be provided, as well as simple finger or stick puppets. I once observed a group of five boys building bridges very intently. They used three soft toy goats to cross their constructions. They were loud in declaiming, *'Who's that going trip trap over MY bridge!'* One boy produced the largest goat and exclaimed, *'Finally, the biggest goat came trip trapping down the hill towards the bridge …!'* One boy stood nearby, hands in pockets, and ruefully observed, *'That bridge will not take the weight of that goat. Besides, you've a troll under there!'*

Some classes also have an ongoing storymaking area. In one school, this was made up like a castle – a story castle (a large cardboard box!). Inside, the teacher had placed some basic equipment – story cloaks, story hats, and a story chair covered in drapes. A story box contained different objects each week, as well as story maps for each story that had been learned and 'blank' maps for new creations. The story castle was an area where children could play at retelling a well-known story, innovating on a story or making up new stories.

It would appear that the more children play at a story, the more it becomes a powerful force in their minds. Echoes of such stories often reappear in children's imaginative play and writing many months later. One September, a reception class had been working with an early story of mine called '*Little Daisy*' that features the following line: **'There they met a cat, a lean cat, a mean cat'**. One very young boy, who was still four in May, dictated a story that featured the following line: *'there they met a dinosaur, a kind dinosaur'*. In another class, a child was creating a pirate story and included, *'There he met a pirate, a wooden-legged pirate'*. This syntactical echo appeared eight months later. It is unlikely that such an unusual construction could have come from anywhere other than the original tale.

- Create a storytelling environment in the classroom.
- Make sure that toys and costumes and a role-play area are made available so that children can role-play story.
- Create a special story area.
- Provide story equipment such as maps, costumes, toys, etc.
- Use traditional tales, tales from the story bank as well as picture books.
- Learn, map and orally retell before reading.
- Purchase blank Big Books for creating class story books, children's innovations and inventions. These are available from madeleinelindley.com (also an excellent supplier for Big Books for use with shared reading).

Independent retelling

As well as 'participation' and 'communal' retelling, there is a third possibility for storytelling. Children who are read to and whose language is developing at an expected rate will soon be ready to begin moving into retelling in their own words and not needing to retell 'word for word'. Teachers should experiment with this, so that all children learn many stories word for word but also develop some in their own words. For some children, this happens during the reception year or during Year 1. For many, it is later.

The teacher tells a new story on several occasions. Activities may be built around the story to provide visual support, kinaesthetic representation as well as making the story memorable and meaningful. For instance, the children might draw or paint scenes, act the story out, recreate the story in the sand area using models or sequence pictures of the main events in the story.

To move into an independent retelling, the teacher explains that the children can retell the story in their own words – it does help if each time the teacher tells the story there is some variation in the retelling and this is pointed out! The children listen to a retelling and then draw their own story map. It might be better to draw a class map, as some children may miss out crucial details and others may overcrowd their maps. Once the maps are drawn, experiment by putting the children straight into pairs, facing each other. They then try retelling the story. They should use their maps to help them. It can help to explain that they do not have to remember the story word for word, but that they should just to 'have a go' and not worry.

Over a few days, the pairs should retell their story if they show an inclination to do so – usually, retelling allows the brain to move from trying to remember the plot to becoming more fluent with the sentences. Some children will automatically learn the tale and perform it in 'mirror' fashion. Others may work by 'toing and froing' the tale.

Perfection is not required. Many good retellings will include hesitations, incomplete sentences and a string of 'ands' to link ideas. All this is part of the children's building of confidence and competence with language. Enjoy their storytelling and praise their embellishments and inventions. Plan fruitful interventions.

- Have some stories that children retell in their own words.

A note about story partners, circles and adults

Once the children are very familiar with the story, move on to story partners and circles. Story circles, where the tale is spoken in a smaller group or in turn, are very useful for those children who do not join in with the initial retellings. It is handy if an adult sits beside reluctant participants to encourage or work with them as their story partner. Your task is to help the child move from **dependence** to **interdependence** to **independence.**

Retelling a story with a partner needs to be modelled by the teacher, demonstrating how to face your partner and work in tandem. There are different ways to work together and those who struggle may benefit from working with a chosen friend or an adult. Try:

1. Retelling like a mirror, saying the words and doing the actions at the same time.

2. Taking turns to say bits – a sentence or part of a sentence.

3. Telling half or the whole of the story and handing over.

Ideally, the partner should be ready to help with a prompt when in listening mode. Pairs should be in a position where they can see the class map or their own story map. It is worth listening in to see if they are retelling the tale or if they have slipped into 'and then … and then'. If they have, they need to return to communal retelling for the time being.

Threes can also work well as long as the children cooperate without leaving one child out! Stories should be rehearsed and developed using the story maps. Once partners are used to working in harmony, they are invited to lead the class or retell to other children in another class. If a pair or 'solo' teller retells a story, use the class as a 'whispered backing group'. Whenever pairs or threes share their stories, it is useful to clap and always comment on 'what was good' about the way in which the tale was told (clearly, expressively, etc.) or the language used or the story itself.

If this is to take off and begin to transform classrooms and schools, one aspect is crucial. All the adults need to be fully committed. Classroom assistants are an invaluable part of the classroom storymaking team. As we have said, often they have a key role in supporting reluctant children on the carpet. They may also identify and draw off small groups or even individuals so that they can retell in a smaller setting. Children who do not join in with the whole-class work nearly always benefit from working in a smaller group. Therefore, all the adults involved should know the story.

- Ensure all adults know the story.
- Develop story circles and partners.

Involving families

See Chapter 10 for how schools have involved all the children's families in the storytelling process and doubled the language acquisition of the children, as well as increased parents' confidence in supporting their children's learning.

Finally – a few words of warning

A good story is not just a bunch of connectives! Indeed, a good story is an experience; primarily felt as images in the mind – they are metaphors. One of the recent key influences on language development in primary schools has been the identification of language features such as connectives and different clause structures indicate proficiency at a certain level. Storytelling is more than just ensuring children use connectives. First and foremost, they need a story to tell – language is the vehicle for communicating the story.

Having said that, it is true that the ability to use a range of connectives means that a child can more easily argue, reason, persuade, justify, explain, organise thoughts and order events, as well as recount and narrate. Connectives enable fluency and connection in language. If teachers use storymaking without becoming overly self-conscious in their emphasis on language features, then most, if not all, children will develop their linguistic competence as a natural matter of course.

Not everyone can script or select a good story for Talk for Writing. A key member of staff needs to be sent each text for 'vetting' – considering the suitability of the text as well as such things as accuracy. Across a school, this soon provides an overview and staff can begin to consider what features are being revisited and where progress is being built into the texts. Remember, though, that progress is not about the length of the story. It is more about the breadth of language structures and uses being experienced. Indeed, if a story has too much detail, there may not be enough room for innovation.

It is tempting to 'sing-song' a repetitive story. Be wary of this, for if it is too rhythmic some children hear the beat but not the meaning. Keep investing the words with expression.

One key barrier to learning stories, rhymes – indeed many things – is the problem of attendance. Where children attend a setting daily, rapid progress is possible. However, where children's attendance is not regular, progress can be slowed. It is for this reason that 'getting the parents on board' is crucial. In an ideal world, much of what we are talking about would be happening at home. However, it is worth noting that only about half of pre-school aged children are read a bedtime story on a regular basis. In some settings this might well be zero. We know that children who are read to have an enormous advantage, as it develops their language, the habit of listening, concentration as well as abstract thought. It is a key indicator of educational success. See Chapter 10 for ideas on how to use the approach to involve families effectively.

- Have someone who collects in all the stories to check for accuracy, suitability and progress across a school.
- Gradually resource each story.
- Make sure that children's retelling does not become a meaningless chant – invest each story with expression and meaning.
- Work hard to ensure good attendance.
- Involve parents so that children experience the stories and rhymes at school, nursery and at home.

CHAPTER

6

Innovation

When to change the story

Once children have become familiar with a story, then the teacher moves into **innovating** – adapting and altering a well-known tale to create something new. Many children will do this quite naturally and play at making alterations to amuse themselves. This should be encouraged. It also seems to happen in cases where children enjoy gaining control over events and manipulating them in their own ways.

While the teacher sets up situations for children to formally be taught, there should also be daily opportunities for children to play at stories – dressing up boxes, sand trays, fuzzy felts, models, outside areas, playground story maps, and so on. This can provide an opportunity to retell a story (imitation) but also innovate and change a story – perhaps by simply swapping over different animals to help pull up the enormous turnip or a different creature to hide beneath the troll's bridge. Playing alongside children in an informal manner can provide the catalyst to children's own innovative play. The skilful practitioner calls upon previous stories and revisits language patterns to help create something new.

Before innovating, it is important to loiter with the original version until it is embedded in the children's 'long-term working memory', as it is impossible to innovate if the original is not well known. This means that the children should not be rushed on to innovation until they know the original really well. The idea is to embed the story so that every child can retell it with confidence. If you rush into innovation, some children will not have internalised the sentence patterns and they will resort to retelling the story in their own everyday *oral* language – generally, with the main ideas linked by 'and then'. Watch out for this, as the idea is to help the children 'talk like a book' – to be able to retell as if they had been read the same story many times and taken the original to heart, complete and in story language.

19
VIDEO

The innovation stage

While retelling in their own words does not matter in terms of a child knowing and loving a story, if you loiter longer with a tale you will find that their innovations will sound more 'like a book' because they will recycle the story language, with a few simple changes. With some children, this shift into story language and standard sentence patterns is immediate. With others, it may take time. While we would suggest that you loiter with a story, there is no point in 'doing it to death'. The retelling and learning and developing of stories must be a thing of joy. The last thing that we want is for children to feel that they are 'getting it wrong' or to have a sense of failure. Try to avoid a sense of 'correction' by using simple recasting, *'Let's do that bit again together'*. Keep it light and fun. Nursery children may well find it hard to retell a story in Standard English, as they have yet to acquire those patterns – just enjoy their retelling as it happens and keep encouraging them by being an enthusiastic listener. The patterns will gradually emerge over time.

It is helpful to remember that most stories are innovations, as there are only a few basic plots but an infinite number of stories can be told based on those plots. Many of the early traditional tales are very similar, as they involve a character leaving home and setting out on a journey into the world usually to be confronted by obstacles that have to be overcome. These, of course, match the child's stage of development and are necessary to the young child who is venturing away from the comfort of home into the world of playgroups, nursery and school. The tales match the child's concerns. The stage of innovation also echoes how we acquire language through innovating on well-known patterns to generate new combinations.

Changing the story

There are many different ways in which teachers help children innovate. Some of this will happen in a playful manner, as children may not be able to help themselves chipping in with possible alterations to a tale. Such moments should be seized upon and encouraged.

However, generally speaking, there comes a point when the teacher leads the children as a class or in groups through the process of changing the class map to create a new class version that is then retold. Settle the children on the carpet and talk the story through, pausing where you have decided to make changes. Some teachers like to 'cross out' parts of the story and draw new images directly onto the class map. For instance, the 'horse' might become a 'duck' in *The Gingerbread Man*'. This will mean that you will end up with a map that is rather messy but it shows what was in the story originally and where you have made changes. It helps to use a different colour for the changes. You could then create a totally new map, complete with the new ideas.

Figure 7. Altered story map 'The Enormous Leek'.

Another tactic is to pin the old map to one side of your flipchart and draw a new version. On the new map, draw in the changes that you want. Again using a different colour will help the children see the differences. Make the sections that have been changed stand out, as the children will be referring to the map when they do their own. A teaching assistant will log the changes the children suggest in a 'save it' box. This is important because when the children come to innovate on their maps, they will have a bank of ideas to draw upon.

A further approach is to use Post-its as illustrated on the video. It is handy to have a variety of Post-its of different sizes and shapes – they come in the shape of arrows as well as mini speech bubbles. Cover over the key aspects on the original map that you want to change.

As you make changes to the story, keep retelling with everyone joining in so that the new class version comes alive. Make sure that you have thought through what will be changed before the session – for your first story, keep this simple and limited. With the first few stories, just make basic changes – names of characters, a few key animals or settings. Keep it very simple so that the *'The Enormous Turnip'* becomes an enormous carrot and the characters trying to pull up the carrot become a variety of zoo animals. This way, the children will find it easy to succeed and, at the same time, they will be getting the idea of taking the known story and altering it to create a new version.

20 VIDEO

Using Post-it notes to innovate before shared writing

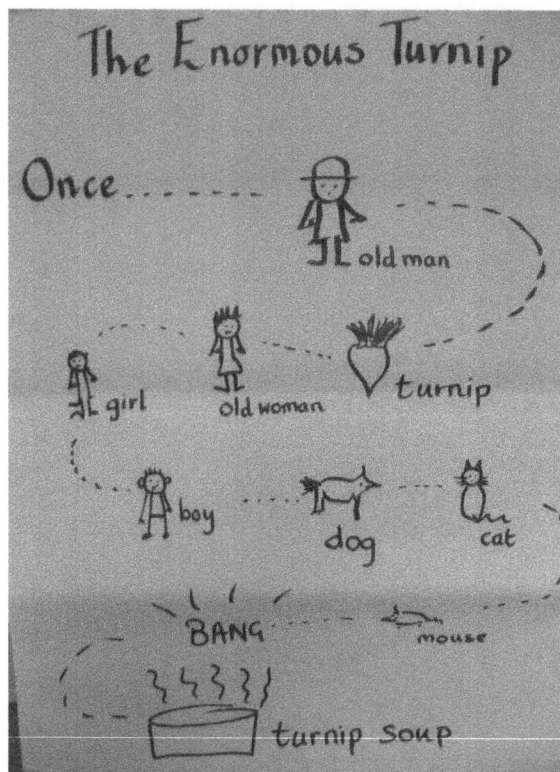

Figure 8.1. Original story map, The Enormous Turnip.

Decide beforehand which aspects are to be changed. You can ask the children for ideas. It is also useful to have some form of back up in case ideas run dry. So, provide alternatives for them to choose from. Use a special story bag or box. Inside, place either cards with images

Figure 8.2. Re-drawn story map, The Enormous Leek.

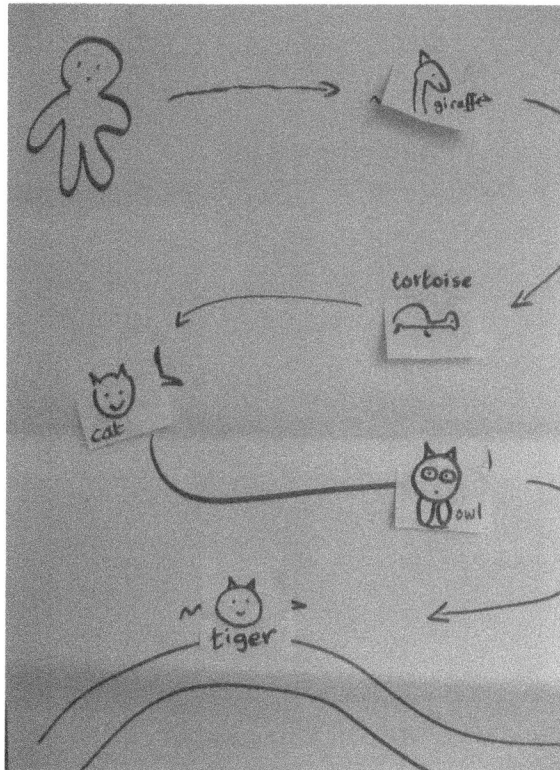

Figure 9. Story map altered with Post-it notes.

on (such as characters, animals or objects) or have toys to select from ... or, in the case of alternatives for a turnip, you can use garden vegetables such as carrots and potatoes. Children can then choose from the 'bank' of toys or cards. Similarly, as young children may find it hard to come up with ideas, it is worth having a story bag or box. Set the alternatives out on the writing table so that everyone can view what the choice is.

I have always enjoyed using story dice. You can buy these but most of them are too small and the images hard to decipher. Make your own by using a square cardboard box. On each face place an image – then roll! You could have a set of dice relevant to each story – one for characters, one for different settings, one for different types of weather, and so on.

Another simple but fun idea is to use story stones. These are literally stones collected from the beach. You can draw onto them and varnish – or write words onto them. These could be used with different drawstring bags – one for animals, one for objects, one for settings, one for characters, and so on. When embellishing, you could have a bag of adjectives, adverbs or verbs and decide whether they would work in a sentence.

Recently, I was in Wilkinson's and spotted a pack of what looked like lollipop sticks in the gardening department – fifty 'birch seedling labels' in the 'get gardening' section. These would be ideal. Write onto

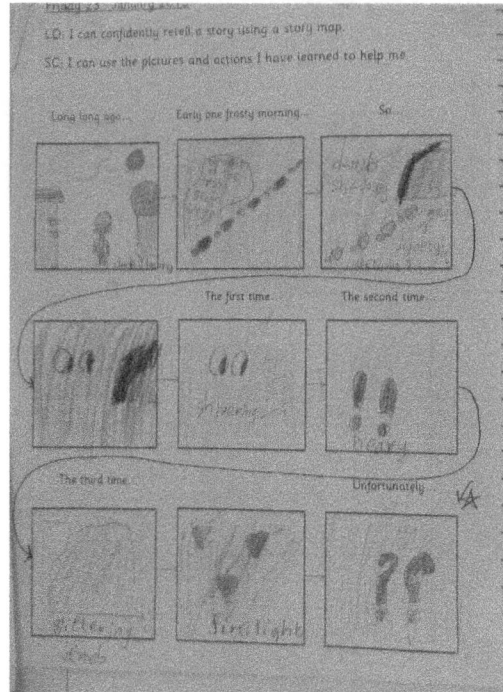

Figure 10. Example of a simple, drawn story map.

each stick an alternative for a story and pop them into different pots. Children come out and randomly select a stick, which gives them a new character or setting! You could colour the ends of the sticks to show what is on them – red for new character, green for new setting, and so on.

One way into innovating is to use small squares on the original map. These show where you want to make simple changes.

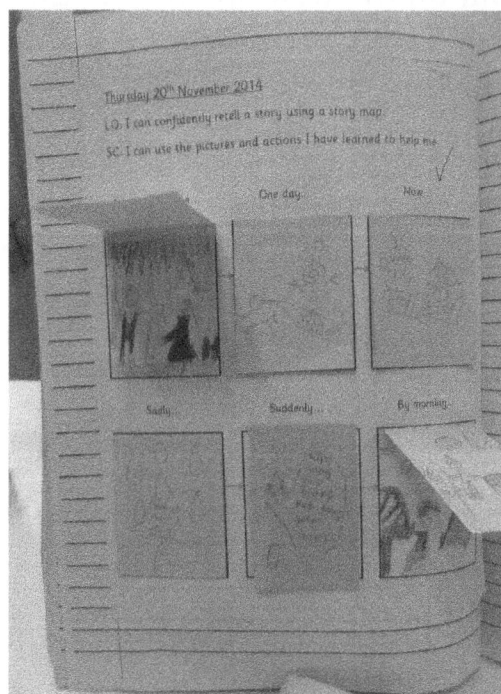

Figure 11. Example of a drawn story map which incorporates Post-it notes.

When innovating, show a new map but have the boxes blank for the new ideas. You can then provide the children with a similar map complete with blank boxes for them to draw in their new ideas.

If we look at a simple example of this early stage of innovation, you can see that the story 'Let Me Come In' has had a few changes to create a new version shown on the right. This is called simple substitution.

Let Me Come In	*Let Me Come In*
Once upon a time, there was a little old **lady** who lived on her own **by** the **sea**.	Once upon a time, there was a little old *granny* who lived on her own *in* the *forest*.
One cold, **wintry** night she sat by the fire, wishing for company.	One cold, *snowy* night she sat by the fire, wishing for company.
At that moment, there was a knock at the door and a teeny, tiny voice said:	At that moment, there was a knock at the door and a teeny, tiny voice said:
'Little old Gran, little old Gran, let me come in for the wind, it is cold and there's snow on the tip of my nose.'	'Little old Gran, little old Gran, let me come in for the wind, it is cold and there's snow on the tip of my nose.'
Gran looked outside and what did she see – but a **mouse**!	Gran looked outside and what did she see – but a *tiger*!
'Go away, go away, no **mice** today!' scolded the little old Gran.	'Go away, go away, no *tigers* today!' scolded the little old Gran
So the frozen **mouse ran** into the snow.	So the frozen *tiger crept* into the snow.

As the children gain in confidence, become more playful and adventurous in the way in which you innovate. Most teachers begin by just changing the name of a character, the animals, the places and the key objects, using simple substitution. However, as the year progresses, embellish and alter in different and more creative ways. Try adding more detail or extra scenes. Put in how a character feels or what they are thinking:

- add description of a character, place or special object;

- add in a new scene;

- reveal the character's feelings;

- add in what the character is thinking;

- use speech bubbles to show new speech.

Very young children can be led into innovation by using floor story mats and toys. I once saw a lovely version of the gingerbread man set out on a story mat. The child had a box of alternative animals and simply swapped these over so that a new version had been created. As he was doing this, unaware that I was watching, he was telling the story and verbalising his thoughts. Altering stories in this way makes the language and events concrete. A story becomes physical and can be manipulated and changed to represent something new. Of course, this will need modelling by an adult in a light and playful way. On a story project with nursery teachers, one teacher told the others: *'Oh, it's easy. I just get the story mat and toys and set them out. Then I get a group round me and I play at the story, swapping toys over and retelling the new version. Then I ask the children who would like to have a turn and we all start playing at changing the story together.'*

Story mats are an important piece of equipment. These are long strips of cloth, about a metre long and perhaps thirty centimetres wide. Children like it if there are a few different coloured ones – green for fields, brown for forests, blue for the sea. These should be rolled up tidily and stored away in a story box or trunk. You then need some small, plastic story boxes. In each one, there is a collection of different toys – zoo animals, farm animals, sea creatures, pirates, and so on. You also have a special box that contains the toys and finger puppets for the current story. This means that the children play at the tale they are learning, and can change the story by choosing different animals or invent a new story.

The children choose a mat and box, then set themselves up by rolling the mat out. They innovate on a story on their own or play in pairs or small groups so that innovation becomes an automatic activity.

Choosing new ideas

So, begin by changing the class map/version and retelling a new class version. This can be retold a number of times but, if you strike the right note, the children will be ready to change their maps and retell their new versions. After a while, this becomes a tried-and-tested routine.

It is often easiest if the children draw their own new map, with their ideas for changes. This is supported by providing the 'banked' ideas, or by using cards to choose from, or even a box of toys to select. Some teachers have found this should be staged to make it easy for the children.

Sit with a group and begin with each child taking turns to choose a new name for the main character. Then use cards or toys to choose new animals, objects or settings for the story. These may be stored in a set of 'story boxes' – one each for animals, settings, characters, and objects. At first, keep the changes VERY simple so that no one gets muddled and everyone is successful. How the children choose new ideas depends somewhat on the story. If you are doing '*The Enormous Turnip*', this lends itself to choosing from goats, sheep, horses, cows or some other grazing animal – and, of course, you will need a fierce alternative to the troll such as a giant, a wolf, a fox, a goblin or an ogre. Older children can draw or write their choices onto simple grids.

Draw and retell

Once the children have made or thought through their own ways of changing the story, they need to draw a new map. Model drawing a new map or making changes to a map so that it is made clear and simple.

Keep the class version to hand so the children can instantly see the underlying pattern. Some children benefit from having a smaller version of the class map to hand and, if this is very clearly drawn, it helps them to see where they need to draw their changes. This could be shown using empty boxes or colour.

Use colour to make it clear which pieces need changing so that they really stand out. For instance, the map could be drawn in black but with anything that can be changed drawn in red. Obviously, the amount of scaffolding and support that you provide relates to what the children need to be a success. Gradually over time, scaffolding may be withdrawn as children become more independent.

Once changes have been thought about, the children draw their own new map with their new ideas. It helps to stage this bit by bit. They say their opening, draw it and then take turns to retell their opening. In this way, the story gradually develops. It is worth working hard at these sorts of routines with the first few stories in order to establish a routine that soon becomes familiar and, in the long run, will therefore need less support from an adult.

Once the maps have been redrawn, the children need a chance to retell their own version a number of times. They can do this in pairs, facing each other and taking it in turns. You may wish to train them in 'how to be a good storyteller' and 'how to listen to a story'. Model working as a pair so that children have seen how this needs to be done. Rehearse it until the class can work in this way successfully.

How to be a good storyteller	How to listen to a story
• speak clearly • look at your audience • use a big voice so everyone can hear • get everyone to join in • use your story map	• look at the storyteller • join in when they want you to • keep still • see what is happening in your head

Children work in pairs with a friend or you could use lollypop sticks to randomly choose pairs. As the children mature, they need to learn how to work with different children; ringing the changes helps children broaden their social sphere and develop the habits of working with anyone in the class.

Have children retell their version to the group or to the whole class. Teachers use the following props to help with this:

- storytelling chair or throne

- story hats

- story cloaks

- magic flying story carpet to sit upon

- story light or candle

- story microphone

- story stones to hold

- story shell to listen to

- story bag or boxes for props.

Some children may need the lure of being able to retell in a pair or three for support. A quieter child might have the task of holding a puppet or object or toy at the relevant moment in a story. When listening to stories, it is a good time to rehearse the importance of the role of the listener as well as how to tell a story. At St. George's in Battersea, children are encouraged to use a 'confident, big voice'. Make sure that you model good behaviour by settling everyone and not starting until everyone is paying full attention. You may have to draw adults in as well so that they do not move around making noises or chatting, as a child telling a story has to be given respect and attention.

Very young children in nursery or at the start of the reception year may benefit from working on their first innovation as a group, guided by an adult as illustrated on the video. The group might use a roll of lining paper so everyone can contribute to drawing the map. This can be held up and then, with the children standing behind the map, the story can be started and finished by the adult, each child saying 'their bit' in turn.

However you move into innovation, the basic idea is quite simple. Draw a new class version and retell it as a class. Then children draw their new version and retell it – this is known as **draw and retell**.

Types of innovation

You could decide to leave the innovation totally open and see what happens. Very small children will be using toys and drawing to create new versions. These may well draw on all sorts of aspects of their lives. Again, this needs to be modelled by an adult or you can play alongside a child to develop fresh versions. This can be left very open and children who have been read to at home and lead lives full of conversation and rich experiences will have much more inner 'story material' to draw upon. These early innovations are great fun.

However, some children will have far less to draw upon and this means that you have to provide a bank of possibilities. Over time, every child will develop a bank of options. This will be built up through being read to, drama, classroom experiences and the stories and poems that the children become familiar with and adapt. Many teachers provide story cards and objects to help innovations, stored away in story boxes or bags.

Over time, a hierarchy has been developed that attempts to categorise the basic ways you can innovate on a story:

Simple substitution

Simple substitution means changing a few basic words – names of characters, types of animal, places or objects, so that 'The Enormous Turnip' becomes 'The Enormous Carrot'. Instead of *the little old man, the little old lady, the little boy, the little girl, the dog, the cat* and *the mouse* helping to pull the turnip up, you could instead include *a giraffe, a monkey, a hippo* or *an enormous dinosaur*! On the film clips, you can see Charlie retelling 'The Enormous Turnip'. In his version, he has used the names of all his friends!

In essence, the children retell the same story as the original but the substitutions allow them to create something new. They experience the satisfaction of making up their own tale while embedding the structures for future manipulation and creative use.

21 VIDEO

Moving from imitation to innovation

22 VIDEO

Charlie innovating on a story orally

New versions should be shared, discussed, drawn as new maps and then children may practise in story circles or retell in pairs. Items or cards plucked from a story box may help children make simple choices. At first, limit what can be changed, as it is our experience that some children want to alter everything and then the story falls apart as the child cannot always recall all the changes!

Addition

Addition means taking the basic story, perhaps carrying out some simple substitutions and then extending the tale by embellishing. This could involve adding extra description so that '*early one morning*' becomes '*early one sunny morning*'. This might involve adding dialogue, further events, description or characters. The teacher will have to model this and encourage the children to embellish their tales.

Many teachers find this a useful place to introduce adjectives, so that the original model has been purposefully written without any adjectives and then at the innovation stage these are added in. Start with adding in single words – adjectives and adverbs. Move on to choosing more powerful verbs (*dashed* rather than *went*) as well as extending sentences by using conjunctions. Try experimenting with alliteration, as this can be great fun and produce surprising results. Just ask the children, '*Can we think of a word that starts with the same sound?*' This is ideal for choosing slightly off-the-wall adjectives. It is the difference between '*the fabulous forest*' or '*the ferocious forest*' and '*the deep forest*'. Eventually, add in extra sentences and events:

- simple additions, e.g. *one day* = *one sunny day*;
- adding in more description – adjectives, adverbs, powerful verbs, similes;
- adding in more dialogue;
- adding in new characters;
- adding in extra things happening;
- adding in extra detail to bring scenes alive.

If you are moving into writing the story down, then it is best to keep additions simple and keep close to the original model. However, if the story is just an oral version, play around with the innovations and see what happens. Here is an example of the story '*Let Me Come In*' with simple substitutions and simple additions on the left-hand side. However, there is a more elaborate addition to the right.

Let Me Come In	*Let Me Come In*
Once upon a time, there was a little old **kind** granny who lived on her own by the **deep, dark** forest. One cold, snowy night she sat by the **blazing** fire, wishing for company. At that moment, there was a **sharp** knock at the **old** door and a teeny, tiny, **squeaky** voice said: 'Little old Gran, little old Gran, let me come in for the wind, it is cold and there's snow on the tip of my nose.' Gran looked outside and what did she see – but an **enormous, growling** tiger! 'Go away, go away, no tigers today!' scolded the little old Gran. So the frozen tiger crept into the **swirling** snow.	Once upon a time, there was a **kind old** granny who lived on her own **at the edge of an enormous forest**. One cold night, **when the snow swirled down like confetti,** she sat by the **roaring** fire, **warming her bony hands and** wishing for company. At that **very** moment, there was a **loud** knock at the **wooden cottage** door and a teeny, tiny voice **whispered from the darkness outside**: 'Little old Gran, little old Gran, let me come in for the wind, it is cold and there's snow on the tip of my nose.' Gran **peered** outside and **at first she could only see the snow and the silver moon high above - but then she saw who had been knocking –** it was a tiger! 'Go away, go away, no tigers today!' scolded the little old Gran, **shaking her finger**. So the **poor,** frozen tiger **crept** off into the snow, **with nowhere else to go**.

Alteration

So far, we have looked at making changes that do not really alter the original story. However, an 'alteration' is a change that involves making a change to a story that then has consequences. You may find that a substitution will lead to an alteration. For instance, if you introduce a horse into the story '*Little Charlie*', you may well find that will influence what goes into Charlie's bag! You cannot put hay in because grannies do not eat hay but a horse might well want an apple! Children might:

- change the setting – the forest becomes an estate;
- alter the nature of a character – the bad wolf becomes kindly;
- alter key events or include new ones;
- include extra characters;
- change dialogue;
- change the plot pattern in some way;
- alter the ending or the opening;
- modernise a tale.

Encourage children to play with story ideas by making big changes and see what happens. Alteration begins to shift the children into being more creative and inventive. Here is an example of the story *'Let Me Come In'* being retold in a playful manner. The children have just taken the basic idea but have moved away from the original and made their own way in. I made this one up with reception children in the summer term. I began by saying something along the lines of, *'Let's make up our own story a bit like that one. Now, who can we have instead of the little old lady? Where do they live? Is it snowing or shall we have some other sort of weather?'*

> **Once upon a time,**
> **there was a pirate called Pete**
> **who sailed on the Seven Seas**
> **in a ship called the Jolly Roger.**
>
> **Late one night, Pete**
> **was settling down to sleep.**
> **outside the storm battered the boat,**
> **the wind blew,**
> **the rain poured down**
> **and the thunder rumbled**
> **like a giant's belly.**
>
> **Pete began to snore**
> **so loudly that his parrot Polly**
> **said, 'Be quiet!'**

> At that moment,
> there was a loud bang on the door
> and a booming, looming voice
> said, 'Let me come in,
> for the storm is too loud
> and I'm soaking **wet**!'

Sequels and prequels

Many good stories offer up the chance to write about what happened before or what happens next. For instance, *'Mr Gumpy's Outing'* actually ends with the words, *'Come again another day.'* This is a direct invitation into writing the story of what happens the next time the animals and the children come to visit.

Combination

A small boy called Declan in Sheffield suggested a further possibility. His idea was to have *'The Little Red Hen'* helping to pull up an *'enormous turnip'*. So, try combining two stories:

> *'Who will help me pull up the turnip?'*
> *said the Little Red Hen.*
> *'Not I,' said the bull ...*

Obviously, blending story patterns can be much more sophisticated than this. Keep a list of the oral stories that the class gets to know as well as the bank of favourite picture books. You will find that increasingly children will innovate by drawing on ideas from other tales, especially if you remind them of this possibility.

It is worth working on different parts of the stories orally. You might want to take the opening and orally rehearse. Then see if it can be developed any further. Let the children work on their openings alone, then in pairs. Hear some different ideas. At first, all of this will be quite limited but, after a while, the children will become increasingly adventurous.

The above possibilities for innovation provide a simple way of considering how a known story might be used as a basis for creating something new. It is always worth thinking carefully about the children's development and what might be suitable, without underestimating what can be achieved. Innovations may be class, group, paired or individual. The usual approach is to create a new class or group version by altering a map. This new version can be told and retold.

WHAT HAS WORKED IN INNOVATION?

- You have to know the story really well. If you do not know the story well, then innovating will prove to be difficult.
- You cannot innovate on a story if the children don't know it well – it has to be internalised through plenty of over-learning.
- Different ways to change the story:
  - use Post-it notes on the class map;
  - roll dice – cubes with a pocket or small boxes with images on each face to randomly select new characters, objects, animals or settings;
  - use a story box or bag and pull out different characters, puppets, toys, pictures, etc.
- Discuss key parts of the story and make them obvious, e.g. opening, dilemma/problem, good/bad characters.
- Change the map directly, using a different colour so changes stand out – then make a new map.
- Use a 'blank' map that has the structure but take the detail out so there are just empty boxes that need to be filled in.
- Think with the children about how they can use the story in their play – and other activities, e.g. paintings, model-making, sand tray, small-world play.
- Try varying how to innovate in the following ways:
  - simple substitution – just change over a few things such as characters' names or the setting;
  - addition – add in adjectives or similes but also be playful and add in extra detail or events;
  - be playful with the innovations to allow for some wild ideas;
  - make some big alterations and see where the story goes.

Bristol Nursery and Reception Story Project teachers

- Turn the new version into a class Big Book or display it as a Wall Story with children's illustrations.
- The teacher talks the children through their decisions about how they will alter the original.
- Children draw their new version as a story map.
- Retell in pairs until they have refined their story.
- Hear some as a class.

Retell and write

New stories are shared and told to other children, other classes, parents – and of course may be recorded. This might be by an adult or older 'story buddy' scribing, using a dictaphone or DVD camera, or of course a child may 'write' their new version. This may appear as mark-making when drawing the map.

Once children begin to be taught handwriting/phonics, they will be increasingly able to represent what they wish to say in a way that others can read. Generally, this happens in a reception class, although some nursery children will be able to write simple words and some nurseries successfully involve children in writing, as illustrated in the video from St. George's, Battersea.

There is much controversy about when to encourage children to start holding a pen correctly. Most nursery children can do so by the end of the year if someone shows them how. You may want to look at the video clips on this issue and decide your policy.

The teacher stages the writing over a number of days, with a little more added a bit at a time. It helps if you present each child with a simple booklet. This should have space for a drawing and lines for them to write upon. This is staged by using a new page for each section of a story so that the children can write and illustrate. Before the children write, the teacher uses shared and guided writing to model how to turn the class oral version into writing.

Pin the map to one side of the flipchart so it is clearly visible. Pin up a large copy of the story spelling card or any other such tricky word-spelling reminder. All say the first sentence together. You then take each word in turn and write it down, carefully modelling the school handwriting style. It helps to use handwriting guidelines (Prontaprint sells flipchart paper with guidelines) so that your handwriting is well formed. Ask the children to sound out rapidly any words where phonics can be used – with the others, use the spelling card or just write it down. Keep rereading. As this can be fairly steady in terms of pacing, stage the writing section by section over, say, a week. You will have to make a judgement about this, based on holding children's attention span. Try to write with care – because you are modelling the attention and care they will need when writing. However, try to also keep the session interactive and fun. As you are slowing language down and fixing it on the page, you will find that some changes to the oral version can be made to improve further what has been learned orally.

As you are writing, you may wish to use other strategies to teach:

22 VIDEO
Charlie innovating on a story orally

24 VIDEO
Lisa Powell doing simple shared writing with nursery children at St. George's, Battersea

25 VIDEO
Nursery teacher Lisa Powell explains her approach to encouraging the children to start writing

26 VIDEO
Nursery teacher Julia Whitehorn helping children enjoy phonics for spelling and early writing at Warren Farm School, Birmingham

27 VIDEO
Nursery children playing at writing at Yew Tree Community School

- make a mistake and ask the children to check for you;

- extend a sentence by using a conjunction such as 'and, but, or, so, when, while', etc.;

- add in extra description by using an adjective or a simile;

- use 'better' or 'stronger' words by changing, for example, *'he went down the road'* to *'he crept down the road'*;

- model oral rehearsal and rereading;

- before every sentence is made up, reread the previous one so that one sentence flows into another;

- experiment by using alliteration.

Keep each day's class writing and display it along a wall so that the children can clearly see the class story growing daily. These can be illustrated. Or – turn the shared writing into a Big Book for reading.

Guided writing involves working with a small group who have similar needs. Ideally, this will be at a proper guided table (horseshoe shaped) in a quiet area. It is best if this can be held in an area away from the noise of the classroom so that everyone can concentrate.

You will see this on the film of the guided session at St. George's. Begin by making sure that the children have the equipment that they need – a sharp pencil, writing book with where to start indicated, handwriting reminder, sound/spelling card and any other prompts such as banks of possibilities.

A guided session allows the teacher to prompt the children towards independence. *'What do you need to do next?' 'How can you help yourself now?'* It is also a time for one-to-one intervention, supporting the children in moving forwards. Try not to dominate by talking loudly all the time. Orally rehearse the opening sentence with everyone saying their own sentence aloud. Let them write for a while. Most of the interventions can be whispered so that you do not disturb everyone else. However, where a generally useful point needs to be made, then you can raise your voice or even invite everyone in to 'help with the writing'. The focus for such sessions will very much depend on the children. In some groups, you will be focusing on sounding out and writing simple labels carefully, 'on the line', or using a spelling card. Others will be orally rehearsing a sentence and then writing it down, using finger spaces. Others will write at more length and you may be working on more complicated spelling, embellishing ideas with adjectives, extending sentences by using conjunctions. Issues may arise such as shifts in tense. Everyone will need to read aloud what has been written so we can hear whether it 'sounds right'. So, some children may still be saying

28 VIDEO
The importance of teaching basic writing skills systematically

their story and drawing, with the teacher perhaps scribing some ideas; some will be drawing and writing a word or simple labelling; some will write sentences and, by the end of the year, more confident reception children will be writing several pages of story.

Of course, writing is underpinned by a strong phonic programme, complete with tricky words. Each story has a spelling card for generic words that should be spelled accurately from the start. It is worth remembering that if children keep writing 'wuns', then this becomes increasingly embedded. Young children should be developing spelling at a considerable rate during the reception year, as well as daily practice of fine and gross motor skills so that pencil grip is developed to secure handwriting.

Finally, many practitioners believe that young children cannot innovate. This is simply not true and innovation at a simple level can be modelled and encouraged from the earliest age. It is worth remembering that it is quite natural for children to innovate as part of language acquisition – it is a natural human activity. However, some children will be more happy making changes than others. Over time, this gradually changes. Often it helps if the children drive the choice of different props or models to go into a story. The more the children are in charge of their story work, the more likely they are to take the whole process to heart.

FINALLY – HOW DO YOU KNOW IT IS WORKING?

- Some children able to retell very quickly – do not underestimate their capabilities.
- Children's confidence built rapidly.
- Parents showing an interest and asking what is happening, as children are going home retelling and talking about the stories.
- Evidence in children's play of them independently retelling or using memorable phrases and vocabulary from the stories. This is especially noticeable where props, toys and costumes from the story are made available.
- Increased use of language.
- The process helps struggling children engage and make progress.
- You can see the impact of the stories in the children's use of language but also in their cooperative play. They are more likely to play together because they have a common, imaginative experience to engage in and manipulate through play.
- Children choose to re-enact and play at the story.
- Many children choose to change the story quite naturally and playfully, innovating through play. It helps to provide a story box or bag with alternative characters, etc.

Bristol Nursery and Reception Story Project teachers

- Use shared writing to model how to turn the oral version into writing.
- Pin the map up and the spelling card so they are clearly visible.
- Take each word in turn and write it down carefully, modelling the school handwriting style.
- Keep rereading.
- Keep the session interactive and fun.
- Use guided writing to support groups with their early writing.

CHAPTER

7

Invention: Moving from imitation to independent invention

(This chapter is supported by the Invention overview – see page 14)

29
VIDEO

Moving from
innovation to
invention

From imitation to innovation to invention

Invention means to independently make up a totally new story. It is worth remembering that the whole intention of Talk for Writing is to provide children with the confidence, language and ideas that will help them create their own stories, drawing not only on what has been taught but also their own lives and concerns.

Imitation feeds the child's imagination with ideas as well as language. **Innovation** develops the ability to take what we know and use it to make something new. Both phases develop confidence in children as story creators. The stage of **innovation** is carefully scaffolded so that the teacher models how to alter a known story, changing the map and retelling a new version. The children are then supported in changing their maps and creating their own new versions. These are drawn, retold and usually shared in pairs, round story circles and performed for the whole class.

So we carefully plan for children to learn new stories and then manipulate the patterns that they know to create new versions – in the same way that language learning works! The third phase of **invention** follows on quite naturally, as it involves children creating a more independent version of the text. This has to be modelled and will involve drawing another map, deciding on what might happen and preparing for writing by retelling. Some children's inventions will be very simple and others more elaborate. All should be valued and celebrated. In the main, young children tend to do another version of the story that they have been working on. However, if you model using the underlying pattern but become more playful, then the children will follow your lead. The aim is for this phase to be increasingly about the children being more independent so that you have **moved them from dependence towards independence** across the three phases:

Imitation	Children learn and explore a story, internalising the language patterns and ideas.
Innovation	The teacher models how to create a new version. Children develop their own new version, making changes to the original.
Invention	Children work more independently to create their own new version.

It can help to draw the underlying pattern of the original story and have blank boxes for new ideas – different characters or settings or events. At the start of the reception year, it is probably sensible to stick reasonably closely to the original so that you are aiming for a more independent innovation. However, as the children gain in confidence, you can move away and begin drawing on different stories and picture books and real life to create.

Here is a lovely invention. It arose at Christmas time after the children had learned a version of 'The Hungry Caterpillar' that involved a Father Christmas who eats too much and gets stuck in the chimney. The innovations had involved using the same story pattern but the children had just changed the food. One of the girls took the basic idea and underlying pattern and made up a different version for her invention, which the teacher wrote down:

> Once upon a time, there was a little boy called Anna who found some fantastic multi-coloured glass in the sand pit.
>
> On Monday, she put on the glasses and everything turned sunshine yellow because sand got stuck in the glasses.
>
> On Tuesday, she put on the glasses and everything turned jungle green because a leaf fell into the sand pit.
>
> On Wednesday, she put on the glasses and everything turned fire engine red because she saw a red crab hiding under the sand.
>
> Finally, she accidentally dropped her glasses and they broke.
>
> Nothing was the same again.

This next example is an invention by a reception boy in February. He wrote his story following on from working with Mini Grey's 'Traction Man is Here'. The teacher proposed that the children could make up 'any story' they want about Traction Man for their invention. First, they made up a class story and then the children either drew and told their new invention, or those who could went on to write their version:

> One day Traction Man was out for a walk 'let me check what my muther paked for me'. 'a drink, some food and my cote'. Next, he went to the parck he saw a magick ring he put the ring in 'boom,'! and then, he was in Jungle not eny Jungle a rain Jungle 'oh no,' he put the ring again and was back 'I will stay home'.

There is much in this little story, not least that we can see the pay off from plenty of shared reading and daily shared writing. He has begun to pick up on the conventions of speech marks and is trying his hand at a range of punctuation. He draws on the story but also a recent trip to the park, having a packed lunch or a picnic as well as a magic ring for magical travel (which may well have been taken from a reading scheme book)!

This next invention came from a reception girl who had drawn her story and was more than ready to tell me it. I scribed directly onto the map, constantly rereading so that she could maintain the thread of her tale. It soon became obvious that the class had been learning and innovating on 'The Three Bears'. The repetition of 'he walked and he walked and he walked' clearly came from an earlier story called 'Little Charlie'. It is a simple example of a child drawing on several known stories to create a new invention:

> Once upon a time there was a little (girl) boy called Geoffrey. He walked and he walked and he walked until he came to a cottage. He knocked on the door, tap, tap, tap and went straight in. He saw not one, not two not three not four but five steaming sweet potatoes. First he tried the big one but it was too hot. Next he tried the middle-sized one but it was too cold. Finally, he tried the baby-sized one and it was just right. So, he ate it all up. After that, he went to sit down. First he tried the big chair but it was too (soft) cosy. Next he tried the middle-sized one but it was too warm. Finally he tried the bay-sized chair and it was just right. CRACK! Suddenly the chair broke!

At that point, her stamina broke as well and it seemed like a good moment to end. As she told me the story, I could hear the rhythm of the learned imitation and the emphasis and expression that the teacher had given their retelling. Laying down solid known patterns is vital. If the children's innovations and inventions do not possess such story patterns, then it means that the original has not been sufficiently well embedded.

One useful strategy is to use the story mountain pattern and to create what years ago I dubbed 'five sentence stories'. Obviously, you do not have to stick to five sentences and if you did it would make for rather brief and dull tales. However, fixing the notion of an introduction, a build up, dilemma, resolution and ending as a basic pattern can be very helpful. If you draw a mountain pattern and Velcro on the key connectives, it will help to make the pattern memorable and may be used to teach and during play.

Here are two inventions that arose from using Russian Dolls and the story mountain pattern. The basic idea of the original story was that the tiniest doll gets lost but everything has to be all right in the end. I introduced this invention to the class by reminding them of the original story that they had learned and innovated. We talked through the story mountain pattern and then discussed ideas. We began by talking through some essentials, such as who has the tiny doll and where does it get lost or left behind. This gave everyone ideas for their opening and build up. We then decided that the tiny doll would meet a scary creature. In the class invention, we had a dragon and some of the children recycled the same idea. However, there were other ideas such as a tiger, a lion, a fox and troll. In all of this, the children were often drawing on incidents and ideas from all sorts of stories that they had told and read. The trickiest part of the story was to work out how the doll might escape the clutches of the monster. In the class story, we had a friendly pigeon swooping down, plucking up the doll and flying home. The children discussed and shared other possible escape plans. I used shared writing to turn the basic ideas into a whole story. It was fairly brief but I made sure that the written class version was on five sheets of flipchart paper, clearly echoing the intended underlying structure. Just before writing, I asked the children to retell their own story and we heard several. As they were Year 1 children, almost everyone was able to settle straight into writing. Here are two examples.

Story structure	The original imitation	Alex's story
Opening: we meet the main character and the scene is set	One snowy night, a little girl called Emily was playing with her Russian Dolls.	One sdormy night I went to a castle.
Build up: the story begins – something happens	Just then, she went downstairs to get a drink of milk and dropped the baby doll.	I dropt my doll calld danial on the stes

Story structure	The original imitation	Alex's story
Dilemma: something terrible happens!	Suddenly, a dragon appeared. It had green scales, a long tail and fiery breath.	Suddnle! a dragon. crept acoss the room the dragon spotid the doll stecht his hed dack and brevd fier agen and agen
Resolution: the problem is sorted out in some way	Luckily, Emily ran back and grabbed the baby doll.	Suddnle a Giat stampt and eet him up
Ending: everything is okay in the end	Finally, the dragon flew away with nothing and Emily fell fast asleep.	then it was time to go home and then I fand him on the stes he was very bernt

Alex's friend Peter also used the same pattern that I had modelled. Here you can see that working independently, Peter has used the same structure:

Story structure	Possible language features	Peter's story
Opening: we meet the main character and the scene is set	Once upon a time/One day/morning/night plus the weather – sunny, snowy, stormy, etc.	One sunny Sunday a little boy called Tom was playing in a cave with some dolls.
Build up: the story begins – something happens	so, next, first, just then, then, after that	Just then his Mum called him so Tom went to her but for got the babey doll but the doll wosent sceard. So he ran further into the cold cave.
Dilemma: something terrible happens!	suddenly, unfortunately, at that moment	Suddenly he saw a blaysing fire. He started to walk sloley then he saw a dragon. 'Hello' said the doll but he shoodoon have. Cos the dragon terned his head on him and opened his mouth to start breathing fire.

Story structure	Possible language features	Peter's story
Resolution: the problem is sorted out in some way	luckily, so, but	But the doll jumpt out of the way onto the dragons foot.
Ending: everything is okay in the end	finally, then, in the end	

Indeed, as children begin to acquire simple and obvious underlying structures, they can create an endless number of stories. The most basic pattern is the story mountain problem/resolution pattern. Children also soon grasp cumulative stories such as 'The-Hungry-Caterpillar' pattern, where every day (or again and again) something happens and increases until there is some sort of explosive ending! Other patterns include stories that start with a warning not to do something, which the main character then disobeys leading to the inevitable problem and resolution. One of the most common basic patterns for small children is the journey story. A character sets off to go somewhere, meets various problems on the way but in the end reaches the destination safely. Other stories involve wishes that go wrong, getting lost or losing something precious and then finding it again, as well as stories in which a character changes. Knowing these patterns helps teachers to work on basic story inventions, as they know where the story is going.

Story type	Pattern	Examples
Cumulative	A very strong repetitive patterning – typical of some picture books but also used often in traditional tales, for instance, where three brothers all carry out the same task.	*'The Very Hungry Caterpillar'*, *'There was an Old Woman who Swallowed a Fly'*, *'The Enormous Turnip'*
Journey	A character travels in search of something or someone – or to find something or someone. Either from A to B or there and back again as in *'The Hobbit'*.	*'The Gingerbread Man'*, *'Rosie's Walk'*, *'The Three Billy Goats Gruff'*
Story mountain – monsters!	Everything is all right until a threat arises. Eventually this is overcome.	*'Little Red Riding Hood'*, *'Jack and the Beanstalk'*

Story type	Pattern	Examples
Wishing	A story involving someone who wishes for something but usually there is a barrier that has to be overcome. A variation is where a character is granted a wish or several wishes but wastes them.	*'The Three Wishes'*
Warning	The main character is warned not to do something or go somewhere – ignores the warning and gets into trouble.	*'The Minpins'*
Visiting other worlds	These stories involve a character travelling through a magical portal from one world, or time, to another.	*'Mr Benn'*
Character change	A character is transformed in some way – rags to riches, ugly to beauty, timid to brave. Occasionally, the transformation involves changing 'form' or personality. In some stories a character learns so much that their views or feelings are transformed.	*'Cinderella'*, *'Not now, Bernard'*
Lost and found	A character finds or loses something of value.	*'Owl Babies'*

The early stages of imitation and innovation, as well as plenty of picture books, feed the mind with language and ideas. The constant retelling and careful scaffolding of new versions also develops confidence in the young learner. Ultimately, these things enable a child to increasingly draw upon what they know about story in order to invent more and more sophisticated and playful tales.

Attitudes	Confidence, motivation – becoming a storyteller.
Language	Vocabulary, turns of phrase, sentence patterns, ways to open and end – all that is needed to tell a good story.

Story structures	Big structures that help to create whole stories – journey stories, lost and found, wishing tales, etc.
Story banks	Possible characters, settings, animals, objects, things that happen, things that go wrong, how to sort things out, possible endings.

- After innovating, lead children into more independent inventions where they develop their own versions.
- Model how to draw and retell a new version.
- Model how to turn the new version into writing as appropriate.
- Encourage children to increasingly draw on all the stories that they know.
- Publish and celebrate inventions.

Listening to invention

Two key driving forces for language learning are purpose and audience. For a story to be told, we need three things – a teller, a story and a listener. Without the listener, not much will occur. One can only imagine what it must be like for babies and toddlers who try to communicate with their mother to be met by a blank stare or the back of a mobile phone! In the end, the child gives up. There is insufficient reward – not enough feedback. Language is mainly a two-way process. Even when talking to myself, I am still talking to myself. Someone is listening!

When little children start telling stories, they will just often rattle on talking as they play. Gradually, this will become more purposeful as long as we are a good audience for what they have to say. It is crucial that adults involved with young children express their interest in what children are saying, as this encourages them to say more, to add the next event, as well as experimenting and enjoying the whole business of inventing stories.

I remember watching a nursery teacher listening to a child making up a story. Every time he spoke, she widened her eyes, smiled expressively and made a comment such as, 'Oh no – *what happened then?*' It occurred to me that perhaps this was the most attention the little boy had ever had in his life. He grinned and added more on to the story each time she showed such obvious delight in his ideas.

Although what he was saying was fragmentary, nonetheless a story was developing, which was especially obvious when he said, *'clip clop clip clop!'* The teacher gasped, *'What is it?'* – *'It's a Billy Goat!'* exclaimed the child. Of course, she also had to wait while he stared at the story stone that he was holding, waiting for something to pop into his mind, as he fed off his knowledge of *'The Three Billy Goats Gruff'*.

> • All adults need to be enthusiastic and expressive listeners, valuing what children say and leaving them space to think.

The importance of play and invention

If classrooms and outdoor spaces are set up to the possibilities of developing imaginative play and story worlds are created, then children will pretend and invent (see page 88). This invention can be scaffolded by blank story maps.

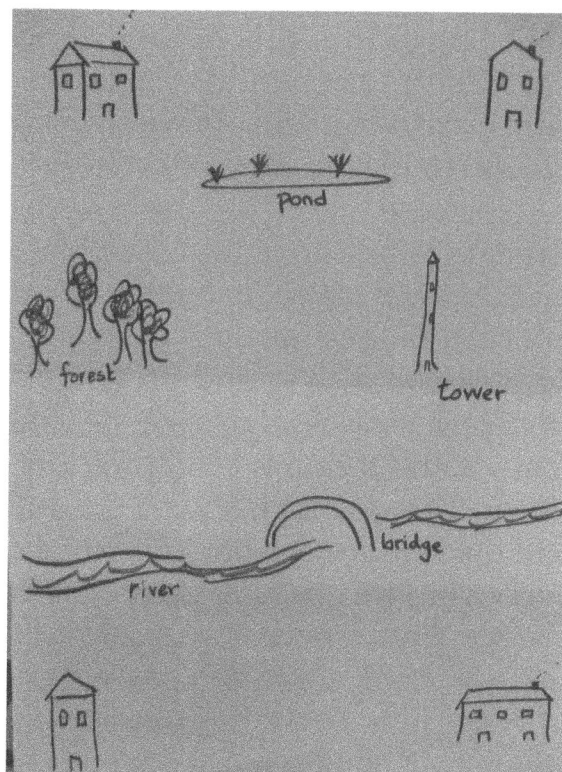

Figure 12. Example of a blank story map.

30
VIDEO

Independent
invention of
a story

As the bank of stories and rhymes that the children know well begins to build, the children will increasingly draw upon it to create their own made-up stories. Their inner 'bank' will include oral stories, picture books, Big Books, TV stories, family stories and the story of their lives. All of these provide an imaginative and real world that can be drawn upon to make something new. Watch the girl from St Thomas of Canterbury in Salford tell her story and delight in her storytelling skills in Video clip 30.

On the very first story project that I co-led, practitioners were reluctant to move into story invention, believing that children would not be able to make a story up! They taught children to retell stories and then helped them make simple innovations but avoided the whole business of invention completely. Indeed, they left this until the summer term, despite my best efforts! This is strange because children make stories up all the time through play. My children used to call this 'tending' (*'Daddy we're "tending"'*). Pretending is something that all children do and indeed in some ways we carry this on through adult life. In my role as a presenter, I stand up and pretend, adopting a certain manner. When I am at home, I am a slightly different person. The ability to pretend helps us be like chameleons, adapting how we talk and behave to different audiences and purposes. Pretending also helps us understand how other people might think and feel. It helps us experience things that we have yet to meet or relive our lives, perhaps altering our story. It is this ability to pretend that helps us imagine and enact different possibilities and this lies at the heart of problem-solving and creativity. The ability to pretend is fundamental: to come up with ideas; to dream new possibilities; to live in them; to see them through.

Do not underestimate what the children will be able to do. They are little story-machines and will make up endless stories whether you like it or not! Children's play hinges around 'pretending' and this is story. As soon as a child picks up a twig and pretends that it is a car, then a story has begun. Their stories may well be fragmentary glimpses, a sequence of events without much structure, but this sort of play is the very stuff of story. There will be a massive difference between the invented stories and the retold tales but in many ways it is the made-up stories that are of most interest. Where do the ideas come from? Where did the language come from? Why is a child endlessly telling stories about a mouse that got stuck? You will see echoes of the stories and picture books and classroom activities appearing in children's inventions throughout their lives, and what we feed their minds is all 'copy' for stories.

Practitioners working in a nursery for children with language deprivation have noticed how after several terms of story learning, their children's inventions begin to develop and grow – sometimes quite rapidly, littered with images, ideas and language features taken directly from the stories that they have learned and played. However, most children can be invited to make up stories right from the very start. These will be fragmentary and rambling but that is fine. Enjoy their inventions; enjoy what their imagination offers – and they will be encouraged to tell more.

Becoming intimate with a bank of stories feeds the imagination with ideas as well as giving children the language patterns that they need to express themselves. You cannot create out of nothing. One nursery teacher reported how when children were inventing stories they would often pause and look round them as if seeking an idea. She noticed that they would see something in the room and then immediately use it in the next part of the story that was being told. This observation shows how children will use the concrete experiences to hand – what is immediate and surrounds them – as part of their own storytelling equipment. In the end, they will internalise this bank of possibilities but then they will have to develop the ability to 'look round' inside their minds to find the ideas.

This 'seeking after ideas' involves a special sort of 'staring'. Initially, a child will look round for something to prompt what might happen next. I once was in a nursery and a child was stuck for what would happen next. He looked round and noticed the dolls house. Inside, he could see a tiny toilet. At once, his face broke into a grin and he said rather triumphantly, *and then there was a toilet!'* and hooted with laughter.

When thinking inside their mind for the next idea, the child's face often seems to fix and a stare appears. The eyes look outwards but their vision is inwards, seeking round the realms of their mind for a thought, an idea, a seed of possibility. The more we can grow the bank of ideas and the ability to access an idea, the more their retellings and inventions will flow.

This thinking brings back a memory. It was a reception class where the play was almost entirely driven by the children. No farm set out, no garage to play with, no story sack of costumes, no beads to thread, no porridge to stir, no beanstalks growing, no tadpoles swimming, no role-play area ready for tea. There was nothing in the room that would tempt me into play. It made me wonder how on earth the adults imagined they would be able to feed the children's imagination.

We have to set up enticing play opportunities. The cunning teacher will broaden a child's inclinations to play in one way – inviting them into other forms of exploration and challenge. Play can be habitual, recycling the same language and thought processes. The cunning teacher will also notice when children are deeply engaged and judge whether to leave well alone or there is an opportunity to participate and challenge the thinking – modelling language, deepening under-standing and offering an unexpected challenge or surprise. *'Are there other ways to sort the seeds? What would happen if we made the tower taller but with a wider base? Can the monkey still see us if we hide him behind the cushion? When we add more stones into the container, what happens to the water? We drew rings round the puddle and now the puddle is smaller, so where did the water go?'*

Of course, you may well spend hours proudly setting out your pirate ship, complete with little pirate figures, a cloth of blue for the sea, parrots and mini treasure chests with the idea of making toilet roll palm trees and then find that it is ignored as an enormous cardboard box is being turned into a ship. However, if children are to develop a range of skills and deepen understanding, it is important to think about the range of opportunities that need to be experienced.

Make the classroom into an Aladdin's Cave of possibilities. Imagine for a moment a child who comes from a small flat. There are no books. There are no toys. There are no pencils or paper or crayons, let alone playdough. There is wall-to-wall TV. This child needs to come into the Aladdin's Cave of possibilities in a nursery or reception class. There should be a toy farm, zoo animals, fuzzy felts, a story castle, knights and dragons, princesses, hats to wear, costumes, masks, puppets, model-making, outdoor play, sand trays, watery worlds, beads to thread, porridge to make, songs and rhymes and picture books. It is our job to open up the world.

And that stirs another memory of a reception class in London, which the head swore was fantastic, but to my eye looked dingy, dirty and unloved. The door to the outside led onto a shabby corridor where mosquitoes hovered. There was a torn up black bin bag that a child had painted upon but it had dried and flaked everywhere creating a snow of paint flakes. There were four easels. One child whizzed round and splashed paint crazily across each one and then wandered off. He picked up a fluffy monkey that looked as if it could do with a good wash and wandered, occasionally thumping other children. Perhaps I caught them on a bad day, though if that is what they are used to, it still haunts me. I often recall the child 'swinging a monkey', obviously bored, searching for something worthwhile to do.

My 'swinging a monkey' story reminds me of a trip to an old people's ward where all the old folk had been corralled into a circle facing inwards. There was a hideous silence and they sat there, barely moving, no one speaking. I sat quietly by my mother-in-law. In the end, one of them spoke. A slow, desperate voice said, *'This is awful. We must do something.'* Let your rooms be Aladdin's Caves and give all your energy to teaching and working with the children to broaden their world and strengthen their learning. Let our classrooms not be awful places.

- Make sure that the classrooms are an Aladdin's Cave of possibilities; an invitation to play; plentiful with possibilities for pretending; where stories can be learned, developed and created.

Progress in invention

Of course, everyone is seeking progress and 'mastery' in learning. Educators talk about 'stretching' children and in my mind I see them like rubber bands and hope they won't snap! Our evidence is seen across England and in other parts of the world where 'talking the text' evidently helps children develop their language and confidence.

The following is the transcript of a four-year-old boy in his first month of being in school when asked, '*Can you tell me a story?*':

> *Once upon a time, there was um a little girl. There's a boy with a teddy … A little … What you doing?... he said, 'I will have chips and beans'. And the bear said, 'Marshmallow pie'. That's what they're reading there. [Points to a group that are reading. He is listening in to what they are saying and taking parts to use in his story!]*
>
> *A little nasty girl came in and sat on their table and she said, 'You're coming with me' … The dog said, it will … come with her … It looked like so much fun. The dog will come with her … And then … She this was the girl gave the bear back and she said, 'It was only a bag … of a sack'.*

To listen in to a group sharing a book with an adult and to steal ideas from it strikes me as masterful! Here he is after a whole year of Talk for Writing, in the summer term when he is five years old:

> *One upon a time there were three bears. One morning Mother Bear said, 'There's … What should we have for breakfast?'*
>
> *'Porridge!' said Little Bear. So, she made some porridge.*
>
> *'The porridge is ready', said Mother Bear. So, they all tucked in.*
>
> *'If Goldilocks comes knock, knock, knock on the door, tell her to come later because I'm trying to read', said father Bear. Knock, knock — that was the door. It was a sad King … and … The three bears said, 'What's the matter?' and the King told them. 'So, let's …' 'Do you like porridge?' said Mother Bear.*

'Yes'.

'Well, we're having some for breakfast so you can have some'. 'Ok but after that, I'll have to go back to my palace'.

After … When he had finished, he went back to his palace and when…. Another knock on the door came … And then … Goldilocks came.

'Hello Goldilocks', Father Bear said, 'I hope you won't make any noise, will you?' Father Bear said, 'Last time you were dreadful'. [It's a different story] 'I won't be noisy', said Goldilocks, 'but I will be nice to Baby Bear'. So they played and then Goldilocks noticed the time. 'I'd better go back home'. And that's the end.

The progress is evident and the new story is full of wit ('*Last time you were dreadful!*'). Of course, 'the telling is the writing' for many young children, as their transcriptional skills will probably not yet match their ability to compose.

Let us take one more example – a four-year-old girl from Sheffield. When asked '*Can you tell me a story*' and then '*Can you make up a story*', the recording is blank apart from a few sounds . Possibly she has no words of English, perhaps she lacks confidence, or perhaps she has never been read to. We do not know. All we know is that when asked to tell a story, she finds this impossible. Further evidence would have to be gleaned from observing her playing. If we move to the summer term and the same two questions are asked, we get a different picture. This time she is able to retell the whole of '*The Three Bears*', lasting over three minutes, as well as inventing a simple story that ran as follows:

Once upon a time, there was a bear, a warm bear.
He was called Linny.

Then he goed to the shops but suddenly a pirate came.

So a fish, a kind fish came to save him.

Then they goed to the castle.

Then they had ice cream.

Then they lived…. happily ever after.

It is a neat little invention that follows the story mountain basic shape. We have a main character who sets off to the shops but meets a villain. However, there is a 'Gandalf' figure – the kind fish – who rescues him. Linny and the fish then make their way to the castle where they eat ice cream before living happily ever after. What strikes me as unusual about

7 VIDEO

Baseline questions

the story is the shape – it has the ingredients of a full blown narrative, the structure is there, including a resolution and ending ... and all of this possibly in a second language. So, in one year, she has moved from silence to being able to retell a known tale in standard English and invent a small but beautifully shaped tale of her own.

To develop invention in the early years, a simple system will need to be established and developed. It will comprise of four key elements, the first of which we have already discussed:

- Invention following on from innovation and imitation.
- Weekly whole-class/group inventions.
- Daily individual inventions.
- Daily invention through play.

Invention: Ideas for inventions and the movement from telling to writing

Weekly inventions

Plan a story invention session ('*Let's make a story up*') at least once a week. Inventions may be led by the teacher or an assistant, working with the whole class, in groups or individually. This can be stimulated by using a story bag or box, which might include objects, models or images such as character cards or story cubes (roll the cube and on each face there is a different character, setting or event).

There are different ways to capture the story – it might just be spoken aloud and left at that. However, stories might be instantly turned into a map so that it can be retold on other occasions, gradually building more events or embellishment. On some occasions, the teacher might choose to write the story down as it develops – either on a flipchart in front of the children or in a class 'storybook' held on the lap. At the start of the year, map the stories, as this shows children how to invent and draw. In a reception class, by about October, it would be worth moving into writing stories down because by then the children should have enough phonics to be able to appreciate the spelling and handwriting. Do not pause on every word, as this will slow the pace. However, you might pause occasionally for help with 'sounding out' and 'tricky words', as you feel appropriate. Remember to keep the focus very much on making the story up.

Class stories can be retold, made into Big Books, wall stories, mini-booklets or recorded and made into audio CDs or filmed as DVDs. Of course, they can be performed to other classes or in assembly. As long as the teacher has in mind the basic story mountain shape, then it is simple enough to help a class or group of children create a tale.

I like to settle the children down on the carpet and make sure that everyone can see me. With a flipchart to hand, I'll tune the children into listening, perhaps by using a rainmaker or with a rhyme or inter-active chant. Then we can begin:

By the hairs on my chinny-chin-chin, Let the story begin

Hold the story mountain pattern in your head. Begin by getting the children to help you introduce a main character in a certain place. Then decide, based on the children's ideas, what the character is doing before something goes wrong – you'll need a dilemma or challenge which will then have to be 'sorted out' before the main characters can get home and live 'happily ever after'.

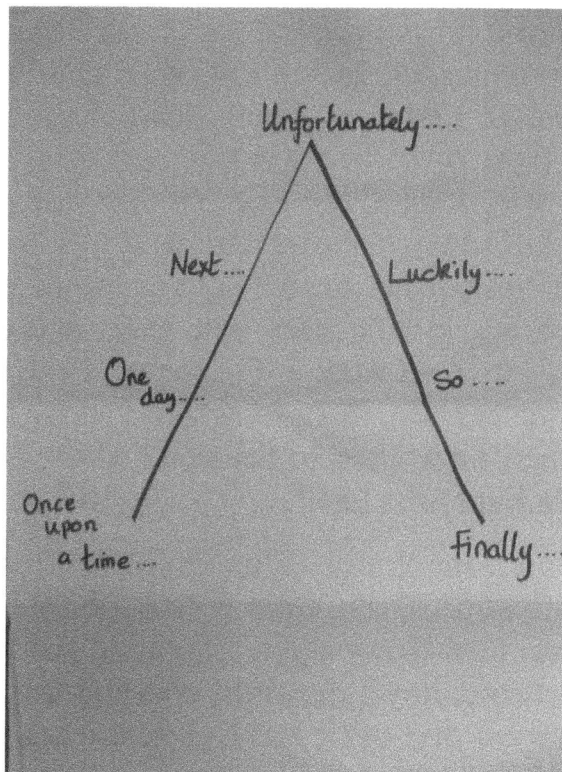

Figure 13. The story mountain pattern with story steps.

a. Start with an opening that introduces a character – '*Once upon a time, there was …*' Ask for some ideas: '*We could have a little girl, a little boy or an animal.*' Once you have agreed on the main character, add on a 'who' clause to say where the character lives, e.g. '*Once upon a time, there was a little bear who lived in a cave.*'

b. Now get the story going by deciding 'when' the story takes place: '*One day/morning/afternoon/night*'. This can be added to by thinking about the weather: '*cold/hot/sunny/rainy/snowy.* You might now have, '*Once upon a time, there was a little bear who lived in a cave. One snowy night …*' Now ask the children to complete the idea – '*What happened? What did the little bear do?*': '*Once upon a time, there was a little bear who lived in a cave. One snowy night little bear went for a walk in the forest.*'

c. Now you could spend time asking what happened next and get a sequence of things that the main character does. To help structure this, use 'first', 'next' and 'after that'. So, the bear might walk down a path and meet an owl, then meet a fox and finally a badger: **'Once upon a time, there was a little bear who lived in a cave. One snowy night, little bear went for a walk in the forest. First, he walked down the path and met an old owl. Next, he walked under the trees and met a red fox. After that, he walked to the pond where he met Mr Badger.'**

d. However, if the story is to have any bite, then you will eventually need a dilemma. Trigger this with a key word such as 'unfortunately'. The dilemma is really hard for children, so it is worth discussing story problems when you tell or read stories. *'What went wrong in that story?'* Listen to some ideas or present them with a choice, e.g. *'Well little bear might get lost or little bear might meet a scary animal. Which shall we have in our story?'* Often, a child will give a different idea (because children like to have their own ideas) and that is all to the good. So, you might now have: **'Once upon a time, there was a little bear who lived in a cave. One snowy night, little bear went for a walk in the forest. First, he walked down the path and met an old owl. Next, he walked under the trees and met a red fox. After that, he walked to the pond where he met Mr Badger. Unfortunately, little bear was lost!'**

e. Now you will need a resolution. This could be heralded by a word such as 'so' or 'luckily'. **'Once upon a time, there was a little bear who lived in a cave. One snowy night, little bear went for a walk in the forest. First, he walked down the path and met an old owl. Next, he walked under the trees and met a red fox. After that, he walked to the pond where he met Mr Badger. Unfortunately, little bear was lost! Luckily, kind Mr Badger took him by his paw and led him all the way home.'**

f. Eventually the story must move to a satisfying ending ('finally') and of course everyone will live **'happily ever after'**: **'Once upon a time, there was a little bear who lived in a cave. One snowy night, little bear went for a walk in the forest. First, he walked down the path and met an old owl. Next, he walked under the trees and met a red fox. After that, he walked to the pond where he met Mr Badger. Unfortunately, little bear was lost! Luckily, kind Mr Badger took him by his paw and led him all the way home. Finally, little bear ran into the cave where his Mummy gave him a big cuddle and they all lived happily ever after.'**

g. Of course, patterns will be borrowed from other stories and recycled and new stories may well feature characters, settings or events previously met elsewhere.

The astute teacher may also select the right tale for the right occasion. One teacher became fed up with the sand tray continually having water poured into it so she invented a story about how this spoilt everyone's play – and as if by magic, the sand tray was never misused again! Stories might be made up to help lonely children or maybe a child who won't share. In this way, some teachers use stories to teach and to heal.

Often all children need is the invitation, '*Let's all make up a story and I'll write it down so we can make a book*', and they are away. In one class I visited, the teacher firmly believed that children could not possibly make up a story. Never one to miss a challenge, I gathered the children onto the carpet and we made up a simple story about a golden umbrella and Captain Fred! Once we had done this as a class, I asked for volunteers to make up a story of their own – virtually every hand shot up. Here is one that I recorded word for word from a small boy:

> *Once upon a time, there was a little boy called Bob and he was going to his friend's and on the way it was dark and Father Christmas was nearly coming and the snow started to fall and he turned home and he quickly ran home to his friend's house. The next day it was Christmas and all the presents and then he went home and his presents in a big Christmas bag.*

You can probably guess what time of year I made that visit!

As I have suggested, many teachers of young children do not believe that their children can make up a story. This must mean that they have never really listened carefully to children playing! Most of the time children are engaged in making up and playing through stories, albeit somewhat fragmented and rudimentary, in their imaginative play. Many teachers delay making up stories, believing that they have to wait. However, the more stories that the class makes up, the more the children will also play at inventing stories for themselves. Inevitably, they will mingle their own life with classroom interests, alongside what they are gleaning from storymaking. Their stories will have characters from TV alongside themselves! It works well to hold regular weekly story inventing sessions. Initially, these will have to be guided by the teacher. You can re-use familiar characters, settings and patterns as well as familiar connectives and sentence patterns. But of course, invention is an opportunity for new ideas, drawing on the children's experiences of stories (read and told) and life.

The alternative to holding a once-weekly story invention session is to do a little bit every day so that the story is built up over a week, little by little. So you might decide to have a ten-minute slot each day when you make up the next part of the story. This would be similar to what teachers do with reading. Every nursery and reception class has a session for reading to the children, so why not have a daily session for making up a story with the children? Either way, you end up with about thirty stories being created in a year!

At first, the teacher will have to guide the story and provide many ideas and choices but gradually over time it is important to withdraw so that the children take more and more responsibility for the inventions. This is the movement from dependence to independence. Remember to keep the story invention simple. Settle the children down and introduce your story ideas or some sort of engaging stimulus. Scaffold their ideas as the story unfolds. It will help if you hold the story mountain pattern in your mind. Young children will come up with random ideas, so try not to be too fussy – anything can happen in stories.

The story of 'The Stone Boy' was made up in a reception class at Alfred Sutton Primary School in Reading and turned into a Big Book for class reading.

The Stone Boy

Once upon a time, there was a little girl called Daisy-Rose who was going to visit her cousin called Nicky. Nicky lives in a tiny cottage in a dark, spooky forest. First Daisy-Rose said 'Bye bye' to her mummy and put on her sparkly pink coat. Next Daisy-Rose crept into the dark, spooky forest, past some giant, magical toadstools.

Around the corner, by the lake was Nicky's tiny cottage. Daisy-Rose rang the doorbell, DING DONG, but nobody opened the door. Nicky had disappeared! It was a mystery! Daisy-Rose found a ticket on the floor. It was for a magic unicorn, so she hopped onto the magic unicorn and it flew to the haunted castle.

It was very spooky and covered in cobwebs. Daisy-Rose was feeling really scared, but feeling a bit brave she knocked loudly on the wooden door. 'Nicky, are you there?', she shouted. Then she slowly opened the door and saw that Nicky had been turned into stone. Daisy-Rose burst into tears and wished for a good witch to turn him back into a real boy.

Suddenly, the good witch appeared in a puff of smoke with her magic book. She looked for the page with the magic spell to turn Nicky back. She found the spell, waved her wand and shouted, 'ANABADABADA' and with a boom of fireworks, Nicky was a real boy.

Nicky and Daisy-Rose thanked the good witch for helping them save Nicky and they said, 'Would you like to come to our disco?' 'Yes', *she said and with another puff of smoke they were safely back at Nicky's cottage, having a disco.*

The End

January - February 2013

The story mountain pattern of problem/resolution will take you a long way. However, you can also draw on other resources for simple plot lines. Try using nursery rhymes. The following can all be retold as stories: *'Humpty Dumpty'*, *'Sing a Song of Sixpence'*, *'Lucy Locket'*, *'Three Blind Mice'*, *'Little Jack Horner'*, *'Jack Spratt'*, *'Simple Simon'*, *'Mary had a Little Lamb'*, *'Hey diddle diddle'*, *'Goosey Goosey Gander'*, *'Little Miss Muffett'*. You can also recycle ideas from picture books as well as from the bank of oral stories and traditional tales. Sometimes it helps to take a class incident and use that to create a story.

Ideas for class or group inventions

- Play – time to daydream, to close your eyes and begin to 'see' a story.

- Use intriguing objects – a shiny button, a lantern, an old map, a key.

- A letter arrives; half a secret message is discovered.

- Drama – acting out and creating a story together.

- Drawing a large story map to use for inventions – draw the map and then ask the children what they think might be happening in the story!

- Use a bag of objects, characters, settings (photos or pictures) – select and then make a story up using the ingredients. Let children choose and then have the fun of making up a story.

- Limit the selection of possibilities so there aren't too many characters to choose from.

- Use a set of character and settings cards to choose 'who' and 'where'.

- Give the 'baddie' a negative characteristic – sad, lonely, angry, mean, spiteful, foolish, cunning, sly.

- Give the main character a positive characteristic – clever, brave, hungry, lonely, hopeful, careful, kind, generous, happy.

- Choose a picture and pin it up – tell the story of what is happening, has just happened and what might happen next. Use pictures, posters, videos, stills.

- Give each child a chance to choose or contribute.

- Everyone likes choosing from story bags and boxes. Hide an object, puppet or picture in a box or bag. Use this as a starting point to develop a story.

- Make sure that the telling process is repetitive to aid early language development – and do not rush what is happening. Make it very clear. Develop a routine and stick to it.

- Have the main connectives on cards with photos of the children doing the actions. Keep drawing on these for basic language consolidation.

- Use story 'equipment', e.g. characters, settings, cards with things that happen, things that go wrong, and ideas for 'putting everything right'.

- This is not the teacher's 'show', so make sure that you take time to listen to and value children's ideas. It does not matter what they come up with – seize any idea and run with it. This will give children confidence to suggest ideas.

- Leave your story equipment (cards, props and map) out for children to use.

- Make durable 'floor maps', using rolls of cloth; these can be accompanied by small boxes containing different toys for different sorts of stories.

- Provide bags with simple puppets.

- Read a favourite picture book and then make up a new story about the main character.

- When making up a story, keep going back to the start as the story is made up so you go over it cumulatively, adding the next section, bit by bit.

- Use signs and actions as well as drawings to represent the emerging story.

- Use simple story structures, e.g. going from one place to another with something scary happening on the way.

- Do not worry if the children's ideas ramble, especially early on as a more 'adult' structure will take years to develop.

- Make sure it ends 'happily ever after', especially if there is something scary in the story.

- Use your voice to make the story come alive as you make it up. Add in simple 'runs', such as: *they slept and they slept and they slept*.

The run gives rhythm and will make the story more memorable and easier to retell.

- Record the story by writing it down in a class storybook on your lap or on a flipchart – or draw the map as it is made up. Remember that drawing and shared writing on a flipchart will make the process slower

- Use a set of dilemma cards to choose a story idea, e.g.

  - Helping someone who has a problem

  - Someone is naughty

  - Helping someone who is lost

  - Going on a journey somewhere

  - Feeling afraid

  - Surprises

  - Getting in trouble

  - Character change stories e.g. Cinderella – poor to rich/angry to calm/sad to happy/lonely to befriended/mean to generous/silly to wise/wrong to right

  - Trying hard to do something

  - Taking something from one place to another

  - Looking for something

  - Visiting someone or a special place

  - Lost stories

  - Stuck in the mud – or stuck anywhere and getting out

  - Helping and rescuing

  - Going to a forbidden place

  - *Warning stories – disobeying the warning*

  - *Overcoming the monster stories*

- Reuse a familiar plot pattern, nursery rhyme or picture book idea.

- Have a weekly class or group invention session.
- Or, have a ten-minute story invention session every day so that a little bit more is added to the story daily over a week.
- Start by drawing a map of the class stories.
- Move on to recording the stories through shared writing.

Daily inventions through play

As has already been noted, children should be inventing stories every day through their play. If the classroom is set up with costumes and toys, opportunities to play at story will occur naturally, especially where the adults intervene in the children's play, encouraging stories to grow. Story language and images can be recycled, experimented with and transformed.

Very young children find making stories up much easier if they have toys to hold and move around. Practitioners have noticed that children often look round the room for something that might appear in their story. This may be because they do not yet have a sufficiently strong internal, imaginative bank of characters, settings, objects and possibilities, so they have to use something external. Gradually, you may notice that they draw on their internal abstract world and characters and runs of language will appear from different stories and rhymes. You may well find Mr Gumpy climbing a beanstalk and chasing a ginger-bread man!

As we have already noted, story is central to much of what happens in play. Children may well on entry to a nursery or reception class play in isolation or parallel. Gradually, they will move towards more inter-active play and story invention where they begin to use each other's ideas, bouncing off possibilities and moving the play forwards. This can be modelled and encouraged so that their stories become increas-ingly co-constructed. Once the children have a common, shared experi-ence of a class story, they are more likely to play together because they have a common, imaginative experience to enter and use for play. Story binds us together.

Take a good look at the classroom and outside space and think about where you can create opportunities for children to play at stories and make stories up. This may involve creating a specific story space. There should be an area for role-play where there are costumes as well as toys. Are there fuzzy felts or puppets with a mini theatre? Different areas with small-world play will invite story. However you organise the room, a key element in encouraging story invention will be the importance that the adults give this when modelling play.

One school uses long rolls of coloured cloth and mini tubs of toys. The children choose a roll and tub and set themselves up. The roll of cloth becomes the story map. An adult settles down with the children and together a story can be retold or invented. Then the adult gradu-ally withdraws as the children play at stories themselves. The adult's role is to trigger a story, to model storytelling, using the key language features that have been decided as well as to listen and enjoy. Gentle questioning may also extend a child's thinking: '*Oooh, what happens now?'* will usually elicit further events. A further role for adults is to make suggestions for stories so that they open up possibilities for the story to take off in new directions. This does not mean taking over the story but gently suggesting a new avenue: *'Does the lion chase them away?'* Often children will reject such intrusions by firmly stating what will happen!

If we play well with children and are skilled story inventors ourselves, then they will follow our lead. In its simplest form, I recall a reception class in South Wales. The teacher settled with a group and a hat box. Inside the hat box she had placed a few objects and a finger puppet of a mouse. *'Now, I'm going to make up a story and I want you all to help me.'* So she took out the mouse and began to tell a story about a mouse going to visit the Queen. After the mouse had set off for London, she paused and asked a child to look in the box for *'who little mouse met on her way'*. The child pulled out a toy cow. The teacher then asked, *'And what did the cow say to the little mouse?'* *'Where are you going'*, mooed the child, solemnly in a deep cow voice! *'I'm going to London to visit the Queen,'* replied the mouse. *'May I come too?'* replied the cow (with everyone giggling) and off they set. They *'walked and they walked and they walked until ...'* and then another animal was chosen. Once the story had been completed, the teacher left the hat box with the children and they took it in turns to be the mouse. Nothing could have been easier. Each week, the 'story hat box' would have different puppets and toys, so that the challenge is varied.

Regular shared writing of class and group stories will encourage children to take an interest in writing their own inventions. Small children love to make little books and write down their own stories, drawing on familiar oral and picture stories. The more that the teacher models this, the more children will take to this activity by choice. Of course, daily handwriting, phonics for spelling and sentence writing is essential to help children develop stamina and succeed.

Every teacher and teaching assistant should carry a notepad and be in the habit of capturing stories as they happen. These can then be shared later on with the class. It is useful to have a specific space for storymaking. A table could be devoted to drawing maps, retelling into a handheld recorder (such as Easi-Speak from TTS) as well as dictating to an adult scribe.

Skilful and gentle questioning at the point of composition helps young children develop their telling, especially by providing a sense of being an interested listener to the tale. Relationships and connections can be made between stories that have been read or told, as well as class events as they become interwoven into a new story. One four-year-old eyed me with gentle concern and informed me, *'I've got a wish in my pocket.'* Of course, this was too much to resist – what was the wish and what would happen? Did anyone else have a wish in their pocket? Suddenly, stories began to emerge concerning wishes. The cunning teacher is always on the lookout for creative moments such as these.

When I worked in teacher training, I ran a PGCE that consisted mainly of mature students. One of the weekly tasks was to explore the difference between what children could do orally and how this compared with their writing. One student came across a boy called Oliver in a Year 1 class. It was September 1990 and when asked to write Oliver took some time to produce, *'The clivdlmn er cliecpin ckcs'* ('The children are collecting conkers'). This was a labour of love with Oliver carving away at the page, taking thirty minutes to complete the single sentence. Of course, from our standpoint now we can see that teaching him phonics for spelling might have been a useful thing but what strikes me most is the contrast with his oral retelling. For the student then asked Oliver to make up a story and tell it and so he did. He called his story *'The Magic Box'* and the teacher recorded it. She gave him the same amount of time, half an hour.

The Magic Box

Once upon a time, there was a little boy called Oliver and one day he was at the seaside building a sandcastle and then when he was digging he found a map. He took it to his parents. 'Look what I've found!' he said. His parents luckily were divers because this map showed a very magic box under the sea. They said that they would go under the sea.

Then the next day came and then they went under the sea and then they saw a whale. They had to swim fast to the cave. Then they got in they saw a big box with what must have been a thousand padlocks on it. The boy's father was called Frederick and he took his knight sword out and then cut the padlocks. He opened it. Then thousands of flashings of lightning and mist came out and the mist showed them another map and then it fell out. They looked at it and it showed them to another box and it showed them that wasn't the magic box.

So they followed the map and this time a shark came along so they had to swim fast because this was a killer shark. They had to swim even faster and then suddenly they saw a whale coming their way so they went to dive away upwards. The little boy's mother went downwards and the little boy's father went upwards. Then the whale and the shark banged against each other, which was unfortunate for the *shark because the whale had his mouth open. So that was the end of the shark.*

They swam to the cave and they saw an even bigger chest with even more padlocks about a trillion or something. so the little boy's father got his knife out and cut the padlocks but this time only half of them he could cut and then he had to get a more special knife which was hidden in the cave that was with the map. So he cut those padlocks and then he opened the box and then all the magic came out flashes of lightning showing sort of pictures of a hundred years ago and Egypt and Jesus and then a magic sort of see-through bag came out on a tray and then they saw some magic water inside. He untied it. All the water came out then everything came in colours in the wrong colours and then it came on to the sea and the sea was purple. So they swam up to shore very quickly and only there were the ones that had colours on - none of the fish had - but they had colours all over, but their faces hadn't, thank goodness.

Then they took the treasure chest with them and that was covered in colours now and the little boy saw them and then suddenly a sort of angel pirate thing came out of the box and he took his cutlass out and tried to fight the man and the man took his sword out and an arrow gun he had then they started fighting. He shot the arrow gun at the pirate sort of man and then he dropped down dead this time forever. Then they took the magic box home and opened it again. He wished for something and then it came true. He wished to be king of all the worlds and he was. He was sitting on a throne by the sea and he was holding his arrow gun and then they lived happily ever after.

Oliver followed this mighty piece of storytelling by proceeding to ask the student various questions. These ran as follows:

Now where did the man find the map?
What happened to the whale and the shark?
How did the man open the chest?
How did the man kill the pirate forever?

Perhaps he was checking to see if my student had been paying attention! Certainly, the idea of asking questions had come from somewhere. The most striking thing that has stayed with me for twenty-five years is the contrast between what he can write down in thirty minutes and what he can say in that time. His oral composition far outstrips his transcriptional ability. Indeed, if we never capture and value children's oral compositions, we only know the tip of the iceberg. They may be small but inside every child there is a wealth that so often remains unvoiced, unrecognised, unknown and undervalued. Now Oliver still had some time left, so he proceeded to tell a further story of similar length involving two men called David and Martin swimming underwater and finding a lava pit!

A final idea for invention: Talk for Writing consultant Carol Satterthwaite suggests using carpet tiles. The idea is simple enough. Paste or fix the tiles along the wall in a snake pattern rather like a pathway.

The carpet tiles are the scenes from a story. Now provide laminated cards that have Velcro on the back. On each card there are drawings that might be of characters, settings, objects, animals or events. The children then use these to make a story up or to sequence the story that you are working on. You could have two carpet tile story snakes – one for the current story and another for inventions. An alternative would be to fix the carpet tiles to the wall in the shape of a story mountain. By each section, provide key vocabulary such as 'once upon a time … who …', 'one day', 'unfortunately', 'luckily', 'finally'. Alternatively, the key connectives could be provided on cards to fix in the relevant places. Use talking tins to remind children what the words say.

- Set up story play situations so that children play daily at making up new stories.
- Intervene in story play to open up possibilities.
- Use plenty of shared writing so that children want to be writers.
- Set up writing areas so that pencils and paper, mini booklets and maps are available for early writing and mapping.

Individual story inventions and dramatising

The classroom and outside area should be set up so that children can play at making up new stories on a daily basis. The invitation to playful creation may be enhanced using a similar approach to that developed in the USA by Vivian Gussin Paley, and championed in the UK by Make-Believe Arts and Trisha Lee. A positive evaluation of this work was carried out by the Open University and can be found in a 2013 'Evaluation Report of MakeBelieve Arts Helicopter Technique of Storytelling and Story Acting' [http://oro.open.ac.uk/38391/1/MBA%20Final%20Report%20.pdf]. More details of the approach can be found through the MakeBelieve website as well as the various books of Vivian Gussin Paley, which ought to be read by all early years practitioners, if only for their humanity.

Some nurseries and reception classes have established a routine where every day it is someone's turn to be the 'storyteller'. This might involve sitting in a special area (such as a 'story castle'). The adult encourages the child to invent a new story, using questioning to gently help the story unfold. Showing genuine pleasure and interest is the teacher's most powerful ingredient. The adult writes down what the child says in the child's own words. This is crucial because if the language is changed, the message to the child may be that they 'got it wrong' and fear of being 'incorrect' will inhibit creativity; it is also a record of their language development.

The inconsistencies and immaturities in what the child says indicate what the teacher needs to continually model and may be built into the next story to be learned. The slipups tell us what to model. If a child only uses 'and' as a conjunction, then the teacher now knows that a story is required that makes repetitive use of 'so', 'but' and 'next'. Of course, some oral readjustments are often made as the story emerges. However fragmentary the story might be, it ought to be accepted and valued.

The story develops and the teacher writes down the child's words as fast as possible, occasionally re-reading what has happened so far. This helps the child make connections between incidents. At the start of the year, the first few stories may well be skimpy but the more stories that children hear from their peers, the more stories and rhymes they learn and the more we read with them, then the larger their bank of possibilities and language. Gradually, the stories grow!

The second part to this simple routine involves 'dramatising' the child's story. At another point in the day, the teacher moves the action over to the 'story-stage' – this is just an area where stories can be acted out. You can create a simple space for dramatising stories by using a carpet, four corners made out of objects or tape to create a story space. The adult reads the child's story aloud and classmates perform the story. Much discussion takes place alongside the performing.

Again, at first, the dramatising might be rather hesitant but gradually confidence grows. Props, costumes and toys can all be used to enhance a retelling. If the children's stories are jotted in a special storybook and dated, this acts as a simple record of their story language development over time. Of course, children's own stories may well involve them playing out some inner concern or worry. Conflicts may arise. Cruel tyrants may need to be defeated. We are not psychiatrists, so leave the natural functions of play and story to work on the children's inner worlds. The words, *let's pretend* are an invitation to manipulate, control and explore the world and ourselves ...

Ideas for organising story inventions through play

- Make durable 'floor maps', using rolls of cloth; these might be accompanied by small boxes with different toys for different sorts of stories.

- Provide bags with simple puppets.

- Create a story space where children can go to invent stories. Provide paper for maps or mark-making as well as story bags/boxes, toys, puppets, blank maps.

- Draw half a new story and tell it to the children. Then ask them to help you make up the rest of the story – many children LOVE this idea.

- If you model plenty of mapping and writing, the children will also draw and make marks – as long as the equipment is provided.

- 'Blu-tack' up characters and settings for children to select and stick onto a map.

- Have a roll of wallpaper/tough lining paper – move along the paper physically – drawing and telling the tale as you go. Invite the children to join in.

- Each child can add the next part of the story – drawing onto the wallpaper map.

- Use the sand tray – draw a map in the sand with your fingers and use objects or small toys. Move these around and make stories up. Then leave the children to it!

- Use string on the floor to mark out a story journey. Provide toys and model how to make a story up, with children joining in. Then stand back.

Join in with storymaking and invention. Make suggestions to open up the possibilities. Avoid over-questioning to 'test' children but use prompting or questioning to help a story develop.

- Create a routine so that every day several children have a chance to tell their story to an adult and have it recorded.
- These stories are shared daily with the class and acted out as enjoyable, social experiences.

From telling into writing

Within weeks of entering a reception class, children will have already begun the important business of developing transcriptional skills such as holding and controlling a pencil, as well as developing phonemic awareness and starting the phonic programme.

Much effort and time has been spent carefully outlining the teaching of phonics in England. This is crucial for spelling. If a child cannot say a word and hear its constituent sounds clearly – and doesn't know which letters might represent these, then early spelling will surely remain a mystery. The faster that this becomes automatic and subterranean so that a child can spell without thinking, the more space the child's brain has to focus on composition.

Early on, children's stories and ideas can be dictated to an adult or recorded using a dictaphone. Once the teacher has modelled sufficient story maps, children will use mapping and drawing as an early but highly effective form of recording ideas and stories. Indeed, when using a map to retell a tale, it often appears as if the child is 'reading' the map. The maps are an early form of writing and reading.

As transcription skills develop, children should move into writing. Develop good writing habits by keeping a close eye on pencil grip and letter formation! The children's maps will soon contain words as labels. Sentences will follow. All of this should be modelled and the children's early writing taught in small groups, preferably in a quiet area so that there is time to think and learn how to take care.

Similar time and attention needs to be given to the development of language, especially story language because of its crucial role as a primary mode of thought. Indeed, composition should exceed transcription. However, in many reception classes the development of composition is slow. By contrast, in Talk for Writing classes, children know a communal story within the first two or three weeks of entering school. Remember, many children arrive in school virtually three years behind where they might have been in terms of language development. There is no time to be wasted.

By the end of the reception year, some children will be able to write whole stories down. They may be writing the original, an innovation or invention. Given the complex demands on a young child in terms of pencil control, phonics for spelling as well as developing composition, very young children should not be asked to write a story down unless they can easily tell their story. If a tale has been developed orally first, it means that a large chunk of cognitive space has been released so that when they write, the children's attention is focused upon transcription rather than trying to cope with the demands of composition at the same time as transcription. In other words, the idea of developing composition orally first makes the act of writing easier for an emerging

28
VIDEO

The importance of teaching basic writing skills systematically writer. Draw and retell before writing. Common tricky spellings such as 'once' should be provided on a spelling card. Before moving into writing, make sure that you have generated with the children different possibilities for new characters, settings, animals, objects and events. Simple lists of these should be displayed so that the children do not get stuck for an idea.

Preschool children also enjoy being writers. To encourage very young children to play at writing, they need to witness adults writing with enthusiasm – stories may be recorded as well as all other sorts of writing – reminders, notes, messages, signs, information, and so on. By using a flipchart, writing may be modelled with the children joining in and helping. The transcription will usually be the adult's job while the children make suggestions for what might be written down. Children may also enjoy 'sharing the pen' to write letters; try simple words and even add in punctuation.

In nursery settings where adults write, and where reading is a common feature, then, as long as pencils and paper are provided, many children will automatically begin to 'play write' themselves. Ideally, these early pieces of 'writing' should be valued and read back to an adult who demonstrates obvious interest and pleasure. They may be displayed or turned into a book and celebrated by reading to others. Over time, children's 'pretend' writing takes on the form of letter shapes and as they are taught phonics/handwriting, words will gradually emerge.

As children in the nursery start to show interest in drawing, mark-making and writing, it is important to provide pencils with a triangular grip and gently show them to hold the pencil correctly. Teaching children to start at the top and move to the bottom as well as round the circle both in large actions and small is helpful as a basis for letter formation. Drawing train tracks and roads from left to right is also a playful way to encourage children to 'stay inside the lines'. By the end of nursery, most children are able to write their own name. Some young children have also been introduced to letters and sounds with simple segmentation of cvc words as a common feature. Indeed, in nurseries, we have seen children writing simple words such as 'push' or 'shop' as well as reading words, sentences and simple books with adult support. All of this happens with great joy and is a natural part of early learning.

Shared writing is carried out with the whole class. It should feel like **joint composition** with the children helping as much as possible. Key aspects to keep modelling are:

- say the sentence aloud before writing it down (oral rehearsal);
- tweak the sentence, if need be, to improve it;

- write it down;

- reread what you have written.

Keep rereading the story as it develops so that the composition is cumulative – with new sentences arising straight out of the previous one. Further points include:

- help children generate possibilities and accept the most effective;

- maintain a pace that engages – brisk, contrasted by pausing for 'thinking time' and 'talk partners';

- write whole stories and not just openings.

- try having a 'running story' that is added to over a number of days;

- plan together by story mapping – then orally retell before turning the map into a story;

- demonstrate how to use a sound mat or spelling card for key spellings.

Guided writing should be an opportunity for children to record their stories. Small groups, with similar needs, are brought together. Some groups may be retelling and mapping their innovations. Others might be at the stage of including simple labels, while other groups may be writing sentences. By the end of the year, many reception children will write whole texts. This may be done over a number of days, bit by bit. The teacher works closely with the group, encouraging them towards independence: *'Now, how can you help yourself'*, *'What do you need to do next'* and *'Let's read it through together and have a think about how it sounds'* are the staple of such sessions. They are an opportunity for individual input at the point of composition, picking up on misconceptions and teaching as needed. Use sound mats, sentence checkers, spelling cards and other simple supports to help children succeed in their writing.

To end, it is worth pointing out that what matters most is that everyone succeeds, in their own unique way. This simple idea may seem contrary to the direction of the education system but the idea that a five-year-old can fail seems to me totally perverse. We have to start with the child, where they are and then proceed forwards, pressing on.

28
VIDEO

The importance of teaching basic writing skills systematically

Teachers' learning

When teachers begin Talk for Writing, there is a certain amount of 'imitation' of the teaching process. This usually begins with a training session in which a trainer will take the teachers through the three 'I's.

Some time will be spent having a go at chorally retelling a story. The teachers then need to go and try this out. Inevitably, you start by retelling the learned story in the same way as you learned, often using the same rhythm and sound as the trainer. One teacher once told me that when she started story work, she could hear my voice coming out of her mouth! After a number of retellings I faded away and she was telling the story in her own way. This is the oral tradition, the passing on of a story 'by word of mouth'. Of course, the children's own retellings will have the emphasis and rhythm of their teacher.

> * Use **shared writing** to teach the whole class, modelling writing skills.
> * Use **guided writing** to work with children with similar needs to develop positive writing attitudes and skills.
> * Provide a spelling card for each story containing common, tricky words.

Initially, teachers help children to learn stories using a few key strategies, such as using a map, using actions and constant retelling, underpinned by other activities that help children understand the story. Most of these suggestions will have arisen through the training. However, as confidence grows, the teacher will begin to reflect on the learning and gradually develop new ideas and strategies. The teacher is now beginning to 'innovate', increasingly making it their own approach. Occasionally, teachers will invent utterly new approaches that need to be passed on to others. In this way, Talk for Writing continually grows and develops. It is not a fixed system. Over the years, I have spent hours watching teachers and children, learning from them – and listening to what they say has worked, for which I am most grateful. The most worthwhile projects have been where clusters of schools and teachers work together over time, deepening understanding and refining their practice.

Here is an example of useful advice drawn from a group of teachers in the Neath Port Talbot area – Donna, Lynne, Kath, Julia, Denise, Dawn, Maya, Christina and Helen. We should all be grateful to Mandy and the local authority literacy team for their leadership, encouragement and vision.

* To learn the actions, play *'Simon Says'*, e.g. Simon says 'who' and they all do action.

* Build three-dimensional maps out of junk and paper or outside using big apparatus.

- Do story bit by bit and film each part, putting the sections together so that you have a whole film.

- Perform a story on location – we did '*The Three Billy Goats Gruff*' on the bridge in the river and anyone passing by had to answer a riddle or the troll might catch them!

- For some reason the idea of doing lots of writing has caught on because I kept saying, 'So we write and we write and we write'.

- Have a long map on the ground – and have flaps that come over the main map to show simple innovations such as new characters. We did an innovation on '*The Three Bears*' – '*The Three Scary Sisters*'.

- We made long maps like zigzag books.

- You can see progress in the maps – the sequence of events becomes clearer. In Year 1, it can help to have simple boxes to draw each scene.

- Learn stories in triangles.

- You can hear the impact of imitation when the children make up their own stories in their intonation, e.g. 'unfortunately'.

- The process provides motivation for learning because everyone succeeds.

- Some very weak writers can do great retellings.

- Learning poetry chorally creates a '*web of remembered words and phrases to use in stories and our writing*'.

- I have one boy with very considerable problems and I really didn't believe he could retell '*The Three Bears*' but he could! This makes me wonder about how else I can vary my teaching to help him learn.

- Put tricky, common spellings on the map.

- Use colour for time words so that 'first' is always red, 'next' is always blue, 'after that' is always green and 'finally' is always purple.

- I have a storymaking area with a bank of maps, cloaks and a storytelling chair. My class now constantly play at retelling and innovations.

- It is not about chanting but about telling.

- For inventions, we just settle down and I say, '*Now who can tell me about our adventures?*' and a story starts to emerge with us as the main characters.

We've had so much fun!

Part 2
Involving families

CHAPTER 9

Why involving parents matters

'If we want good outcomes for children, then we must look to the role of parents as their children's educators.' – Dr Gillian Pugh, evidence to the House of Commons Select Committee on Education and Employment, 2000.

'If parents engage with their children's education, the attainment of the child will increase by 15% no matter what the social background of the family.' – Professor Charles Desforges, 2003

'The home learning environment has a greater influence on a child's intellectual and social development than parental occupation, education or income. What parents do is more important than who they are, and a home learning environment that is supportive of learning can counteract the effects of disadvantage in the early years.' – The EPPE Project, Edward Melhuish and colleagues, 2008

'Nothing can be achieved without working with parents. All our recommendations are about enabling parents to achieve the aspirations that they have for their children.' – Frank Field, 'The Foundation Years: Preventing Poor Children becoming Poor Adults', The Report of the Independent Review on Poverty and Life Chances, 2010

'Mothers and fathers are their children's first and most important educators ... What happens in this home environment has more influence on future achievement than innate ability, material circumstances or the quality of pre-school and school provision.' – DfE, 'Supporting Families in the Foundation Years', 2011

'An awful lot of words to tell us what we already know.' My mother's blunt comment on my brother's first family-health research paper comes to mind when attempting to sum up what research tells us about the importance of involving families in their children's developing literacy. Unequivocally and unsurprisingly, research shows that families really do matter. What else needs saying? Below, I have attempted to summarise not only what we know, how we know it and what type of involvement works best, but also what governments in the UK in recent years have done as a result of this information, and how much notice practitioners are taking of the implications of all this.

Awareness of just how central parents are to a child's education is not new. Apparently, sometime in the first century AD, the Roman rhetorician Quintilian advised that as soon as a child was born, the parent must 'make sure that the nurses speak properly' and 'devote the keenest possible care, from the moment he becomes a parent, to fostering the promise of an orator to be'. Two millennia or so later, the US government asked a panel of child-development experts to draw up a programme to help communities meet the needs of disadvantaged pre-school children. Their report became the blueprint for Project Head Start, launched in 1965 to support low-income families with children from three to school age. In 1994, Early Head Start was added on, aimed at families with infants and toddlers on the basis of evidence from research and practice which illustrated that early intervention through high-quality programmes enhances children's physical, social, emotional and cognitive development. Sure Start (see page 154), launched in the UK in 1998, is based on Head Start.

Every parent really does matter

When the Labour Party came to power in the UK in 1997, 'education, education, education' was very much on the agenda. The key issue was what needed to be done to make a real difference to literacy standards in England. As much as these things can be measured over time, research carried out by the National Foundation for Educational Research had shown that literacy standards had remained relatively unchanged for fifty years – a surprising finding given the very wide range of teaching approaches since 1948. It also contradicts the myth, much promoted by the popular press (always failing to grasp the difference between illiteracy and functional literacy), that we were hurtling towards illiteracy: declining from some mythical golden age when the whole country waited agog for the next instalment of Dickens' latest novel. In reality, the education system had been doing very well for the majority of children but failing what researchers powerfully referred to as 'the long tail of underachievement' – a significant minority who were doing badly when compared with children in other Western countries.

The National Literacy Strategy, launched in 1998, and building on the previous Conservative government's National Literacy Project, did improve things. Literacy standards began to rise. In England in 1997, only 67% of eleven-year-olds reached Level 4 or above in Reading but by 2000 that number had risen impressively to 83%. However, the government target was 85%, thus relative success was presented as failure in a culture that was increasingly becoming target driven. After that, results began to plateau – thus the 2010 result was still 83%: the government's desired year-on-year progress did not materialise. Although results recently have begun to climb – the 2014 and 2015 results reaching 89%, is there a limit to what teachers alone can achieve by pedalling harder in a more focused direction?

The first emphasis of the Strategy was on primary schools. Most strangely, in the light of the overwhelming research to the contrary, speaking and listening was not included in the initial literacy focus – reading and writing were the order of the day. However, throughout, there was an emphasis on involving family. The importance of securing parental involvement was outlined in the 1997 White Paper, 'Excellence in Schools' (DfEE, 1997), which ushered in the Strategy. At this point, the Strategy focused on providing parents with information, giving them a voice and encouraging parental partnerships with schools. Meanwhile, the new government started funding a number of literacy-related research overviews to establish the direction in which to move.

One piece of research that contributed to the understanding that families were key was the strikingly titled 'The Early Catastrophe – The 30 Million Word Gap by Age 3', published in 1995 by two American research professors Betty Hart and Todd Risley. Their findings have reverberated around our understanding of the importance of the home to children's literacy development ever since. Their longitudinal study (repeated observations of the same variables over long periods of time) involved observing forty-two young children in their homes from 7–9 months to three years to determine which factors in early experience might account for the development of vocabulary skills.

Unsurprisingly, what they found was a parallel between the language the children heard at home and the language they could use: language in – language out. But what lies behind the headline is the magnitude of the difference. Their estimate of a 30-million-word gap is based on the fact that, in words heard, the average child on welfare was having half as much experience per hour as the average working-class child and less than one-third that of the average child in a professional family. When you extrapolate the actual figures for a fourteen-hour waking day over three years, you can reach the 30-million-word gap. Not only did the children on welfare have much smaller vocabularies, but they also added words much more slowly, which would suggest an ever-widening gap. Moreover, the children on welfare on average heard twice as many negative as positive communications; children with professional parents on average experienced six positive communications to every one negative, which encouraged them to communicate. As the researchers hauntingly expressed it, 'Cognitively, experience is sequential: experiences in infancy establish habits of seeking, noticing, and incorporating new and more complex experiences, as well as schemas for categorizing and thinking about experiences.' In many ways, this research has been the linchpin of understanding how much talking to children matters. These findings have recently been echoed in a book entitled *Learning to Write, Reading to Learn: Genre, Knowledge and Pedagogy in the Sydney School* by James Martin and David Rose.

Interestingly, in 2009, Meredith L. Rowe, an assistant professor of human psychology at the University of Chicago had attempted to identify what home behaviours might have led to this inequality of language acquisition and how it could be remedied. The researchers (Rowe and Goldin-Meadow, 2009) videotaped fifty children from the full range of social backgrounds to see how they interacted with their parents when they were fourteen months old and assessed their vocabulary skills at this early stage of language production. They discovered that, although there was **no relation** between the word types parents used and the word types their fourteen-month-old children used, the children from the higher income backgrounds frequently used gesture to communicate because their parents frequently used gesture to communicate with them. The same children and their families were then videotaped forty months later when the children were four and a half. There was a correlation between the level of gesture used at fourteen months and the size of vocabulary children achieved at four and a half years, which suggests that gesture to reinforce the meaning of words is key to early language acquisition. (Such research may help explain why the Talk for Writing approach has proved so successful – because of its emphasis on actions to help children understand and internalise language.)

In the same year as the National Literacy Strategy was launched in England, the government also launched Sure Start across the UK, the cornerstone of its drive to tackle child poverty and social exclusion. Sure Start is run through local programmes in the most deprived regions of the country. It aims to achieve better outcomes for children, parents and communities by increasing the availability of childcare for all children; improving children's health, education and emotional development; and supporting parents in their role alongside developing employment aspirations. One of the ways in which Sure Start centres work is by providing children with high quality play and learning experiences; children's early language development is a key determinant of Sure Start's success. The logic of focusing on the home was reinforced in 2002 when the Organisation for Economic Cooperation and Development (OECD) issued a report showing that, 'Being more enthusiastic about reading and a frequent reader was more of an advantage, on its own, than having well-educated parents in good jobs.' Its research showed that children from deprived backgrounds performed better in tests than those from more affluent homes if they enjoyed reading books, newspapers and comics in their spare time. The study, which covered thirty-one countries, found encouraging children to read for pleasure could compensate for social problems that would usually affect their academic performance. Their findings have been reiterated by PIRLS (the Progress in International Reading Literacy Study conducted in England in 2011 and published in 2012): 'After controlling for socio- economic background, children whose parents regularly read to them in the first year of primary school score on average 14 points higher in reading tests at age 15.'

Sadly, Sure Start, though still in existence, has been greatly cutback by the endless years of austerity that followed the 2008 recession. Local authority spending cuts resulted in a 20% fall in the number of children using Sure Start centres between 2014 and 2018, with the most dramatic decline occurring in some of England's poorest areas. The charity Action for Children estimates that 1.8 million children used Sure Start centres in England in 2017-18 – down from 2.2 million four years earlier – a direct consequence, it says, of a 62% cut in council early years' service spending since 2010. At their peak in 2010, there were 3,600 Sure Start centres. According to The Sutton Trust, between 500 and 1,000 Sure Start centres have closed totally in England since 2010 and many have greatly reduced the number of children that they support. This is particularly concerning because, at the time of updating this book (April 2020), the children whose education will be damaged most by the Coronavirus lockdown that has closed schools is those children who should have benefitted from Sure Start but never received this essential support in the name of austerity.

In 1999, the then Department for Education and Employment (DfEE) had funded the Centre for Research on the Wider Benefits of Learning, based at the Institute of Education and led by Professor Leon Feinstein, as part of its efforts to reduce social exclusion. Many of their findings were based on the 1970 British Cohort Study, which followed the lives of 17,000 people in the UK across the decades. Their findings grabbed the headlines in 2002 when it was suggested that the socio-economic attainment gap was evident in children as young as twenty-two months. Just before their second birthday, children were given four simple tasks to see how their skills were developing: the ability to point to different facial features when asked; putting on and taking off a pair of shoes; stacking a pile of coloured bricks; and drawing lines and circles on a piece of paper, as opposed to simple scribbles. It was discovered that the children with professional-class parents were far better at completing the tasks than children of working-class parents. A difference in income of £100 a week was equal to a 3% improvement in the ability to do the tasks. Children whose parents were educated to at least A-level standard were 14% above those whose parents were not. This reinforced the 30-million-word-gap findings about the centrality of early years to future attainment.

A few months later, Professor Charles Desforges and Alberto Abouchaar published their much-cited literature review of what research could tell us about *The Impact of Parental Involvement, Parental Support and Family Education on Pupil Achievement and Adjustment* (2003). This had been commissioned by what had, by its publication date, become the Department for Education and Skills (you rather hope they keep the old name plates for when they come round again) to inform the development of policy intended to close the social class gap in achievement. The findings of this review contributed significantly to the development of *Every Parent Matters* in 2007, in which the government set out the vital role of parents in improving their child's life chances. The key conclusion drawn by Desforges was striking: 'Parental involvement in the form of "at-home good parenting" has a significant positive effect on children's achievement and adjustment even after all other factors shaping attainment have been taken out of the equation. In the primary age range, the impact caused by different levels of parental involvement is much bigger than differences associated with variations in the quality of schools. The scale of the impact is evident across all social classes and all ethnic groups.' He summed his finding up in these telling words: '*If parents engage with their children's education, the attainment of the child will increase by 15% no matter what the social background of the family.*'

In other words, teachers pedalling faster in the right direction will not make as much difference as parental involvement. But it also drew two more very important conclusions. First, that parents indirectly influenced their child through shaping their child's self-concept as a learner and through setting high aspirations. Secondly, different levels of parental involvement are associated with social class, poverty and health, and also with parental perception of their role and their levels of confidence. As the report expressed it, 'Some parents are put off by feeling put down by schools and teachers.' This significant sentence is the focus of a later section of this chapter.

In the same year, Michael Fullan from the University of Toronto published his final evaluation of the National Literacy and Numeracy Strategies, entitled *Watching and Learning 3* (Earl et al., 2003). Although he was focusing on classroom practice, and concluded that teaching had improved substantially since the Strategies were introduced, the executive summary included a section on reaching out to the community beyond school: 'The government is well aware of the importance of involving parents in efforts to improve children's learning ... To close the gap between high and low performing children, however, may require more attention to out-of-school influences on pupil attainment.'

The more you look at the research, the more you draw the conclusion that Quintilian was right. If you want to raise standards, support parents in supporting their children's linguistic development from the moment they are born. This growing wealth of evidence that what happens in the home in the early years of a child's life is key to that child's future development, encouraged the government to fund the National Literacy Trust's *Talk to Your Baby* initiative. This provided practical advice and encouragement to families and professionals alike about the importance of early communication in children's development. *Talk to Your Baby* no longer exists but, fortunately its very useful resources can still be downloaded from the NLT website. In 2012, early years practitioner Dr Cathy Hamer, who managed the campaign, carried out a research review for the National Childbirth Trust on the importance of parent–child communication from birth. Her key findings are as follows:

1. *Language development is influenced by the child's communication environment. Parents give their babies and young child an advantage when they talk with them, read with them, listen and respond to their babbles, gestures and words. More conversations increase the advantage for children in terms of their language development.*

2. *Children's language development at the age of two (their understanding and use of vocabulary and two or three word sentences) is very strongly associated with their performance on entering primary school.*

3. *There is a strong association between a child's social background and their readiness for school as measured by their scores on school entry assessments. However, the communication environment is a more dominant predictor of early language than social background. Therefore, aiming to improve the home learning and in particular the communication environment for young children in less advantaged social groups through support for parents is considered an important strategy for addressing social inequalities in educational attainment.*

The full report is downloadable from www.literacytrust.org.uk.

What type of involvement works best

It was and is clear what would make the biggest difference: supporting families to support the literacy of their children has the highest leverage. Exactly how best to do this is not so clear. This was the focus of The Effective Provision of Pre-School Education (EPPE) Project (1999–2004 and later extended to 2014), again funded by the DfEE. EPPE was a large-scale longitudinal study of 3,000 children, which followed their progress from the age of three. It found that while parents' social class and levels of education make a difference, 'The home learning environment has a greater influence on a child's intellectual and social development than parental occupation, education or income. What parents do is more important than who they are, and a home learning environment that is supportive of learning can counteract the effects of disadvantage in the early years.'

This research also identified a range of activities for three- to seven-year-olds that were associated with positive outcomes, including:

- playing with letters and numbers, emphasising the alphabet, reading with the child;

- teaching songs and nursery rhymes, painting and drawing;

- and visiting the library.

This list is unsurprising, but it's reassuring to know that the things you thought would be useful were indeed useful. It also found significant differences in the types of home-learning activities that parents undertake with boys compared with girls. Significantly, more girls' parents had reported activities such as reading, teaching songs and nursery rhymes, suggesting that this may explain some of the variation in outcomes of boys and girls when they enter primary school.

What sort of involvement works best was also the focus of 'Parental Involvement and Student Achievement: A Meta-Analysis', published in 2005 as part of the Harvard Family Research Project (Jeynes, 2005). It analysed what could be learnt from seventy-seven pieces of research about which aspects of parental involvement help student education and which aspects are the most important. The findings underline the importance of parental involvement and that this influence comes both from voluntary involvement and parental programmes. This research concludes that schools should 'adopt strategies to enhance parental engagement in their children's schooling'... and 'familiarise themselves with the facets of parental involvement that can help the most, so that they can guide parents on what steps they can take to become more involved'. Included within this recommendation was talking and reading with your child, as well as encouraging high expectations.

In 2007, another Harvard Family Research Project, 'Family Involvement in School and Low-Income Children's Literacy Performance', built on this understanding (Dearing et al., 2007). It examined whether changes in family educational involvement between kindergarten and fifth grade (age five to ten years) affected literacy achievement, with a focus on families participating in events at their children's school. Their findings were significant. If families who were initially uninvolved in the school became more involved, their children's literacy improved. Importantly, even one or two additional involvement activities per year were associated with meaningful improvements for children. Again, this was shown to be more significant than family income, maternal level of education or the child's ethnicity. Moreover, family involvement in school matters most for children at greatest risk, where the parent has low education and low income. When family involvement levels were high, the achievement gap could be wiped out.

Such research underlines the importance of early years settings creating an educational environment that increases the involvement of families and sustains it across primary schooling. Importantly, they emphasise that increases in family involvement are most likely to occur among lower-income families when schools not only reach out to families and invite them to become involved, but also when schools help these families overcome barriers to involvement, for example child care. A useful overview of all the research on the importance of families and the home environment to literacy was compiled by Angelica Bonci for the National Literacy Trust in 2008 and subsequently updated. This can be downloaded from http://files.eric.ed.gov/fulltext/ED521654.pdf.

Overcoming the barriers to involvement

'Some parents are put off by feeling put down by schools and teachers.' The importance of Desforge's statement cannot be over-emphasised. It is easy to say that we must support families in supporting the literacy of their children and overcome the barriers to their involvement. Knowing exactly how best to do this is not so easy. The long tail of underachievement brings with it a legacy of children who felt they were failures at school becoming the parents of school children themselves and often, understandably, feeling that though they want to help their children they are not certain how to do so. Some parents shy away from engaging with schools because of their negative childhood experiences of school.

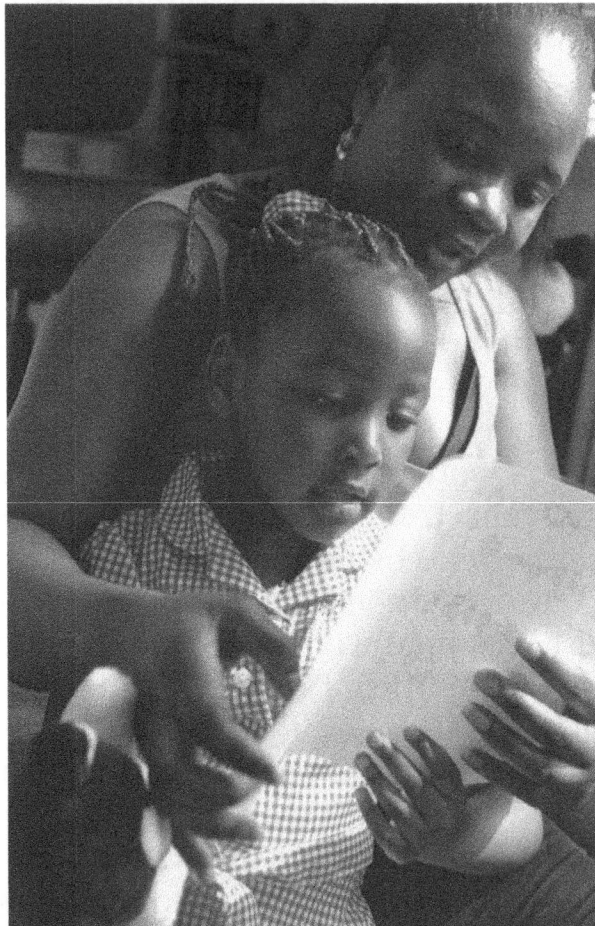

Figure 15. A parent at Lowedges sharing a storymap with her child. Picture: Linda Busses.

All early years settings and schools will say that they make parents welcome, because they know they should and it makes sense; together they can make a difference. But is involving parents at the centre of their culture? In a few establishments, the old chalk line denoting 'no parent past this point' is still alive and well in the minds of the powers that be and dictates the level of parental involvement. As one teaching assistant in a reception class explained to me in 2010, 'Parental involvement is an ideological issue in this school.' There was a surface welcome but parents were quickly ushered off site to enable the professionals to get on with the job.

Early in 2007, two researchers from Warwick University, Professor Alma Harris and Dr Janet Goodall, with funding from the Department for Education and Skills, released the results of 'Engaging Parents in Raising Achievement – Do Parents Know they Matter?' This was not only an extensive review of what the literature could tell us about the link between parental engagement and pupil achievement but also looked into what could be learnt from encouraging schools to trial new ways of engaging parents in schools, particularly those parents seen as 'hard to reach'. Thus they included in-depth case studies with thirty schools over a twelve-month period to measure the impact of different forms of parental engagement upon pupil achievement and behaviour. This resulted in three key findings:

- *Parental engagement is a powerful lever for raising student achievement in schools. Where parents and teachers work together to improve learning, the gains in achievement are significant.*

- *Parents have the greatest influence on the achievement of pupils through supporting their learning in the home rather than supporting activities in the school. It is their support of learning within the home environment that makes the maximum difference to achievement.*

- *Parental engagement is heavily linked to socio-economic status, as well as parental experience of education. Parents of certain ethnic and social groups are less likely to engage with the school. Schools that offer bespoke forms of support to these parents (i.e. literacy classes, parenting skill support) are more likely to engage them in their children's learning.*

The implications of this research are important because they suggest that there are effective ways in which schools can engage parents more fully in learning and that engaging all parents, but particularly the 'hard to reach parents', has a positive impact on achievement. Here are their practical suggestions:

- *Parental engagement must be a priority – rather than a bolt-on extra. It needs to be fully embedded and integrated in teaching and learning plans if it is to make a difference to achievement.*

- *Communication with parents should be two-way. Schools need to be clear about the aims of all communication with parents and to be prepared to listen to parents' needs.*

- *Sustaining the engagement of parents as well as reaching those parents who are less engaged, should be built into forward planning.*

- *Engaging 'hard to reach' parents has a significant impact on raising achievement and a positive effect on behaviour in schools. However engaging 'hard to reach parents' requires bespoke strategies that meet the need of the particular parent group.*

- *Schools should consider the uses of new technologies in engaging parents but with caution. Schools need to be clear about what they aim to achieve, as technology is not an end in itself. The main aim is to engage parents in learning, as this is the most powerful way of raising achievement even in the most challenging contexts.*

In 2008, the education department, now-bedecked in the rainbow colours of the rebranded Department for Children, Schools and Families (DCSF), published 'The Impact of Parental Involvement on Children's Education' (DCSF, 2008a) as part of its 'Every Parent Matters' agenda. This focused on overcoming the barriers to parental involvement as well as reiterating its importance. The key findings reflect the research overviews that led up to the policy:

- *Parental involvement in children's education from an early age has a significant effect on educational achievement, and continues to do so into adolescence and adulthood.*

- *The quality and content of fathers' involvement matter more for children's outcomes than the quantity of time fathers spend with their children.*

- *Family learning can also provide a range of benefits for parents and children including improvements in reading, writing and numeracy as well as greater parental confidence in helping their child at home.*

- *The attitudes and aspirations of parents and of children themselves predict later educational achievement. International evidence suggests that parents with high aspirations are also more involved in their children's education.*

It very much focused on the outcomes of The Effective Provision of Pre-School Education (EPPE; see page 158), but it also raised the important question of what are the challenges to becoming more involved? A 2007 parental survey had found work commitments to be the key barrier (identified by 44%). Child-care issues were identified by 7%, and lack of time by 6%. It also suggested that difficulties with basic literacy and numeracy skills could be a key barrier. Analysis of longitudinal data on adults (using the British Cohort Study and the National Child Development Study) had looked at how parents' literacy and numeracy levels can affect children. This study indicated that children of parents with the poorest grasp of literacy and numeracy were at a substantial disadvantage in relation to their own reading and maths development compared with children who have parents with good literacy/numeracy.

The time barrier may be easing. According to Angelica Bonci's literature review for the National Literacy Trust in 2008, the time parents in Britain spend with their children has increased steadily since the 1960s. Research suggests that the average time spent in child-related activities had risen from less than thirty minutes in the 1970s to more than an hour a day in the 1990s. This is thought to be the result of parents increasingly seeing time spent with their children as important, but it is also suggested that changes in technology may have eased domestic work. The amount of time that fathers spend with their young children has also risen dramatically over the past twenty years, which is encouraging.

Is the current emphasis still on involving families?

It had seemed like full steam ahead and then the government changed. With the arrival of the Conservative-led coalition government, the rainbow colours of the DCSF were quickly in the bin and the Department for Education (DfE) reverted to its plain old name. Doubtless every child, every family mattered, but not as much to politicians as being credited with being the party that made the difference.

In many ways, on the surface, the focus on family remained the same. But beneath the surface of the grand words and grand statements summed up in the following paragraphs lies the stark fact that the funding was not there to support the words. The Government's austerity policy hit the poorest hardest. You only have to look at the rapid decline in Sure Start funding, explained on page 155, to see the sad reality behind the grand words.

To return to the words of the DfE website on its Early Years vision: 'The Government is committed to "co-producing" this vision, and working collaboratively on the detailed policy and implementation questions which will follow. We want a system that is led by the professionals who understand how best to deliver these services – we have been working closely with experts in the early years sector to produce our publication, collaborating on a new vision for the crucial foundation years of each child's life. This partnership is what we are calling co-production, and we hope to see it continue and gain in strength after publication.'

Perhaps, initially, these were not empty words. In the summer of 2010, three early-years-related independent commissions were set up to guide the creation of the vision, two led by Labour MPs and the third by Dame Clare Tickell, the Chief Executive of Action for Children. The first commission, led by Frank Field, had the important task of providing an independent review on poverty and life chances. By December of that year, Field published 'The Foundation Years: Preventing Poor Children becoming Poor Adults', which had two overarching recommendations:

- *To prevent poor children from becoming poor adults the Review proposes establishing a set of Life Chances Indicators that will measure how successful we are as a country in making life's outcomes more equal for all children.*

● *To drive this policy of raising life chances the Review proposes
establishing the first pillar of a new tripartite education system:
the Foundation Years, covering the period conception to five. The
Foundation Years will then lead into the school years, leading to
further, higher and continuing education.*

In early 2011, the second commission, led by Graham Allen, MP,
delivered its report, 'Early Intervention: The Next Steps'. The covering
letter included within the report is important because of the emphasis
it puts on a cooperative approach based on the best of evidence, as its
first three recommendations make clear:

1. *The cross-party co-operation that has characterised this issue
   should continue and be actively developed. All parties should pub-
   licly accept the core message of Early Intervention, acknowledge
   that the culture of late intervention is both expensive and ineffec-
   tive, and ensure that Early Intervention plays a more central part
   in UK policy and practice.*

2. *All parties should commit to the central objective of Early Intervention
   to provide a social and emotional bedrock for the current and future
   generations of babies, children and young people by helping them and
   their parents (or other main caregivers) before problems arise.*

3. *With the encouragement of the Government, the best and most
   rigorously proven Early Intervention programmes should be
   pulled together using the best methodology and science available,
   to promote their wider use.*

The third review, led by Clare Tickell, looked into the efficacy of
the statutory curriculum for this age group, known before and, mirac-
ulously, after the review as the Early Years Foundation Stage (EYFS).
In July 2011, the DfE published the 'Families in the Foundation
Years' evidence pack full of the sources that informed the development of its Foundation Stage policy and, in the same year, published
'Supporting Families in the Foundation Years' (DfE, 2011a, 2011b).
This describes the system needed to make the vision a reality and
explains the role of commissioners, leaders and practitioners across
the range of services for families in these years. Its foreword will
sound familiar:

*The first few years of a child's life are fundamentally important. Evi-
dence tells us that they shape children's future development, and influence how well children do at school, their on-going health and wellbeing
and their achievements later in life ...*

It is now very clear that early help and intervention is crucial if we want to support families to get out of a cycle of poor outcomes that repeats itself over and over through the generations.

That means every service that families and young children come into contact with being clear how they can best support child development, in the broadest sense, so that children reach school-age ready to take advantage of all the opportunities available to them. It also means putting parents and children at the heart of services while freeing up professionals to do what works and is best for their local community rather than focusing on central prescription.

When you read the opening paragraph of the section of this document called 'Parents and families at the heart of services', you can again see how powerful the research has been in shaping the vision:

Mothers and fathers are their children's first and most important educators. From the moment of birth, the relationship between parents, between parents and their child, and the activities they do together affect later development, giving children the trust, attitude and skills which help them to learn and engage positively with the world. What happens in this home environment has more influence on future achievement than innate ability, material circumstances or the quality of pre-school and school provision. When fathers and mothers talk, play, read, paint, investigate numbers and shapes or sing with their children it has a positive effect on children's later development. Mothers' and fathers' involvement in reading is the most important determinant of their child's early language and literacy skills.

A later section states significantly, 'The last twenty years have brought much positive change, and there is a consensus that we should do more ...' It is encouraging to see that the efforts and progress of the past twenty years are acknowledged and that there is agreement on the way forward. This issue literally can transform the life chances of children and should never be a political football.

The difference a unified approach can make is all the more striking when you compare what has happened to the EYFS curriculum as a result of the independent Tickell Review, with what has happened to the primary curriculum in England as a result of the change of government. It would have been nice if the new primary curriculum had also been co-produced or even had a single primary expert on the working party. The new draft primary curriculum is so different from its predecessor that it is clear co-production was not the order of the day there.

It was, therefore, excellent to see that the 2012 statutory framework for the early years foundation stage and its updated version in 2014 was remarkably like the previous government's one – even the colour scheme for the strands is the same, which must have been a great relief for all those who'd just got their heads round the previous version and colour-coded everything accordingly. You could see that they were remarkably similar.

In October 2019, the DFE opened consultation on its Early Years Foundation Stage. This consultation closed at the end of January 2020.

The key proposed changes are:

- **Curriculum** – *Communication & Language* will have a focus on oral language and vocabulary acquisition; Literacy will have a new Early Learning Goal (ELG) on comprehension;

- **Communication & Language (C&L)** is to be threaded through all areas of learning as it underpins all seven areas of learning;

- **Assessment** – the reforms propose the removal of the 'exceeded' criteria. Teachers will still be required to stretch higher achieving children and will need to provide a narrative in relation to this to parents and Y1 teachers.

The DfE plans to launch the finalised version of the Early Years Foundation Stage requirements in September 2021. This will be accompanied by a rewrite of *Development Matters* which offers non-statutory guidance on their implementation. If schools so chose, they could volunteer to implement the new Early Learning Goals in 2020, though doubtless all such decisions would have been affected by the Corona virus school shutdown in that year.

Reactions to the consultation proposals varied. For example, on November 11, 2019, Nursery World said, "Early years experts have criticised the latest EYFS revisions, saying the proposed educational programmes and Goals are 'muddled' and developmentally inappropriate for young children." There seems to be general agreement that as the consultation progressed, the proposals were improved.

One particular concern was voiced by Beatrice Merrick, chief executive of Early Education, "It is our view, for example, that the Government's key focus on Communication and Language is best shown by keeping three ELGs in C&L, not reducing them to two while adding one to Literacy.

"This change is also likely to lead to an increase in the number of disadvantaged children not reaching the Good Level of Development, as the data show the Literacy goals are already pitched too high, further increasing the perceived equality gap while making no actual difference to children's outcomes."

A different perspective was presented by early years consultant Jan Dubiel, who welcomed the review saying, "We do need to celebrate what we have but also understand that it is not static, and as we understand more about the nature of learning and what children need to learn most, then that should be incorporated into the document.

"It ultimately comes down to interpretation and it is really important that people see the changes in context with the EYFS. The Characteristics of Effective Learning are still very much in place and are a very strong part of the EYFS."

What the practitioners tell us

Much education research is based on pulling together what is happening in practice; much of what practitioners do is influenced by what researchers have found – but it is still useful to look at what the practitioners say about parental involvement.

Figure 16. A parent at Lowedges sharing a storymap with her child. Picture: Linda Busses.

In 2007 and 2008, I worked in partnership with a wide range of leading early years organisations and consultants to create the Early Reading Connects family involvement toolkit as part of the then government-funded National Reading Campaign. We met many times and people shared their knowledge generously, which enabled us to pool the tremendous expertise that was represented. We knew it made sense to organise our ideas within the statutory framework for the early years foundation stage, but one of the key things to establish first were the underpinning principles that would guide our recommendations for how early years practitioners could work effectively with parents, carers and the wider family. The four principles agreed were as follows:

- *Work in real partnership with families by building meaningful relationships with children and parents.*

- *Build trust, respect and understanding by valuing the reading and literacy that underpins different families' cultures.*

- *Support parents in building positive relationships with their children – enhancing the esteem of parents, children and practitioners.*

- *Help build confidence so that mums and dads feel able to support their children and are fully aware of how much difference their support can make.*

In essence, these are all about relationships, relationships, relationships. Building positive relationships is clearly the key. Although there is no longer government funding to support this initiative, the excellent Early Reading Connects family involvement toolkit which this group created, full of practical advice from early years practitioners to other early years practitioners about how to involve families, can still be downloaded from www.literacytrust.org.uk.

The positive relationships section of the document (in purple to match the framework) includes useful advice:

- *Personal contact is always best. Talk to key parents to get them engaged and then get them to recruit others.*

- *Find time to talk to mum or dad so you can find out more about their child and what they do at home to support their child's development.*

- *Home visits are a great way of meeting a family on their turf as well as picking up on parental and child interests.*

- *Ask those who do attend sessions what they want from them and get them to bring others along.*

- *Use visual images. Create a display based on successful events to encourage others to join.*

These recommendations were borne out by the National Literacy Trust's analysis of practice in relation to parental involvement, which pointed to three successful ingredients in getting at-risk parents involved in early language and literacy activities with their very young children based on the activities of organisations like Sure Start, Book Start (the national baby book-giving programme run by the Booktrust) and PEEP (Peers

Early Education Partnership, now called Peeple, which focuses in supporting children in disadvantaged families).

1. *Home visiting to help break down barriers with parents so that talking to them about books and early language can be introduced in a way that is relevant to their own situation. As positive relationships develop – this may take several visits – parents can be persuaded to come along to group activities at a local centre.*

2. *Actually showing parents (modelling) how to communicate with very young children is more effective than simply providing information.*

3. *Shared fun in taking part in literacy activities and talking with their children, encourages parents to try out these activities at home. Over time, parental confidence improves and, as a result, those parents who need to improve their own skills are more likely to take action to do so.*

The significance of the practitioners' focus on building relationships cannot be overstated. When there is an atmosphere of mutual respect and trust, then parents can get the support they need to help their children. As Balqees Iqbal, a family literacy tutor at a primary school in Rochdale explained: 'Mums are learning a lot through these sessions. When we went to school, play wasn't important. And if I'd have come home and told my parents I'd played with paint, or sand or something, they'd have been horrified. But now play is everything. Children learn through play.' As a mum herself, Balqees had benefited from going to family literacy sessions and then decided to train to become a tutor. Her very closeness to the community made her the perfect person to support the mothers who came to her sessions. It is these sorts of considerations along with practical strategies that parents can adopt that are key to building the relationships that make interventions successful.

Helping parents to feel confident about what to do to support their child's learning was therefore at the centre of a study begun in 2010 called the 'Thirty Million Words Project'. This was led by Dr Dana Suskind from the University of Chicago and focused on how the gap could be narrowed. By June 2012, twenty-six families had participated in the eight-week programme, which, like its predecessor in 1965 (see page 152) had involved visiting families in their homes weekly. But this time, rather than focusing on measuring the gap, the emphasis was on how to support parents in order to narrow the gap.

One of the parents involved, Aneisha Newell, explained how the project supported the parents: 'We would sit down and have a talk about some important tips on getting my numbers up [the number of words spoken to a child every hour]. And how we can convert little small activities that you would never think of, such as riding the bus and using that time to actually talk to your child and use more words during that time.' She managed to break the study's record three times over the course of her eight weeks on the programme, once achieving 2,800 words in one hour, three times the average. 'It's not easy, definitely not easy to do, to talk to a child', Newell said. 'Because sometimes you're just like, "Shh okay that's enough, I don't want to answer any more questions. It's peace time."'

The study's results suggest that the strategies the parents were encouraged to use will help their children's literacy and educational achievement because the project demonstrated that their parents now had a significant sustained understanding of their child's language development and how to support it (Suskind and Leffel, 2013).

Significantly, all the indicators are that it is the attitude of mind of the institution that makes all the difference if parents are to be successfully supported and involved. This is summed up by Hilary Grayson who conducted the 'Rapid Review of Parental Engagement and Narrowing the Gap in Attainment for Disadvantaged Children' for the NFER in 2013: 'Schools whose home–school liaison practices have been adjudged "outstanding" or "good" by Ofsted take the approach that no family, however hard-to-reach, is unreachable.' The report summarises the evidence as follows:

- *It is important for parents to be consulted and to feel that their opinions are valued; communications can be tailored to suit parents' individual circumstances.*

- *Parents' greatest expressed need is for advice and emotional support. They prefer services to be offered universally rather than targeted, to reduce stigmatisation; they like to feel they have a choice.*

- *The participation of ethnic minority parents can be increased by making cultural adaptations to programmes, such as providing interpreters or language classes. Sensitivity to the background of intervention participants was also emphasised in sources of evidence about parent support and training, and interventions with families and communities.*

- *Parents appreciate follow-up activity to reinforce the learning gained from participating in interventions.*

- *Holistic interventions involving strong engagement between parents, schools and the wider community are necessary to narrow the attainment gap.*

- *Community-based services are best delivered by a multi-agency team that has a good relationship with service users.*

- *Partnership working between a range of local services offers more opportunities to reach the most vulnerable families, as any service with which they are in contact can refer those families to supportive interventions.*

- *Schools have a key role to play as the coordinators and deliverers of services to improve outcomes.*

Of course, all this is easier said than done. The findings of Field (2010) and Allen (2011) underlined the urgency of focusing help effectively on those who most need it while not stigmatising such help. If parents' experience of school themselves as children was negative, then early years settings and schools have to go out of their way to build bridges and repair the damage done.

So is everything in the garden rosy? Have all our early years settings throughout this period been so immersed in the need to involve parents that it's just a question of business as usual? Not according to 'The Bercow Report: A Review of Services for Children and Young People with Speech, Language and Communication Needs' (2008), which concluded that early intervention is essential to overcoming communication problems that could blight young people's futures. The review states: 'Evidence illustrates that there is insufficient understanding of the centrality of speech, language and communication among policy makers and commissioners nationally and locally, professionals and service providers, and sometimes parents and families themselves. It follows that insufficient priority is attached to addressing SLCN.'

Bercow's conclusions were borne out by research into 'Low Income and Early Cognitive Development in the UK' conducted by Jane Waldfogel and Elizabeth Washbrook for the Sutton Trust published in 2010. They concluded: 'Low income children lag their high income counterparts at school entry by sixteen months in vocabulary. The gap in language is very much larger than gaps in other cognitive skills.' The '30 million word gap' did not appear to be narrowing very much.

Jean Gross, as England's Communication Champion in 2010–11, reiterated such concerns: 'Language skills are a critical factor in social disadvantage and in the intergenerational cycles that perpetuate poverty. Poor language skills are the key reason why, by the age of 22 months, a more able child from a low income home will begin to be overtaken in their developmental levels by an initially less able child from a high-income home – and why by the age of five, the gap has widened still more.'

Her excellent book '*Time to Talk*', published in 2013, includes a chapter on working with parents that includes this worrying paragraph: 'Not all parents know how communication develops and how they can help. For example, surveys conducted in the national year of communication showed that only a quarter of parents knew that on average babies say their first words between 12 and 18 months. They knew much more about walking milestones than about talking milestones. A fifth of parents-to-be believe it is only beneficial to communicate with their baby from the age of three months and one in twenty believe that communicating with their baby is only necessary when they are six months or older.'

Yes, a lot of words to tell us what we probably already knew, but the evidence and the urgency is overwhelming. Perhaps we need to rethink our practice if parents aren't at the very heart of the process. Perhaps we need to make certain that involving parents is presented in a way that appeals to the parents who are most in need of support while not stigmatising them. When Pie and I first set out to see what a difference it would make if schools involved parents in the Talk for Writing storytelling approach, I thought that involving all the parents would be difficult. I was wrong.

If you look at Chapter 10 and the related video clips, you will see how reception teacher Jeanette Smith has used family storytelling to involve **all** her children's families on an estate on the edges of Sheffield, as well as how Katie Hanson did the same in a deprived city centre area of Sheffield with a very different ethnic mix. Equally, Margaret Goodwin, the headteacher of Warren Farm in a similarly deprived area of Birmingham, manages to involve all the parents. Perhaps Jeanette's observations about how schools, through the reporting to parents system, tend to focus on negative communication needs thinking about. As the children get older, our obsession with league tables will have exacerbated a school culture in which many parents feel they are being endlessly told off about their children's failures. This perspective is the focus of an interesting article by education correspondent Valerie Strauss that appeared in the *Washington Post* in February 2013:

> 'Likewise, while everyone wants parents to be engaged with what their children are doing in school, what matters more is the nature of that engagement. There's a big difference between a parent who's focused on what the child is doing – that is, on the learning itself – and a parent who's focused on how well the child is doing. To ask "So, honey, what's your theory about why the Civil War started?" or "If you had written that story, would you have left the character wondering what happened, the way the author did?" represents a kind of engagement that promotes critical thinking and enthusiasm about learning. To ask "Why only a B+ [or a 3 on the rubric]?" is a kind of engagement that undermines both of these things.

'Of course, parents wouldn't be asking the latter questions if the school weren't reducing students to letters and numbers in the first place; they're taking their cue from educators who blur the differences between a focus on learning and a focus on performance, or between intrinsic and extrinsic motivation. Nevertheless, this issue seems to have escaped the notice of just about everyone who writes on the topic of parent involvement.'

Perhaps, we need to think about both our focus and the language we use, so that we do not become buried in the gobbledygook of assessment. 'Is it a bike or a bollocking?' one confused father once memorably asked as he handed me his child's final report from primary school at a secondary transfer meeting. He was right to be confused. I couldn't advise him whether to award or berate his daughter. The report was full of generalising educational waffle about what was being taught and arcane grading systems but you gained no meaningful insight into how his daughter was progressing or feeling; the child was lost in a sea of education speke. We both laughed but it was not funny. Perhaps we need to think more about how schools as well as early years settings appear through the eyes of the parents and how this perspective can help us ensure that parents really are at the heart of the process.

References and further reading

Allen, G. (2011) *Early Intervention: The Next Steps: An Independent Report to Her Majesty's Government*. London: Cabinet Office [https://www.gov.uk/government/uploads/system/uploads/attachment_data/file/284086/early-intervention-next-steps2.pdf].

Beard, R. (2000) *National Literacy Strategy: Review of Research and other Related Evidence*. London: Department for Education and Employment.

Bercow, J. (2008) *The Bercow Report: A Review of Services for Children and Young People (0–19) with Speech, Language and Communication Needs*. London: DCSF Publications [http://dera.ioe.ac.uk/8405/1/7771-dcsf-bercow.pdf].

Blair, T. (2001) Speech when launching Labour's education manifesto at the University of Southampton.

Bonci, A. (2008) *A Research Review: The Importance of Families and the Home Environment* (updated 2010 and 2011) London: National Literary Trust [http://files.eric.ed.gov/fulltext/ED521654.pdf].

Brooks, G. (1998) Trends in standards of literacy in the United Kingdom, 1948–1996, *Topic*, 19: 1–10.

Brooks, G., Pugh, A. and Schagen, I. (1996) *Reading Performance at Nine*. Slough: National Foundation for Educational Research [https://www.nfer.ac.uk/publications/11112/11112.pdf].

Clark, C. (2007) *Why Families Matter to Literacy: A Brief Research Summary*. London: National Literary Trust [http://www.literacytrust .org.uk/assets/0000/2038/Why_families_matter.pdf].

Dearing, E., Kreider, H., Simpkins, S. and Weiss, H. (2007) *Family Involvement in School and Low-Income Children's Literacy Performance*. Cambridge, MA: Harvard Family Research Project [http://www .hfrp.org/publications-resources/publications-series/family-involvement-research-digests/family-involvement-in-school-and-low-income-children-s-literacy-performance].

Department for Children, Schools and Families (2008a) *The Impact of Parental Involvement on Children's Education*.

Department for Children, Schools and Families (2008b) *Statutory Framework for the Early Years Foundation Stage*. London: DCSF.

Department for Education (2011a) *Families in the Foundation Years – Evidence Pack*. London: DfE [https://www.gov.uk/government/ uploads/system/uploads/attachment_data/file/262397/DFE-00214-2011.pdf].

Department for Education (2011b) *Supporting Families in the Foundation Years*. London: DfE [https://www.gov.uk/government/uploads/ system/uploads/attachment_data/file/184868/DFE-01001-2011_ supporting_families_in_the_foundation_years.pdf].

Department for Education (2012) *Statutory Framework for the Early Years Foundation Stage*. London: DfE [http://webarchive.nationalarchives.gov.uk/20130401151715/https://www.education.gov.uk/publications/standard/allpublications/page1/dfe-00023-2012].

Department for Education (2013) *Developing a Vision for Early Years*. London: DfE.

Department for Education and Employment (1997) *Excellence in Schools*. White Paper. London: DfEE Publications.

Department for Education and Skills (2007) *Every Parent Matters*. London: DfES [http://webarchive.nationalarchives.gov.uk/20130401 151715/http://www.education.gov.uk/publications/eOrdering Download/DFES-LKDA-2007.pdf].

Desforges, C. with Abouchaar, A. (2003) *The Impact of Parental Involvement, Parental Support and Family Education on Pupil Achievement and Adjustment: A Literature Review*. London: Department for Education and Skills [http://www.bgfl.org/bgfl/custom/files_uploaded/ uploaded_resources/18617/Desforges.pdf].

Earl, L., Watson, N., Levin, B., Leithwood, K. and Fullan, M. (2003) *Watching and Learning 3: Final Report of the External Evaluation of England's National Literacy and Numeracy Strategies*. Toronto, Ontario: University of Toronto.

Feinstein, L. (2003) Inequality in the early cognitive development of British children in the 1970 cohort, *Economica*, 70: 73–97.

Field, F. (2010) *The Foundation Years: Preventing Poor Children becoming Poor Adults. The Report of the Independent Review on Poverty and Life Chances*. London: Cabinet Office [http://webarchive. nationalarchives.gov.uk/20110120090128/http:/povertyreview. independent.gov.uk/media/20254/poverty-report.pdf].

Grayson, H. (2013) *Rapid Review of Parental Engagement and Narrowing the Gap in Attainment for Disadvantaged Children*. Oxford: NFER/Oxford University Press.

Green, R. and Strong, J. (2009) *Early Reading Connects Family Involvement Toolkit*. London: National Literary Trust.

Gross, J. (2013) *Time to Talk: Implementing Outstanding Practice in Speech, Language and Communication*. Abingdon: Routledge.

Hamer, C. (2012) NCT Research overview: parent–child communication is important from birth, *Perspective – NCT's Journal on Preparing Parents for Birth and Early Childhood*, March, pp. 15–20.

Harris, A. and Goodall, J. (2007) *Engaging Parents in Raising Achievement: Do Parents Know they Matter?* DCSF Research Brief RW004. London: Department of Children, Schools and Families [http://web archive.nationalarchives.gov.uk/20130401151715/http://www. education.gov.uk/publications/eOrderingDownload/DCSF-RBW004. pdf].

Hart, B. and Risley, T.R. (1995 [2003]) The early catastrophe: the 30 million word gap by age 3, *American Educator*, Spring, pp. 4–9.

Jeynes, W.H. (2005) *Parental Involvement and Student Achievement: A Meta-Analysis*. Cambridge, MA: Harvard Family Research Project [http://www.hfrp.org/publications-resources/publications-series/ family-involvement-research-digests/parental-involvement-and-student-achievement-a-meta-analysis].

NCS (undated) *Head Start and Early Head Start – Evidence Based Practice*. Arcata, CA: Northcoast Children's Services [http://ncsheadstart. org/wp-content/uploads/2011/11/EvidenceBasedReport.pdf].

O'Neill, P. (2008) The *Educational Theory of Quintilian* [http://www .newfoundations.com/GALLERY/Quintilian.html].

Organisation for Economic Cooperation and Development (2002) *Reading for Change: Performance and Engagement across Countries*. Paris: OECD [http://www.oecd.org/education/school/programmefor-internationalstudentassessmentpisa/33690904.pdf].

Peters, M., Seeds, K., Goldstein, A. and Coleman, N. (2008) *Parental Involvement in Children's Education 2007*. DCSF Research Report RR034. London: Department of Children, Schools and Families [http:// core.ac.uk/download/pdf/4158077.pdf].

Rose, D. and Martin, J.R. (2012) *Learning to Write, Reading to Learn: Genre, Knowledge and Pedagogy in the Sydney School*. London: Equinox.

Rowe, M. and Goldin-Meadow, S. (2009) Differences in early gesture explain SES disparities in child vocabulary size at school entry, *Science*, 323 (5916): 951–3.

Slavin, R.E. (1997) Success for all: policy implications for British education, paper presented at the *Literary Task Force Conference*, London, 27 February.

Suskind, D. and Leffel, K. (2013) *Thirty Thousand Words Project: A Randomized Controlled Pilot* [http://www.lenafoundation.org/wp-content/uploads/pdf/LENA-Conf-2013/Presentations/LENA-Conference-2013-Dana-Suskind.pdf].

Sylva, K., Melhuish, E., Sammons, P., Siraj-Blatchford, I. and Taggart, B. (2004) *Effective Pre-School Education: Final Report.* London: Institute of Education.

Tickell, C. (2011) *The Early Years: Foundations for Life, Health and Learning. An Independent Report on the Early Years Foundation Stage to Her Majesty's Government.* London: DfE [https://www.gov.uk/government/uploads/system/uploads/attachment_data/file/180919/DFE-00177-2011.pdf].

Twist, L., Sizmur, J., Bartlett, S. and Lynn, L. (2012) *PIRLS 2011: Reading Achievement in England.* Slough: NFER.

Waldfogel, J. and Washbrook, E. (2010) *Low Income and Early Cognitive Development in the UK* [http://www.suttontrust.com/wp-content/uploads/2010/02/Sutton_Trust_Cognitive_Report.pdf].

10

The storytelling process as the key to family involvement

Figure 17. Parents and children storytelling together at Lowedges School, Sheffield. Photograph by Linda Busses – www.pixlb.co.uk

31
VIDEO

ne story-
elling
rocess
s the key
family
volvement

One key focus when I worked at the National Literacy Trust was how to engage and then involve parents in creating a reading culture in the home, with a particular emphasis on those parents whose lack of confidence in reading themselves made them shy away from reading with their children.

This problem was, therefore, very much in my mind when I first saw Pie illustrate the Talk for Writing approach in 2005, quickly getting a large audience of teachers to become expert in showing their children how to become expert at telling 'Little Charlie'. For me, it was a Eureka moment – this was exactly what was needed to get the pattern of language into children's heads (and not just little children's heads but also much older students, and not just with stories but with non-fiction text across the curriculum). But could it also be the perfect way to support parents and carers in storytelling in the home? Once the story was internalised, reading it off the page would pose no problem for child and parent alike, and innovating on the story to make it relevant to your child would be easy. Was this the Trojan Horse that could help involve all parents that I had been looking for?

From that point on, I worked with Pie, first to get the Primary National Strategy to support the development of the Talk for Writing approach in primary schools for fiction and then with local authorities to trial how to spread a non-fiction version of the approach across the primary curriculum. Throughout that time, we were also looking for opportunities to see if we could find the funding to trial and evaluate the difference it would make if you involved families of nursery (Foundation 1) and reception children (Foundation 2) along with their children.

One publisher turned us down on the grounds that the shareholders wouldn't appreciate such research - though their luxurious central office didn't look as if they were short of a penny or two. Others were only interested in the results as a way of selling particular reading schemes.

Fortunately, in 2009 Sheffield Council came to the rescue. Unfortunately, by 2011 the cash crisis brought the project to a sudden halt along with our hopes of getting it properly evaluated. But we are very grateful for what Sheffield Council, plus local consultant Pam Fell (who was asked to accept early retirement during the project) and Professor Jacky Marsh from the University of Sheffield managed to do. We remain permanently indebted to the reception teachers Katie Hanson (Porter Croft School) and Jeanette Smith (Lowedges School) in Sheffield who have taken the idea and made it their own as this chapter and the video illustrate.

The background to the Sheffield Family Storytelling Project

When we started planning the Sheffield Family Storytelling Project, we were very aware of how research emphasises that when parents and carers are involved with their child's learning and support the work carried out in school, children make better progress than when the link between home and school is tenuous. For a number of years prior to the start of this project, Pie's Talk for Writing approach had been used in many of Sheffield's early years settings as a key strategy for helping children to build up a bank of traditional tales, developing their imaginative and linguistic repertoires. The extra ingredient that the project brought was to explore strategies for involving the families in the storytelling process. We wanted to discover if this helped the children make more progress, as well as making the family members themselves feel more confident. We wished to see what would happen if parents, grandparents and other family members were 'trained' and supported in telling the stories that the children were working on in class, so that they could support their children in further developing the stories at home. Would such an approach accelerate the children's language development?

The reception teachers on the project, therefore, set out not just to teach the children to be able to retell the stories in Talk for Writing style but to investigate what would happen if the children's families were involved so that children told the stories at home as well as in school and their families could tell the stories too. The project raised a whole number of interesting questions. If schools involved families in storymaking, would the simplicity and fun of the storytelling approach overcome some parents' lack of confidence in supporting their child's education as they would wish to do? Would helping families join in with an approach that values the spoken word help to break down 'literacy' barriers and provide a way in which more families could gain the confidence to contribute more to their child's learning?

The structure of the project

The project was divided into two parts. The first year was to be a trial to see if the schools could find effective ways of involving the parents and, if they could, there would be a second year in which the approach could be properly evaluated based on what had been found to work in the trial year.

The trial year focused on children in reception classes in a few Sheffield schools in challenging areas linked to poverty as well as, in some cases, language and cultural diversity. The teachers and teaching assistants were asked to record children's storytelling at the start of the year and compare this with what they could do by the end of the year. They were expected to establish a regular, daily routine for storytelling so that the children gradually learned a bank of stories, as well as innovating and inventing their own tales.

We posed the group three questions:

1. How do you get parents and carers involved?

2. What do you do with them?

3. How do you maintain the momentum?

When the group first discussed these questions, they raised related questions of their own:

- How do you help the families to learn the stories?

- How do you encourage parents to come into school for a storytelling workshop?

- How do you keep feeding in new stories?

- Would a DVD or audio CD be of use?

- Is a workshop the best approach?

- If so, what do you do in a workshop?

The simple solution

The most striking finding from the initial trial was how easy it was to involve parents in this approach and not just a few parents but **all** the parents. We still remain astounded by this fact. Anyone who has been engaged with projects to involve parents from challenging areas will know that involving everyone is practically unheard of. My mind was full of all the barriers identified by teachers, family tutors and early years professionals who had tried assorted methods of involving families in reading for many years. I knew that engaging some families would be relatively easy but to engage all of them!

One of the teachers on the project, Jeanette Smith from Lowedges School, had left the first session saying, 'I've waited thirteen years for something like this.' Clearly she set off back to school to see if she could make it work. And so she did. When she fed back to the small group of project teachers what she had done, she stated in a matter-of-fact way that she had involved all her parents. The jaws of those listening dropped. She had came up with the breathtakingly simple idea that the best thing to do would be to work with the children until they had internalised a story and then invite the family members who would be picking their children up from school to arrive a little bit early one day so that the children could perform for their parents before the children asked their parents to join in. And once the parents had been involved with imitating the text, it was even easier to get them involved in innovating the text with the children, as the video of the parents and children combining 'The Little Red Hen' with 'The Enormous Turnip' illustrates. The effectiveness of this simple approach had also been 'discovered' by Katie Hanson at Porter Croft Primary School. No formalities, no complex organisational extras: just pure simplicity. But behind this simplicity lay some key foundations.

The foundations underpinning successful parental involvement in storytelling

When we discussed what had enabled the teachers to involve their parents successfully, four key interrelated ingredients emerged. These are expressed below in the context of reception classes in schools, since it is there that we trialled the approach, but we believe that the underlying ingredients would be similar in any early years setting, though some of the terminology used would be different.

1. **Headteacher involvement:** The most important underlying ingredient is the headteacher's genuine and active support for the project. It is so easy for a 'good idea' to become lost among too many other 'good ideas'. The teacher leading the approach needs to have permission to focus on establishing storytelling both in the class and with the families and community, and to be encouraged to try. One teacher who had not managed to make any progress blamed the snow. All listening were doubtless thinking that it had snowed on their schools as well. Behind the lack of progress lay the fact that the school was sinking beneath a sea of well-intentioned, ill-focused initiatives.

2. **Passionate commitment of teacher:** Commitment on the part of the headteacher is linked directly to the class teacher's own belief in the importance of the project and its potential as a vital ingredient in the children's development. Without a passionate commitment from the teacher, such a project will founder.

3. **Relationships, relationships, relationships:** The third essential ingredient is the quality of the relationship between the teacher, the teaching assistant if there is one, and the families. Getting to know parents and carers so that there is an element of trust is vital to any form of educational setting and home initiative, as emphasised below.

Parents and children innovating on *The Little Red Hen* at Lowedges School, Sheffield

4. **Involve the children in storytelling first:** It soon became clear that before you could involve the families effectively in storytelling, it was important for the children to have internalised a story themselves. This is reflected in the structure of this book: it focuses on how to involve the children in storytelling before focusing on how to involve the families.

What is striking as you watch the video clips and read the quotations below from the two leading schools involved in the project is how similar the solutions of these two teachers were, even though their intakes were very different culturally. Katie Hanson's explanation of how she involved the parents echoes Jeanette's solution; the picture below of Porter Croft parents leading storytelling at later sessions speaks for itself.

Figure 19. Porter Croft parents leading storytelling at later sessions.

'To get the parents involved, we tried a few different approaches. We knew that we wanted to get them in but it was finding the times of day that suited them best; it was finding what the parents wanted from us. So we trialled a few different ideas.

'The thing that really helped us was inviting the parents all in to come and watch the children perform the storytelling. We got the children to write the invites to their parents, which encouraged *the parents to come in because their child had actually invited them in to watch it.*

'We got them in and got them to watch the performance and then sprung it on them that they were now going to be taught by their child how to tell the story. So the children went to their parent and we told the story as a group ... The children then took the story map home with their parents and practised the story again at home.'

Katie's explanation of the impact that involving the parents has made is particularly important because it emphasises how much more quickly the children's language development increased as a result of practising the stories at home as well as in school:

'Having the parents involved in the storytelling sessions has really had a higher impact. We'd already started using the Talk for Writing approach; we'd already seen the impact that it was having on the children, on their story writing and their story telling and their general oral literacy around school.

'Bringing the parents into it meant that they were getting that reinforcement from home and they were taking the story maps home and learning them with parents and it meant that they internalised the story much faster. So, whereas before a story would take us maybe three or four weeks before they had really internalised and understood the story, they would maybe by the end of the second week completely be able to tell the whole story through independently and you can then move on to the innovation much, much faster.'

The difference it makes to the parents – defeating the what-has-he-done-now? syndrome

You only have to listen to the parents from Lowedges School on the video (see clip 33) to see the potential power of this simple approach in helping them forge a closer relationship with their child's nursery and school and, in the process, gaining in confidence themselves. The parents at Porter Croft School, a few miles away in central Sheffield, are mainly from very different cultural backgrounds but, interestingly, the key points drawn out by both teachers are very similar. Katie explains:

33
VIDEO

Parents from Lowedges explain how and why the approach has helped them and their children

'It also helps our parents because quite a lot of our parents don't speak English as a first language. They find things like reading with their child at home quite daunting, things like phonics. They've not gone through the British school system and so it doesn't make a lot of sense to them. And even with workshops, they still approach it with quite a lot of anxiety. They're worried

Figure 20. A parent at Lowedges sharing a storymap with her child. Picture: Linda Busses.

about doing it wrong. Whereas, with the storytelling, you can't do it wrong because a story can do whatever you want the story to do. And I think that has made their involvement with their children much more enjoyable for them. It's a more pleasurable thing – it's not something where they think, "Oh no, we've got to get out the dreaded reading book and read!" We do still send home reading books. We do still encourage home reading – I'm not saying it's replaced that in any way but they now work alongside each other.'

This is exactly the point that Jeanette from Lowedges makes. Her mainly white British working-class parents may feel equally daunted by the education system in their own way but this can be overcome if what they are being invited in to do is fun and supports their child. Jeanette reflects on how schools have a tendency to call parents in to talk about problems:

'I think we probably just don't ask them to do things like story-telling because what we do is ask parents to come in so we can talk about their child's report which, as a parent myself with my boy when he was younger, I hated. I was always thinking, "What has he done now?" Whereas, if someone had said to me when he was younger, "I want you to come in and learn a story. He's learning it – you can learn it", I would have loved it. It's a shared language. Immediately, you can join in with the parents and I prefer that to, "I need to see you about your child," because this is always positive. I don't want to sound clever but it has been fairly easy to get parents in.'

Jeanette also emphasises the importance of understanding the power of this approach to make people feel good about themselves and their child:

'I could have got all our parents here today ... Generally most parents come and once you say, "Your kids will be so proud", that I think is the thing that gets parents in. This is a big unit. We've got fifty-two parents and we get about forty-seven coming in to do storytelling – we nearly couldn't fit them all in out there ... Our parents are like every other parent in the country. They are very supportive of us as a school. I think every parent in the country feels they want to be proud of their children. They want their children to be proud of them.'

Figure 21. Parents limbering up for some storytelling at Lowedges Primary School, Sheffield.

Both teachers emphasise how positive the approach is, and how much fun it can be. This is what makes it so powerful because it gives parents not only the confidence to join in but also the motivation to want to join in. As a result, the family storytelling approach opens up a wealth of opportunities for family involvement, as Katie explains:

'Involving parents in storytelling has made them much more comfortable about coming into school because they know they're coming in to do something that's going to be fun – it's going to be enjoyable. No one is going to be sitting them down and saying, "Oh, do you know what your child did this lunchtime?" It's something they know they will be able to come in and do ... We had a Big Build project a few months ago and we sent a letter home saying, "Parents, can you come in and help us?" Two or three years ago we probably wouldn't have had any parents in but we now get parents coming in the door; we get parents offering to come and help. And parents from other classes who've been through the storytelling process with us and are further up the school will come back and offer their help, even supporting children in class, or coming into the storytelling sessions with the parents or just generally going out and spreading the word for us.'

33
VIDEO

Parents from Lowedges explain how and why the approach has helped them and their children

'It's made it a much more inclusive feeling and now they don't just drop their children at the door and run. They don't just pick them up and run. In the mornings, they'll actually come in for the fifteen minutes where they're welcome to come in to the classroom and work with the children.'

'And at the end of the day we have open story sessions where parents can come in and either join in with the storytelling that we're doing or they can choose to do something with the story sacks on their own with their own individual child or a small group of children. So we try to encourage them to come in and invite them in as much as we can.'

Moving on to innovation and invention

The underlying approach was found to be just the same for involving the parents in innovation and invention. For example, if the story selected for the imitation stage was *'The Gingerbread Man'*, then the children would first have been taught to imitate it and then perform it for their families. The families would then have been invited in to join in and everyone would have gone home with a story map for the *'The Gingerbread Man'* to support telling the story at home.

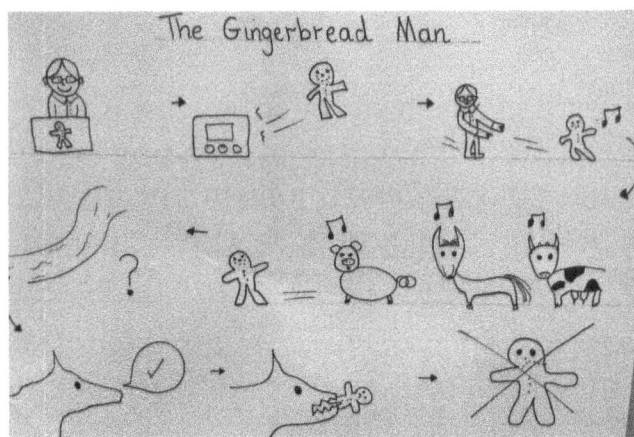

Figure 22. Story map from the nursery class at St. George's School, Battersea.

The innovation stage: Then, in class, the teacher would focus on showing the children how to innovate on the story, as explained in Chapter 6. Once they were good at this, the families would again be invited in at the end of the day to watch what the children could do and to learn how to innovate on the story. As before, a story map would be sent home but this time only with the bare bones of the story in place, leaving the families to decide who the main character would be and what obstacles they would face on their journey.

The invention stage: The teacher would support the children in inventing their own stories based on the underlying pattern of the original as explained in Chapter 7. The parents would be invited in to see a perfor-mance, to join in and to carry on the process at home.

Interestingly, we discovered during the pilot that initially many of the teachers were reluctant to move from the imitation stage to the innova-tion stage because they felt that the children wouldn't cope but, when they actually tried it, they found that the children lapped it up as did the parents. The teachers' lack of confidence in what the children could achieve was thus holding them back as reception teacher Katie honestly admits: 'It's made me realise they are far more capable than I had given them credit for.'

- Secure the headteacher's active support for involving the families in storytelling.
- Help the children imitate a story so they can perform it well.
- Use the informal approach. Ask family members to arrive around fifteen minutes earlier than usual to pick up the children.
- Get the children to perform their story.
- Encourage the children to encourage their parents to join in and praise everyone for contributing.
- Show the parents their child's story maps and transcripts of their early writing so they can see how the process is helping their child.
- Have a copy of the story map for every child to take home.
- Be realistic about what can be achieved initially but set your sights on getting every family involved.

Some advice on involving everyone

The project also focused on how to reach out to the families of **all** the children. The teachers and teaching assistants from the project analysed some barriers to involvement and what had worked to overcome them, and devised the following advice:

- Achieve a constant welcoming atmosphere to build up good relationships.

- Encourage all family members to get involved – from older brothers and sisters to grandparents. You may want to target getting grandparents involved.

- Invite parents who haven't been before by speaking to them or even better getting other parents to speak to them (nothing is more powerful than peer-group recommendation). Play on the fact that parents will want to support their children and that this is a fun way of doing just that.

- Use friendship/extended family links to involve parents/family members who can't attend.

- Once you've got the momentum going, keep on trying to attract the shy/less confident; don't give up on them. Use the buddy approach and get another parent to hook them in.

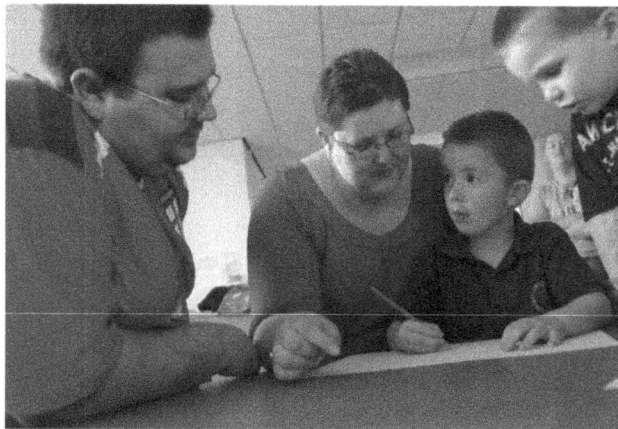

Getting the blokes on board: Ensuring that you involve dads and granddads is often tricky because traditionally it is the mums who come and collect children from school. But many dads at Lowedges turned up to the sessions. Your approach will doubtless depend on the nature of your school community but here is the advice on involving dads and granddads from the pilot schools:

- Make certain you have some male staff/ambassadors involved in the initial session so that any dads or granddads can see other men getting involved.

- Make sessions as practical as possible – give the blokes something to do.

- Once you've engaged a few dads or granddads, ask them to become ambassadors and ask their advice on how to get more men involved. This advice may involve organising separate events for dads (sometimes dads will not attend if they think it will be mum dominated). For example, you could hold the dads' event just before school and the mums' event at the end of the school day (ask the dads' ambassador to find out what time would suit them).

- You may want to talk to the dads at a place where you know they will be – for example, if you have many Muslim children at your school, try setting up a dads' session at the local mosque after prayers so that they understand why it is important to join in the school sessions, and find out what times would suit them. One enterprising school in Lewisham, having failed to involve dads effectively in school events, started organising dads-only sessions down the local pub and it worked a treat (though, of course, this wouldn't suit all cultures).

Involving parents who may lack confidence in speaking English: Lack of confidence plus a lack of knowing what to do can be central to parents' fear of being involved. In the words of a parent in Rochdale who had been brought up in Pakistan and was now attending family learning sessions at her child's school: '*I used to nag, nag, nag but now I know how to help my child.*' Her beaming confidence said it all. The central route in is exactly the same for all parents, but below are some additional ideas for parents for whom English is not their home language.

- First, concentrate on getting the children to perform the story well. It is very important for children who do not speak English at home to start hearing their voice speaking English. This builds confidence.

- Then invite their parents and families in to see the children perform. If the parents are reluctant to take part, encourage the children to invite their parents to join in. This participation will also make the parents more confident with speaking English.

- Try to involve ambassadors from the range of cultures represented in your school. If possible, involve influential members of the local community and get them to understand what you are trying to achieve; they may be able to get everyone else in their community involved.

- Help parents create their own story maps – you may want to send home crayons and paper to help.

- Use older pupils or brothers and sisters to translate and become storytelling buddies.

- If another language(s) is dominant in your school, you may want to set up dual language sessions in, say, Urdu and English or Somali and English. Before the session, seek out an enthusiastic parent(s) who is a confident speaker of both English and whichever mother tongue has been selected and train them in the storytelling techniques so that they can act as interpreter and trainer. You may want to make a CD of the story in English (preferably of their children telling the story) so parents can take it home and practise.

- Encourage the parents to adapt the approach to stories from their culture – for example, change the Gingerbread Man into a Chapatti, or Little Charlie into Little Ali.

18 VIDEO
Katie Hanson explaining the impact of the approach on children learning English as an additional language

- If you have a wide range of additional languages, encourage the children to work with their parents to translate the stories into their home language and ask them to practise both versions at home. This can also provide a great source of entertainment at a session where all the different versions are performed. Sheffield, as part of its Every Child a Talker initiative, put on a marvellous display of 'We're Going on a Bear Hunt' in a wide range of languages.

What was the impact?

The initial trial showed that where successful links had been made, involving storytelling at home as well as in school, there was a powerful impact upon children's language development. For instance, evidence from the *communication, language and literacy section* of the Foundation Profiles in Porter Croft School showed that by the end of the first year of the trial, 75% of children involved in the trial were performing at or above national expectations. This contrasted with the previous years' intakes, where on average only 30% of the children had made similar progress. Now all the children are performing at or above national expectations by the time they leave Year 2. As Katie explains, 'It has allowed them to get the common language of story – and it has allowed parents in.'

This impact builds on what was found by the original 'storytelling' research project. This had focused on involving the children but not their families in storytelling and had shown that the children's language development accelerated and their behaviour improved. The Family Storytelling Project showed a stronger impact. It is worth remembering that all the schools involved served what might typically be described as 'deprived' communities. Where the trial was able to flourish, teachers have become committed to ensuring that this approach gradually feeds into the next class and are developing a whole-school approach.

Before and After measurements

One simple way of measuring impact is to use the *Before and After* approach. The *before* information acts as your cold case baseline, against which you can measure progress.

- Produce, say, four case studies – two boys, two girls. Ask the two questions below before the approach begins:

  - **Can you tell me a story you know?**

  - **Can you make up a story for me?**

  Record their stories or at least transcribe them.

- Ask the same questions some months later after having focused on storytelling in school and with the family at home.

Pupil case study examples from the trial schools
The schools involved in the trial found that initially the children either could not tell a story at all or could only recount some aspects of a story but not tell it coherently, as the two case studies below illustrate. You may want to listen to the audio recording of one child's responses on Video 7.

Pupil A, January 2010

Teacher: *Can you tell me a story?*
Pupil A: *Erm ... can't think ... Don't know.*

Pupil A, six months later, June 2010

Teacher: *Can you tell me a story?*
Pupil A: *Once upon a time there was a little girl who went for a walk in the woods. She walked and she walked and she walked until she saw a house. She went into the house and saw three bowls of soup. She ate the little one. Then the bears came home. They growled at her and she ran home to mummy.*

Pupil B, September 2009

Teacher: *Can you tell me a story?*
Pupil B: *Once there was a princess and she went to a castle. A witch tried to lock her up, but the prince saved her. The princess married the prince and they lived happily ever after.*

Pupil B, nine months later, June 2010

Teacher: *Can you tell me a story?*
Pupil B: *This is the story of little tiger. He was extremely small. Once upon a time, there was a little tiger who lived in the jungle. Early one morning, he woke up and wanted to hunt for some people. So he walked and walked until he found some people. Unfortunately, his mummy came to take him home. Then she put him to bed. He still wanted to hunt for people so he went to find some people, but then his mummy came and took him home to bed. He still likes to hunt people.*

In addition, you may find it useful to:

- Keep a research diary – noting down thoughts/reflections on how the initiative is progressing. Note down when you hear a child using language from the story as well as what worked and what didn't.

- Compare your school's Foundation Stage CLL measurements for the previous year(s) to the results following a year of using this approach.

- Interview some parents after the project has got going asking them to reflect on their feelings before the project and how they feel now. (Professor Jackie Marsh's useful advice was that it was probably best not to try to interview parents before the project, as this could be very intimidating.)

The potential long-term impact

Anyone who has taught children realises very quickly how much home matters and, once a learning culture becomes part of the home culture, how much easier it is for children to learn. The family storytelling project enabled us to show that all parents can become involved in helping to create this learning culture and, over time, this could have a real impact on their children's progress at school. Moreover, this could have a long-term impact within families rather like the domino effect. If children are brought up within a family where storytelling and sharing books are part of their culture, it is something these children will automatically do with their children once they become parents themselves. Over time, this approach could help every home become a language-rich home.

Parental involvement case studies

Below are two case studies from Porter Croft School, Sheffield, showing what a difference involving families through the Talk for Writing approach can make to a school: one from the reception teacher's perspective, the other from the headteacher's perspective.

Case study 1: Involving the families in Talk for Writing works wonders

Katie Hanson, Foundation 2 teacher at Porter Croft School, Sheffield, reflects on how involving families in the Talk for Writing approach has transformed the school

If you had said to me at the beginning of the project, "You will be able to get four-year-old children to structure and invent stories," I would have laughed and said it was impossible. But they can. It's made me realise they are far more capable than I had given them credit for. If you provide the right building blocks and structure, then they can. There has been a complete change in what they can achieve, and in what I expect them to achieve.

In the autumn term of 2009, my school was lucky enough to be selected by Sheffield Council to take part in a project that was investigating what difference it would make if the families of reception children were involved in the Talk for Writing storytelling approach. To enable me to measure progress, I was shown how to ask the children

Figure 24. Katie Hanson, Porter Croft School, Sheffield.

to "Tell me a story" at the beginning of the project and then, several months later, ask the same question. This approach to establishing what they know and what progress they have made has been a real insight. Before, I took it for granted that they could, even though they couldn't. Now I know how to build the foundations so they can become storytellers.

The progress the children are now making needs to be set in context. The national expected level for a four-year-old entering Foundation 2 (previously known as Reception) would be 40–60 months. At Porter Croft, only 17% of children arrive at this level and 25% enter below 30 months. Over half the children live below the poverty line with 75% of them on free school meals. 75% also speak English as an additional language with many having recently arrived with their families in the country. But now our children are leaving Year 2 making progress in line with the national average and leave Year 6 making progress above the national average.

Before the project, trying to teach children to write stories was like building a house without foundations. We were trying to get them to do something that they didn't have the building blocks in place to do. They didn't have the language patterns to be able to tell a story so how could they write it down! The children were very passive. They would listen to stories being read to them but now they are actively involved in telling the story themselves so that the language and all the key storytelling sentence patterns are in their heads. Previously it was all too much. They were trying to remember a story and how to form the letters and leave space between the words. There were just too many things to do. We were setting them up to fail; not just in literacy but in all aspects of school.

Involving the families turned out to be easy. Once the children had fully internalised a story (the imitation stage of Talk for Writing), we invited the families to come in a little early to collect the children who then performed for their families and invited them to join in. This communal storytelling was the first time some of the children and their parents had heard their own voices speaking English.

This approach has gone from strength to strength. Now the families come in and join the storytelling once a half term and the children regularly take story maps home to work with their families on innovating or inventing their own stories. It has been a revelation to many of the parents that you can make your dragon drive a car and enjoy a cup of tea in front of the fire. It's opened up the imagination of many of the parents as well as the children. It's also made homework interactive and enjoyable. Now children learn one story per half term and take home a story map and then innovate or invent their own story. So they share at least four stories a term with their families. They are also encouraged to take home story sacks at any time. The children don't see it as work; they love storytelling and it has become part of the culture of the school: one carpenter dad is making each of the classrooms a storytelling chair.

Family storytelling has not only brought parents into the school but has changed their attitude towards the school. It's opened up the conversation about children and learning. Parents have stopped demanding to see the writing and understand the key role that talk plays in children's development. Parents are now much more confident about how to support their children's learning at home and the children can take the lead in storytelling activities at home, which builds their confidence.

What's made the difference? If you go back three years, children in Years 1 and 2 couldn't write a properly structured story. Now they can talk and write properly structured stories independently. The big difference is the level of oral rehearsal at home as well as at school. The approach has embedded the good language patterns in the children's heads so they can tell a story. It provides them with an explicit language model that is reinforced in the home. It's also made all the teachers become more explicit and careful to model the key connecting phrases for the children so they know how to speak coherently. Foundation children are now writing several pages and, when they leave Foundation 2, they can write stories. Because they have rehearsed a story orally, when they come to write it down or innovate on it they know what they are going to write so they have the space to think about the spelling and how to form the letters and the finger spacing. They can cope with the mechanics because they have the story in their head. This problem would be solved by the Talk for Writing approach alone but, when you add in the parents as well, then the children's immersion in storytelling language increases so they are learning stories much more quickly and then they can start focusing on the writing.

The whole school is taught in Talk for Writing style but family involvement is working its way up the school with the initial cohort, so we now [2013] have family storytelling involvement from foundation to Year 3. At the moment, we are getting the Year 3 teachers acclimatised to having such close parental involvement. The school provides lots of opportunities for teachers to observe each other teaching in Talk for Writing style so we can learn from each other. So recently the Year 3 teacher has been to see how I involve the parents. We support each other: if a new teacher comes, they are shown how to teach the approach. Now we don't accept any barriers to learning. As long as the children attend school, we can help all the children achieve.

The approach has made a huge difference – the children can now express themselves and articulate their ideas. And there has been a whole series of spinoffs. It has resulted in a talk-led curriculum. We have included *Communicate in Print* into our approach to support children with speech and language delays – every word has a picture – just like the text maps for Talk for Writing. Now children who can't read can read their stories by looking at the pictures, which builds their confidence and helps them begin to read. The children also now do *Philosophy for Children*. This gives them stimulus – they can now identify issues that they want to discuss and express their opinions.

Talk for Writing has completely changed the way I teach. It has been the single most significant thing in developing my philosophy of how to teach: it forms the way I do things and makes me a much better teacher. It has helped me take a step backwards and has helped the children become more responsible for their learning. Now there is more dialogue: more two-way speaking and real listening.

Video clip 21 shows Katie teaching her class; Video clip 18 shows Katie explaining the impact of the approach on children learning the English language.

21 VIDEO

Moving from imitation to innovation

Case study 2: From the bottom to the top

Headteacher Jim Dugmore explains how talk for learning has transformed Porter Croft School and achieved a real partnership with parents

Together we are Porter Croft

In 2007, Porter Croft Church of England School in Sheffield, with only 28% of children achieving expected levels, had sunk into the bottom 200 schools in England; a very depressing statistic when you remember that there are around 17,000 primary schools in the country. Although 75% of our intake arrived below the expected level, this was no excuse: a systematic overhaul was desperately needed to improve the life chances of children leaving the school. At the heart of the problem was language deprivation: children entered school with very poor language skills and the school was failing to rectify the problem.

Today, the intake is very similar with pupils from nineteen different ethnic backgrounds speaking twenty-four languages; still around 75% of the intake arrives below expected levels but now they leave with standards at or above the national average. In 2012, 85% of pupils were achieving expected levels and 100% had made two levels of progress since Key Stage 1, putting Porter Croft in the top ten of schools in Sheffield.

What has made the difference? Luckily in 2007, just as the school was recognising that a complete change of direction was necessary, Sheffield local authority had asked Pie Corbett to run a series of training days over more than a year on Talk for Writing. This enabled the school to transform its way of teaching so that today talk is at the heart of the curriculum and underpins the school's ethos.

Anyone entering the school will notice that the children are greeted by all adults working in the school. The centrality of this welcoming ethos is explicit if anyone is seeking work here. The first question at interview is, "Why do you want to work here?" and the importance of modelling good communication and how it can foster inclusivity is stressed. The school motto "Together we are Porter Croft" crystallises what we are striving to achieve. All our teaching, based on the Talk for Writing model, is now highly interactive. Through oral rehearsal, the burden on the children of what to write has been lifted and they can focus on how to write it effectively. This has made a great difference.

How parents now support the school and their child's education

Back in the days before 2007, reading books were not sent home because it was feared that they would just disappear. Involving parents in the storytelling process has opened up the doors to making all parents feel really welcome in the school.

Now real communication has been achieved with parents in a spirit of partnership – a shared conversation about how we can work together to help their child rather than the parent passively receiving a lecture from a professional. All this relies on a sense of trust and the way in was through inviting the parents to join in the storytelling process. Storytelling is the gateway: it has enabled us to establish positive relationships so that parent and teacher alike can share secrets about how we can help each child move forward.

Books and reading are now high profile. Because the storytelling has involved the parents, it has become easy to get parents to volunteer to support reading. The library has been moved from a dark gloomy place to the centre of the school where everyone sees it. Good links have been built with the local library service, including visits from the library bus, which help make reading visible. The spirit of World Book Day spreads out to many assemblies, which are often based on fantastic books. In the mornings, when parents have dropped their children off at school, some stay to help because they know they are welcome. We have an army of translation volunteers and parent ambassadors to ensure all new parents get involved in storytelling.

Back in 2007, Children mumbled looking at the floor if asked to sing or read aloud. Now they and their parents have found their voice because they have found their self-esteem. The children love to perform and there is real electricity in the air. Parents flood in to see and join in performances. The foundation stage graduation afternoon is packed with smiling parents confident that their children will do well.

Talk for Writing works because in essence it is simple and yet has a very high impact. Once you've taught that way and put focused talk at the centre of teaching and learning, you won't go back to any earlier approach.

Appendix 1: Sentence, spelling and story games

Over the years, I have thought a lot about sentences and in particular the words that link ideas together and allow us to add on an extra idea – connectives. Generally speaking, the first conjunction that children acquire is 'and', which happens somewhere in the middle of their third year. At this point, there is an explosion in what a child can say because 'and' is used to create a never-ending stream of utterances and to pause and think about what might be said next! If the teacher does not set out to teach or model other connectives, then by the time the child is in Year 2 they may well be stuck writing stories joined endlessly by 'and then'. However, we can add to the children's repertoire by setting out quite deliberately to teach them a broader range of conjunctions. In nursery and reception, we might decide to model ' because, so, what, when, who, where, why, that which, but, or, that, while, before, after, so, to, if although, whether, unless'.

It is worth thinking a little about connectives*. They are crucial to language development because they help children acquire fluency but also allow them to order, organise, argue, reason, explain, recount and narrate. Our work on Talk for Writing has revealed a simple truth – if children have not heard how a connective is used in a sentence, there is no chance that they will somehow be able to magically do this on their own. They need plenty of practice 'hearing' how a complex sentence works and then 'saying' it … way before ever 'writing' it. The 'hearing' and 'saying' must come first.

Children learn language by hearing words used at least six times in a range of contexts. The words and their attendant sentence patterns may be built into the stories that are orally learned and then read. They may also be used when writing, as well as modelled constantly by the adults in different situations. Such deliberate teaching will ultimately pay off, especially where actions accompany the words that are spoken with emphasis. There should be the gradual and cumulative build up of conjunctions because they allow us all to argue, reason, justify, narrate and explain.

However, children can only operate at their linguistic level. They need to pass through a phase of hearing words and sentences being used many times in different circumstances before attempting to use new structures themselves. They also need to understand what is being said! Errors or immature utterances indicate what cannot yet be managed when speaking. They then pass through a phase of 'having a go' and where an adult sensitively recasts and mirrors back the standard version, this helps the child gain in confidence and polish their speech.

Talk for Writing gives high prominence to the importance of modelling talk, saying this together, learning texts orally and listening enthusiastically. For us, talk lies at the heart of learning and is vital. The words allow us to bring into being ideas that we can then manipulate by using sentences. Without the words, without our story, we are nothing.

Sentence games

An important part of Talk for Writing is the work that is carried out on sentences and spellings. As far as spelling is concerned, a strong phonic programme should be sufficient (including attention to tricky words) but there may be some key words that will be needed for those who are writing. For instance, the word 'once' might as well be learned right from the start!

When playing with a story, the teacher often becomes aware of a sentence pattern that is causing a problem. This might be overcome by 'singing' the line or by simplifying it. However, it is worth isolating sentences and rehearsing them. At the stage of innovation, the same can be done. Take a sentence, say it together and then innovate in various ways, using the children's ideas. For instance:

> *Once upon a time, there was a Little Red Hen who lived on a farm.* (Original story)
> *Once upon a time, there was a Little White Goose who lived on a farm.* (Simple innovation)
> *Once upon a time, there was a little girl called Aya who lived by a stream.* (Slightly more adventurous innovation)

Creative sentences can be invented playfully in poetic writing by using a repeating line and making up plenty of ideas, adding details. Children love this sort of writing because to them the world is quite fresh. I remember my daughter commenting on a school friend by saying, '*I like Katie but she has snails in her ears.*' It turned out that the snails were earrings! Anyway, you could make up lists of playful magic wishes in sentences, e.g. *'I wish I were a furry caterpillar bumping along the road.'* Use objects and images to make up and write sentences describing real things, e.g. *'I can see the hot, yellow candle flame flickering.'*

It is worth paying attention to how we speak in front of children. We need to speak clearly and not rush sentences so that the children can hear the sentence and the distinct words. Be aware of modelling whole sentences. As children become more confident, notice their responses and turn them into whole sentences. These may then be repeated with everyone joining in. Keep this light, playful and be sensitive so that children are encouraged to talk and respond but gradually become familiar with patterns. Talk while learning will be fragmentary as the mind is focused upon learning. However, when we explain or present our ideas, we need sentences to express ourselves so that others can understand our thinking.

> In relation to text type and progress:
> • Begin by speaking/hearing sentences.
> • Use colour and kinaesthetic methods.
> • Start with oral before written.

Game 1 – Mr Copycat

A simple copying game that started with my hand up a puppet! The idea is simple – the puppet says a sentence and the children have to 'repeat what the puppet says'. They have to listen and repeat. Sounds simple enough! Try swapping the puppet over so the child is in charge. Try varying HOW you say the sentence, e.g.

- loudly
- softly
- rhythmically
- musically
- word by word
- syllable by syllable – like-a-ro-bot.

Try different sentence types, e.g.

- long
- short

- simple

- compound

- complex

- 'when' starter

- 'how' starter

- 'where' starter

- instructional

- information

- question.

If you have children who struggle with language, the game can be very revealing. Use the following list of words and sentences. Start with words and then very short, simple sentences. The sentences increase in complexity and linguistic demand. Eventually, you will get to a point where the child cannot imitate the sentence exactly. This will suggest something about their language development and may indicate to you what sorts of syntactical structures they might need to hear more often. The error suggests that the sentence pattern is not yet part of their linguistic bank – so, keep modelling that sort of sentence pattern.

'Mr Copycat' can be deployed to help children get ready for storytelling or writing other text types. For instance, when you are warming up the class before story writing, it might be a good idea to practise certain sentence structures such as openings, 'suddenly' sentences, exclamations, questions and so on.

Notice the children's errors. But also remember that just because they can repeat, it doesn't mean that they can use that sentence structure automatically in their everyday speech – they might just be good copiers!

1. Dog

2. Cat

3. Red

4. Sheep

5. Where?

6. Big car

7. My friend

8. On the table

9. Running along
10. Go over there!
11. Come here.
12. Look at that!
13. Dog is barking
14. The man took the bag.
15. The girl is running.
16. The bus is late.
17. Stop doing that!
18. Where is your reading book?
19. What is the teacher saying?
20. The ship sailed across the sea.
21. I can see a table and a chair.
22. There is a black cat and a white dog.
23. I ate a doughnut last week.
24. The puppet is writing a list with a pencil.
25. The teacher gave the boy a letter.
26. The puppet saw a cat in the house.
27. Ali had a toy and Hamza had a banana.
28. The giant walked across the cave and then he ate his breakfast.
29. The princess cried when she saw the sad farmer.
30. After the king ate his breakfast, he had a cup of tea.
31. While Sal ran home, Bill dug the garden.
32. Before Tina came to school, she watched television.
33. The bumblebee was caught by the crafty cat.
34. Jo ate the apple that the queen had given to her.
35. The king, who was waiting in the castle, ate a sandwich.
36. Aunty Mabel, running as fast as she could, soon came to the lake.
37. Because he had not slept, Bill went home.
38. The prince ran to the cave, wishing that he still had the ring.

39. The bumblebee, the eagle and the old shark soon became the best of friends.

40. While the teacher was talking, the two boys, who had just finished cleaning up the mess, asked if they could help her when she went out to her car.

Game 2 – Louisa's connective game

Once upon a time – one day – first – then – next – after that – after a while – a moment later – the next day – meanwhile – soon – at that moment – suddenly – unfortunately – luckily – so as soon as – now – finally – eventually

Louisa is a Year 2 teacher in North Wales whose class invented this game. It is important to note that the class spend ten to fifteen minutes every day on storytelling. Each class in the school does storytelling while the children are having their milk! When I visited, they were working on *'The Magic Porridge Pot'*. Louisa provided a large story map on a coat hanger. Because the children have heard and told many stories using connectives, they are therefore familiar with the syntactical patterns those connectives produce. They have 'heard it and said it' … and in shared reading and writing they have read it and watched it being written. All this experience helps them play the game.

- Put a range of connectives that might be used in a story on cards.

- Begin by making up the start to a simple story.

- Pause at some point and select a connective from one of the cards.

- The children (or chosen child) have to continue the story using the connective. Let children try rehearsing in pairs before contributing.

- Through playing the game, you will discover that certain connectives are easier to use than others. For instance, most reception children will find 'and' not too hard. However, 'before' will prove more problematical. All of this information tells the teacher something about the child's linguistic development.

- Of course, it all depends on the children's familiarity with the connectives. You may have to prompt them or model how to use a connective. It can help to provide the opening of a sentence. For instance, if you hold up 'when', you might help by saying 'when she …'.

- Start with a simple range of connectives. Over time, add in more. When a new connective is added, model how to say the sentence before expecting the children to be able to invent their own.

- Try stopping mid-sentence and use a conjunction that can introduce another clause.

- Try stopping at the end of a sentence and hold up a connective that could open a new sentence. For instance, try using 'when' words (temporal connectives – *now technically referred to as fronted adverbials!), 'how' words (adverbs) and 'where' words (prepositions).

Game 3 – Gita ran home ...

Provide a sentence opening and a few connectives on cards. The children choose which to say and complete the sentence. Begin very simply: *and – so – when – as – but – because*. Start with '*and*'. A child might say, '*Gita ran home and had tea.*' If the child is comfortable with this, move on to '*so*': '*Gita ran home so she could see her Mum.*' You may need to model examples. Ask the child to repeat the example, joining in. Notice what children can say comfortably and what they cannot. This then tells the teacher what has to be emphasised and modelled. Keep these games fun and enjoy the children's ideas.

Game 4 – Sound and action sentences

When children start to write, make sentence demarcation obvious using sounds and actions, e.g. say '*ping pong*' at the end of sentences. Alternatively,

> *? = ugh (scratch head);   ! = whee bang;   . = bang*

Game 5 – Build a sentence

In this game, you provide a word and the children have to make a sentence. Then try two words! It can help to have something to look at like a big poster or onscreen image. As one teacher said, '*We were dreadful but now we are getting quite good.*' Keep the game lively and fun with little sense of correction or 'getting it wrong'. Constant recasting and mirroring back will help. If children struggle to say a complete sentence, then take their idea, put it into a sentence and all say it together.

Game 6 – Boring sentences

As children develop, you may be able to play this game. Provide a dull sentence and work with the children to make it more interesting.

> **The cat went along the wall.**

Try changing words, adding words in to the sentence and using a conjunction to make the sentence longer.

Game 7 – Teacher as the naughty writer!

Some children may even get to the point where they can distinguish between what makes a sentence and where it goes wrong. Playing the 'naughty teacher' who writes things down incorrectly can be fun, as the children like spotting where the teacher trips up!

Game 8 – Finish

Provide part of a sentence for the children to complete. Where they struggle, pause, prompt and praise.

The old king ...

... and laughed.

Game 9 – Drop in

Provide a sentence and practise adding to it by dropping in adjectives or extra detail. Make this fun.

Game 10 – Join

Provide two simple sentences and join them with simple conjunctions, e.g. '*and, but, so, as, when, but, because*'.

The cart stopped. The farmer got down.
The cart stopped so the farmer got down.

Game 11 – Compare sentences

Provide several sentences that say the same thing. Which is 'better'?

The man got the fish and ate it.
The farmer grabbed the fish and gobbled it up.

Game 12

These exercises are intended to warm-up the mouth, tongue and lips – exercising the muscles and making children more aware of the sounds they can make.

The mouth
Begin by getting the children to open their mouths wide like a frog, then tightening them up like a disapproving aunt and finally making a large, wide grin like a laughing jester. Repeat this ten times.

Now ask the children to pretend that they are at the doctor's surgery and open their mouths wide saying '*argh*', then shrivel them tight and say '*oooo*'. Repeat ten times.

Next, invite the children to give a long slow yawn, feeling the way their mouths open wide and their throats stretch. Then ask them to stick their lips together and push them out, puckering as if to do a stage kiss and saying '*oooo*', followed by drawing their lips right into their mouths and humming. Repeat ten times.

The children can then pretend to chew a tricky toffee, moving their mouths round and round and then opening and closing their mouths like a frog, croaking. Repeat ten times.

The tongue

Once their mouths are warmed up, it's time for the children to exercise their tongues. Ask the class to use their tongues to push their left and then their right cheek ten times each. Then they can waggle their tongues up and down, and side to side making a funny noise. Now get them to try this in their mouths silently. Can they feel the tops and bottoms of their mouths? Ask them to run their tongues along their teeth.

Next, invite the class to move their tongues round and round in their mouths, first one way and then the other, like a wheel spinning and then to stick the tongue in and out rapidly ten times. See who can curl their tongues. The children who can do this can then blow through the tunnel they create.

The lips

Now move onto exercising the lips. Get the children to do five short kisses and then five big kisses in an exaggerated fashion and then push their lips out and pant through them five times. Keeping their lips pushed out, ask them to say '*oooo*', and as they pull them back in to say '*eeee*' like a mouse. Repeat ten times.

Once they have warmed up their lips, you can move on to talking by practising saying vowel sounds with the class. These often disappear in unclear speech. Repeat each vowel aloud in a chant as a class annunciating each one as clearly as possible: *a – e – i – o – u*. Then get the children saying the vowels rapidly like machine gun fire, followed by stretching the vowels out, e.g. so they say the long *ay* sound.

Chant the five vowels in a musical, rhythmic sound: *aeiou, aeiou, aeiou, aeiou, aeiou*, etc. It helps if the children make hand gestures for each vowel, as this makes the vowels more memorable. Now try this little routine as a class chanting together:

T - T - T - T - T - Tay
T - T - T - T - T - Tea

T - T - T - T - T - Tie
T - T - T - T - T - Toe
T - T - T - T - T - Two
M - M - M - M - M - May
M - M - M - M - M - Me
M - M - M - M - M - My
M - M - M - M - M - Mow
M - M - M - M - M - Moo
N - N -N -N -N - Neigh
N - N -N -N -N - Knee
N - N -N -N -N - Nigh
N - N -N -N -N - No
N - N -N -N -N - New

Try repeating this with other sounds, e.g. *b, d, s, f, l, r.*

Spelling games

Every school in England now does daily, systematic phonics for reading. However, not every teacher has realised that it is also important to push phonics into early spelling through segmentation and knowing what letter or letters might represent different sounds. In Talk for Writing, we make sure that children are taught the common tricky words that they will need for the story or type of writing that they are doing. These can be practised and will also be on a spelling card. There will be a different card for different stories so that if some children are writing a version of '*The Little Red Hen*', then there will be a card with words such as 'wheat' and 'corn'. All this runs alongside the phonics and spelling programme but it is worth bearing in mind that learning spellings that we will need adds a purpose to learning.

Here are a few basic spelling games to add to your repertoire. We would suggest that daily spelling is crucial to liberating writing and developing confidence.

- **Systematic, daily phonics** – pushed into writing and reading.

- Link **spelling and handwriting**.

- **Daily** – quickfire segmentation and blending. This could be by 'doing a dalek' and sounding out words with a dalek action, e.g. shop = sh / o / p.

- **Which one** – Write up several versions of a word. Which one is right and how do you know? (*wos – was – woz – waz*).

- **Picture it** – look carefully at a common word. Chant the spelling whilst making actions.

- **Speedwrite** – who can write this word down on their mini board the most times in two minutes?

- **Finish** – cloze procedure with letters missing, e.g. bec _ _ se.

- **Countdown** – choose two vowels and five consonants. How many words can you spell in three minutes?

- **Riddles** – provide a riddle, e.g. 'I'm thinking a word that has three sounds. This think often purrs. They have whiskers.'

- **Muddles** – work hard at common spellings that children muddle up.

- **Shannon's game** – this is the same as hangman except with little ones we see if we can draw a clown's face. Show them the number of letters in the chosen word and provide the first letter, e.g. k _ _ _. They have to guess the letters in the right order. After a while, they may have k i _ _. Now they have to guess the third letter and so on. This game focuses on serial probability – what is likely to come next.

- **Rhyme it** – choose one of the words below and the children have to think of other words that rhyme. You may find having A & C Black's *Rhyming and Spelling Dictionary* helpful! Try using – *train, wheel, bone, light, flies, soap, seed, snail, goat, cream, face, five, bowl, cake, hook, car, sock, back, shout, wood, led, bad, toy, day, gate, see, try, blow, true, game, gave, fine, moon, fool, boast, feet, cap, ash, rat, day, best, ill, bit, line, ring, ink, ship, shot, stop, hump, poke, mug.*

Storytelling games

Game 1 – Make up a story by passing it round a circle.

Game 2 – Retell in pairs word by word, bit by bit or sentence by sentence.

Game 3 – Use a small ball of wool to unravel a tale from one child to another.

Game 4 – Tell a story and stop it at a key moment. Put the children in role. Get them to tell you what they can see, what can they hear or touch, or taste or smell. In this way help them imaginatively enter the world of the story.

Game 5 – In pairs, each child holds a toy. The toys have a conversation.

Game 6 – Create a three-dimensional version of the story in the hall or playground by using everyone to represent things in the story such as a bridge or a pond. Freeze the story and ask each part of the physical story to say what they are feeling or hearing or hoping.

Game 7 – Retell a story with the children using body percussion as you tell the story.

Game 8 – Retell a story and insert sounds:

Sounds and actions

- *arrrr* – eagle's call
- *brrr brrrr brrr* – phone ringing
- *bzzzz* – bee buzzing
- *ch* – chopping sound
- *dooo doooo* – horn beeping
- *eeeee* – mouse or rat squeak
- *ft ft ft ft* – swatting flies
- *gggggg* – engine dying
- *h* – panting
- *itch itch* – scratching noise
- *jjjjjj* – engine starting
- *kk kk kk kk* – stones knocked together, horse's clip-clop
- *lahyyyy lahyyyy* – sheep baaing sound
- *m* – motorbike
- *nnnnnn* – aeroplane sound
- *owww* –pain
- *p p p p* – tap dripping
- *quack* – ducks
- *rrrrrr* – engine sound
- *sssss* – snake hissing
- *shhhh* – waves on the shore
- *thhhh* – low engine
- *u - u - u - u* – ominous bird sound

- *vvvvvv* – low engine, e.g. automatic toothbrush
- *whoooo* – owl hoot
- *x* – cutting sound of scissors through paper
- *yaaaar yaaaar* – rooks or other bird sound
- *zzzzzz* – mosquito

Game 9 – We used to play this game when I was at school. It is a really effective way of encouraging inventive thought and is a fantastic whole-class game. The first person pretends to place something in an imaginary trunk belonging to 'Grandma' and says, '*In Grandma's trunk there is a [name of item].*' The second player then has to repeat what has come before and add in another item. So the first child might say:

In Grandma's trunk there is a brush.

The second player might follow this with:

In Grandma's trunk there is a brush and a shoe.

This carries on with each person adding another item. If someone misses an item or cannot remember an item, they are out of the game. The game keeps going until there is only one player left in the game who is declared the winner.

Game 10 – Turn the words below into cards and use these for making up sentences and stories, e.g. choose a character and a setting and an object. Tell the story of what happened. Many teachers create their own cards to suit the children and the locality.

Opening phrase

Once upon a time	One frosty day
Early one sunny morning	This is the story of
Many years ago	Long, long ago
Once there was	It was a wintry day when

Build-up

After that	As long as	Later that day	Later on	One day
After	As soon as	First	Next day	Since
Although	As	Immediately	Next	So
Anyway	Before/long	Late one night	One afternoon	That afternoon
Till	Until	When	While	Once

Problem

Suddenly	At that moment	Without warning	To his/ her amazement
Unluckily	Accidentally	However	Unfortunately

Resolution

Luckily	Fortunately	So	Amazingly	Unexpectedly

End

Finally	Eventually	In the end	At long last	So it was that

Characters

pirate	teacher	farmer	king
prince	boy	girl	princess
woodcutter	knight	Queen	guard

Settings

cave	hill	cottage	castle	classroom
market	city	forest	sea	river
city	village	park	bridge	train

Things

spinning wheel	stone	secret	book
ring	bucket	wish	message
magic bean	moon	star	box

Main character

boy	girl	prince	princess	farmer
woodcutter	maid	mermaid	hunter	elf

Baddie

ogre	giant	robber	troll	wolf
fox	king	dragon	goblin	thief

Feelings for the main character

kind	gentle	happy	cheerful	gentle
generous	helpful	brave	loyal	wise

Feelings for the baddie

cruel	greedy	mean	selfish	spiteful
sad	lonely	unloved	lost	angry

Things that happen

stolen	lost	ouch!	wish	help!
chase	forbidden	danger	message	a noise

Nursery and reception Talk for Writing language bank

Remember to model the language and sentence structures in everyday class activities.

Introduce:

- Once upon a time ... who ...
- One day/morning/afternoon/night
- First
- Next
- Then
- After that
- Unfortunately
- Luckily
- So
- Finally
- ... happily ever after
- Conjunctions in sentences – and, until, but, so, or, because
- 'Run' (he walked and he walked ...)
- Description – a lean cat, a mean cat ...
- Alliteration
- Adverbs: luckily, unfortunately
- Prepositions: down, into, over, out, onto, under, in front, behind, etc.

Year 1 Talk for Writing language bank

Remember to model the language and sentence structures in everyday class activities.

Consolidate:

- Once upon a time ... who ...
- One day/morning/afternoon/night
- First
- Next
- Then
- After that

- Unfortunately
- Luckily
- So
- Finally
- … happily ever after
- Conjunctions in sentences – and, until, but, so, or, because
- 'Run' (he walked and he walked …) and repetition for effect
- Adjectives for description – a lean cat, a mean cat, etc.
- Alliteration
- Adverbs: luckily, unfortunately, quietly, silently, etc.
- Prepositions: down, into, over, out, onto, under, in front, behind, etc.

Introduce:

- A long while ago
- Soon/as soon as
- So/so that
- At that moment
- Suddenly
- To his/her amazement/surprise
- By the next morning/day/night
- When, while, where, what, who, why, which/that
- Simile using 'like'.

Year 2 Talk for Writing language bank

Remember to model the language and sentence structures in everyday class activities.

Consolidate:

- Once upon a time … who … A long while ago
- One day/morning/afternoon/night

- First
- Next
- Then
- After that
- Soon/as soon as
- To his/her amazement/surprise
- Unfortunately/Suddenly/At that moment
- By the next morning/day/night
- Luckily/so/so that
- Finally … happily ever after
- When, while, where, what, who, why, which/ that
- Simile using 'like'.
- Conjunctions in sentences – and, until, but, so, because, or
- 'Run' (he walked and he walked …)
- Adjectives – for description – a lean cat, a mean cat …
- Alliteration
- Adverbs: luckily, unfortunately, amazingly, quietly, etc.
- Prepositions: down, into, over, out, onto, under, behind, etc.
- Powerful verbs, e.g. crept not went
- Simile using 'like'.

Introduce:

- After a while/a moment later/in a moment
- The next day/morning/night/Meanwhile/at that time…
- so … to … since … if, however, though, although, whether, unless
- Sentence of three to describe, e.g. he wore big boots, a tall hat and a shiny cloak.
- Simile using 'as'.

---

* The term connective is not a grammatical term. It is an umbrella term for conjunctions (joining words) and adverbials. Since both link text together, it is a useful term when teaching very young children.

Appendix 2: The early years story bank

Index of stories

Most of the common traditional tales are readily available. In nursery and reception classes, children should learn *'The Little Red Hen'*, *'The Enormous Turnip'*, *'The Gingerbread Man'* and *'The Three Billy Goats Gruff'*. These are simple, repetitive tales that are easily mapped and taught with actions. Because of their nature, it is easy to create simple innovations by changing characters, settings and key items from the story. Here are various less well-known stories that I have adapted, written or created with teachers or children. The precise origins of some are probably lost in the mists of time, but I would want to credit those teachers, children and storytellers who sowed the story seeds for these tales. Some are well known by storytellers, such as *'Mr Wiggle and Mr Waggle'*, *'Gunny Wolf'*, *'Quackling'*, *'Jack and the Robbers'* and *'Who is the Strongest?'*. Others are new. Some came from surprising places. *'The Baby Mouse'* came to me when teacher Ken Holmes drew my attention to the name of a road, 'Wibbly Wobbly Lane'. It actually exists! If the rhythm of my voice does not suit your voice, then alter the tale. They may be made more demanding or easier, as you see fit. However, remember that they are stories and therefore make sure that you are telling a good version. Do it with joy!

1. *Mr Wiggle and Mr Waggle*

2. *Stuck in the Mud*

3. *Old Mac's Farm*

4. *A Mouse called Maisy*

5. *The Sleepy Bumblebee*

6. *Finding a Friend*

Mr Wiggle and Mr Waggle

Once upon a time, there were two friends
– Mr Wiggle and Mr Waggle.

Mr Wiggle lived in this house
and Mr Waggle lived in that house.

Early one morning, Mr Wiggle decided
to go and visit Mr Waggle,
so he opened up the door – *eeeeeeee!*
popped outside – *POP!*
and closed the door – *eeeeeeeee!*

Then he went up the hill and down the hill, up the hill and down the
hill all the way to Mr Waggle's house.

Where he knocked on the door,
knock, knock!
Do you think Mr Waggle woke up?
No, he did not.

So Mr Wiggle knocked on the door again,
knock, knock!
Do you think Mr Waggle woke up?
No, he did not.
So Mr Wiggle went home ...

Up the hill and down the hill, up the hill and down the hill all the
way home ...

Where he opened up the door – *eeeeeee!*
Popped inside – *POP!*
Closed the door – *eeeeeeee!*
And fell fast asleep.

Shhhhhh!

The next day, Mr Waggle decided
to go and visit Mr Wiggle
so he opened up the door – *eeeeeeee!*
popped outside – *POP!*
and closed the door – eeeeeeeee!

Then he went up the hill and down the hill, up the hill and down the hill all the way to Mr Wiggle's house.

Where he knocked on the door,
knock, knock!
Do you think Mr Wiggle woke up?
No, he did not.

So Mr Waggle knocked on the door again,
knock, knock!
Do you think Mr Wiggle woke up?
No, he did not.
So Mr Waggle went home ...

Up the hill and down the hill, up the hill and down the hill all the way home ...

Where he opened up the door – *eeeeeee!*
Popped inside – *POP!*
Closed the door – *eeeeeeee!*
And fell fast asleep.

Shhhhhh!

Now the next day – Mr Wiggle and Mr Waggle decided to go and visit each other ...
So they opened up the door – *eeeeeeee!*
Popped outside – POP!
And closed the door – eeeeeeeee!

Then they went up the hill and down the hill, up the hill and down the hill until they met in the middle.

[Mr Wiggle and Mr Waggle then have a conversation that you can make up or sing the 'rhyme of the week']

Then they decided to go home.

Bye, bye!

So, they went up the hill and down the hill, up the hill and down the hill all the way home ...

Where they opened up the door – *eeeeeee!*
Popped inside – *POP!*
Closed the door – *eeeeeeee!*
And fell fast asleep.

Shhhhhh!

Bee Bo Bendit
My story is ended.

Retelling © Pie Corbett 2010

Stuck in the Mud

Once upon a time, there was a Farmer called Tom
who had a cow called Daisy.
Early one morning Daisy went into the farmyard
and got stuck in the mud!

'Who will help me pull Daisy out of the mud?' said Farmer Tom.
'I will,' said the horse.
So, they pulled and they pulled and they pulled
but Daisy was stuck fast!

'Who will help us pull Daisy out of the mud?' said Farmer Tom.
'I will,' said the goat.
So, they pulled and they pulled and they pulled
but Daisy was stuck fast!

'Who will help us pull Daisy out of the mud?' said Farmer Tom.
'I will,' said the sheep.
So, they pulled and they pulled and they pulled
but Daisy was stuck fast!

'Who will help us pull Daisy out of the mud?' said Farmer Tom.
'I will,' said the dog.
So, they pulled and they pulled and they pulled
but Daisy was stuck fast!

'Who will help us pull Daisy out of the mud?' said Farmer Tom.
'I will,' said the cat.
So, they pulled and they pulled and they pulled
but Daisy was stuck fast!

'Who will help us pull Daisy out of the mud?' said Farmer Tom.
'I will,' said the rat.
So, they pulled and they pulled and they pulled
but Daisy was stuck fast!

So, the rat and the cat and the dog and the sheep and the goat and the horse and Famer Tom pulled Daisy. They pulled and they pulled and they pulled until out popped Daisy and they all fell down with a BANG!

After that, they all went home and had a cup of tea.

Snip snout – the cow is out!

© Pie Corbett 2010

Old Mac's Farm

Farmer Mac worked on a farm.

Last thing at night,
he went into the barn
and said, 'Good night cows!'
The rain pattered on the roof. *Pitter, patter!*
The wind blew through the grass. *Whooo, whooo!*
The barn door creaked shut. *Eeeeek!*

The cows all mooed,
'We can neither sleep nor slumber!'

So, Farmer Mac said,
'What you need is company.
Here is a cat ... *meow*!'

Then he said, 'Good night cows!'
The rain pattered on the roof. *Pitter, patter!*
The wind blew through the grass. *Whooo, whooo!*
The barn door creaked shut. *Eeeeek!*
The cat said *meow!*

The cows all mooed,
'We can neither sleep nor slumber!'

So, Farmer Mac said,
'What you need is company.
Here is a dog ... *grrrrr!*'

Then he said, 'Good night cows!'
The rain pattered on the roof. *Pitter, patter!*
The wind blew through the grass. *Whooo, whooo!*
The barn door creaked shut. *Eeeeek!*
The cat said *meow!*
The dog went *grrr!*

The cows all mooed,
'We can neither sleep nor slumber!'

So, Farmer Mac said,
'What you need is company.
Here is a ...' [*Keep adding in animals —sheep, horse, donkey, etc.
until:*]

So, Farmer Mac paused
and he thought and he thought and he thought.
Then he – took away the cat – *meow!*
Then he took away the dog – *grrrr!*
etc.

Then he said, 'Good night cows!'
The rain pattered on the roof. *Pitter, patter!*
The wind blew through the grass. *Whooo, whooo!*
The barn door creaked shut. *Eeeeek!*

And the cows
fell fast asleep.

Shhhhhhhh!

Retelling © Pie Corbett 2010

A Mouse Called Maisy

Once upon a time,
there was a little mouse called Maisy
who lived in a small, dark hole in the long, tall grass
at the very end of the meadow.

Late one night, she felt hungry
so she sneaked out of the small, dark hole in the long, tall grass
at the very end of the meadow
and crept into Mrs Valentina's house
to look for some cheese.

First, she looked in the fridge
but there was no cheese there.
Next, she looked on the kitchen table
but there was no cheese there.
After that, she looked under Mrs Valentina's bed.
There she found a teeny, tiny, tasty piece of cheese.

At that moment, Mrs Valentina woke up
because she could hear something scratching,
something scrabbling, something squeaking!

Maisy was standing right in front of her
nibbling that teeny, tiny, tasty piece of cheese.

Mrs Valentina jumped out of bed and screamed!
She chased Maisy
all the way down the stairs,
through the door,
across the meadow,
through the long, tall grass
and all the way home!

© *Pie Corbett and the infant class at the International School of Madrid 2015*

The Sleepy Bumblebee

One sunny day, Mr Bumblebee woke up
and looked out of his hive.
Unfortunately, he could not sleep
because all the dogs were barking.

'Oh no!' buzzed Mr Bumblebee,
'I can't stand this!'

After that, he went to sleep
on a poppy
but he could not sleep
because all the children
were singing.

'Oh no!' buzzed Mr Bumblebee,
'I can't stand this!'

After that, he went to sleep
near a pond
but he could not sleep
because all the ducks
were quacking.

'Oh no!' buzzed Mr Bumblebee,
'I can't stand this!'

After that, he went to sleep
on a willow tree
but he could not sleep
because all the monkeys
were munching bananas.

'Oh no!' buzzed Mr Bumblebee,
'I can't stand this!'

After that, he buzzed off
back to his hive
but he could not sleep
because –
the dogs were barking,
the children were singing,
the ducks were quacking,
and the monkeys were munching.

But just then –
The monkeys chased the ducks
and the ducks chased the children
and the children chased the dogs
and they all ran away!

So Mr Bumblebee fell fast asleep!

Four leaf clover – my story is over

Retelling © Jeanette Smith (Reception teacher, Lowedges Primary, Sheffield) and Pie Corbett 2010

Finding a Friend

Once upon a time, there was a little girl/boy [*insert name of chosen child*] who wanted to find a friend.

Clap! Clap! Clap!
'Here comes a new friend.
Jiggety jog! Jiggety jog!'

Girl: 'Who goes there?'

'It is I, Mr Elephant.'

Girl: 'Mr Elephant – he'll just blow his own trumpet.'

Everyone: 'Open up the door
             and shoo him away.'

Clap! Clap! Clap!
'Here comes a new friend.
Jiggety jog! Jiggety jog!'

Girl: 'Who goes there?'

'It is I, Mr Cheetah.'

Girl: 'Mr Cheetah – he just can't be trusted.'

Everyone: 'Open up the door
             and shoo him away.'

Clap! Clap! Clap!
'Here comes a new friend.
Jiggety jog! Jiggety jog!'

Girl: 'Who goes there?'

'It is I, Mr Giraffe.'

Girl: 'Mr Giraffe – he'll just think he's above me.'

Everyone: 'Open up the door
                    and shoo him away.'

Clap! Clap! Clap!
'Here comes a new friend.
Jiggety jog! Jiggety jog!'

Girl: 'Who goes there?'

'It is I, Mr Chimpanzee.'

Girl: 'Mr Chimpanzee – he'll just monkey about.'

Everyone: 'Open up the door
                    and shoo him away.'

[*Keep adding in more animals as you wish*]

Clap! Clap! Clap!
'Here comes a new friend.
Jiggety jog! Jiggety jog!'

Girl: 'Who goes there?'

'It is I, Mr Rabbit.'

Girl: 'Mr Rabbit – MY – He looks so fine.
                            He can be a friend of mine.'

Everyone: 'Open up the door
                    and let's be friends,
                    Let's be friends.'

Retelling © Pie Corbett 2010

The Baby Mouse

Once upon a time,
there was a baby mouse
who lived in a nice, warm hole

with her Mummy
and Daddy.

Early one morning,
baby mouse
went walking down
the wibbly wobbly lane.
She walked and she walked and she walked
until she was lost!

First, she met a cat.
'I want to go home!'
said the baby mouse
in a teeny, tiny voice.
'Can you help me?'
But the cat shook his head
and went off
to look for some cream.

So, she walked and she walked
and she walked down
the wibbly wobbly lane,
until she met a dog.
'I want to go home!'
said the baby mouse
in a teeny, tiny voice.
'Can you help me?'
But the dog wagged his tail
and went off
to look for a bone.

So, she walked and she walked
and she walked down
the wibbly wobbly lane,
until she met a little grey rat.
'I want to go home!'
said the baby mouse
in a teeny, tiny voice.
'Can you help me?'
But the rat scuttled off
to look for a rotten egg.

By now,
the baby mouse

was tired.
So, she yawned
and she yawned
and she yawned.

She was so tired that
she curled up
in a nice, warm hole
and fell fast asleep ...

And when she woke up,
to her greatest surprise,
guess who was there?
'Where have you been?'
her Mummy asked.

'I got lost
walking down
the wibbly wobbly lane,'
said the baby mouse
in a teeny tiny voice.
'But I seem to have found
my own way home.'

And her Mummy gave her
the biggest cuddle
that a baby mouse
could ever
imagine.

© *Pie Corbett 2015*

The Rainbow Princess

Once upon a time,
there was a beautiful princess
who went out for a walk.

She walked and she walked and she walked
until she came to a pond.

There she met a green frog
who felt sad.

Mr Frog hid in the pond
and did not want to show his face.

'Come with me,'
said the princess,
'and we'll see if we can find you some happiness.'

First, they came to some tall grass:
swishy swashy, swishy swashy.

Next, they came to a path of sharp stones:
ouchy grouchy, ouchy grouchy.

Then, they came to the sea:
splishy splashy, splishy splashy.

After that, they came to a dark forest:
tippy toey, tippy toey.

Finally, it started to rain:
drippy droppy, drippy droppy.

Up in the sky, they saw a rainbow,
So Mr Frog and the Princess
walked and they walked
and they walked
until they came
to the end of the rainbow,
where they found a pond
and in the pond
they met
little Miss Frog
and she too felt lonely.

So Mr Frog leaped
into the pond
with a mighty
SPLASH
and those two frogs
lived happily together
in a pond
at the end of the rainbow.

And as for the princess,
well, she walked home

with a smile
as bright as a rainbow.

© *Pie Corbett with Banbury teachers*

Little Jack

Once upon a time,
there was a boy called Jack
who lived in a fishing village.

Early one morning,
his mother said,
'Take this basket of food
to your grandma for tea.'
Into the basket,
she put two shiny mackerel,
a crab and a beautiful clam shell.

Jack set off.
He walked and he walked and he walked,
until he came to a bridge.
There he met a cat –
a lean cat, a mean cat.
'I'm hungry,' said the cat. 'What have you got in your basket?'
'I've got – not one, but two shiny mackerel and a crab,'
said Jack but he kept the shell hidden.
'I'll have one mackerel,' said the cat
and she ate it all up.

Next, Jack walked and he walked and he walked,
until he came to a post office.
There he met a dog –
a thin dog, a slim dog.
'I'm hungry,' said the dog. 'What have you got in your basket?'
'I've got – one shiny mackerel and a crab,'
said Jack but he kept the shell hidden.
'I'll have the mackerel,' said the dog
and he ate it all up.

Next, Jack walked and he walked and he walked,
until he came to a corner shop.
There he met a pixie – a naughty pixie.
'I'm hungry,' said the pixie. 'What have you got in your basket?'

'I've got a crab,' said Jack
but he kept the shell hidden.
'I'll have it,' said the pixie,
and off he ran.

Next Jack walked and he walked and he walked,
until he came to grandma's house.
'I'm hungry,' said grandma.
'What have you got in your basket?'
She opened the basket
and found nothing
but a beautiful clam shell.
Jack held it to her ear.
She listened and she listened and she listened
but all she could hear
was the beautiful sound of the sea.

Luckily,
she had jam
and bread for tea.

© *Pie Corbett 2015*

Gunny Wolf

Once upon a time,
there was a little girl/boy
called [*choose someone's name*]
who lived on the edge
of a deep, dark wood.

Every day, her Mother told her,
'Do not go into the woods
or Gunny Wolf might get you!'

Do you think she listened?
No, she did not!

One sunny day, she went walking
through the woods.

First, she saw
some pretty white flowers

so she stooped down to pick them up
and sang a little song:
'*Tray blah, kum kwa.*
 Tray blah, kum kwa.'

Next, she saw
some pretty blue flowers
so she stooped down to pick them up
and sang a little song:
'*Tray blah, kum kwa.*
 Tray blah, kum kwa.'

After that, she saw
some pretty red flowers
so she stooped down to pick them up
and sang a little song:
'*Tray blah, kum kwa.*
 Tray blah, kum kwa.'

Finally, she saw
some pretty pink flowers
so she stooped down to pick them up
and sang a little song:
'*Tray blah, kum kwa.*
 Tray blah, kum kwa.'

But, at that moment,
out of the woods came
Gunny Wolf
pad, pad, padding,
with his red eyes flashing
and his white teeth snapping
and he gave a hungry growl –
gggrrrrrrrrrr.

Quick as a click,
the little girl began to sing
her song:
'*Tray blah, kum kwa.*
 Tray blah, kum kwa.'

Immediately, Gunny Wolf closed his eyes
and began to fall asleep.

So the little girl
took not one, not two but three steps
past the pink flowers
towards the house.

But as soon as she stopped singing
Gunny Wolf woke up
and gave a hungry growl –
gggrrrrrrrrr.

Quick as a click,
the little girl began to sing
her song:
'*Tray blah, kum kwa.*
 Tray blah, kum kwa.'

Immediately, Gunny Wolf closed his eyes
and began to fall asleep.

So the little girl
took not one, not two but three steps
past the red flowers
towards the house.

But as soon as she stopped singing
Gunny Wolf woke up
and gave a hungry growl –
gggrrrrrrrrr.

Quick as a click,
the little girl began to sing
her song,
'*Tray blah, kum kwa.*
 Tray blah, kum kwa.'

Immediately, Gunny Wolf closed his eyes
and began to fall asleep

So the little girl
took not one, not two but three steps
past the blue flowers
towards the house.

But as soon as she stopped singing
Gunny Wolf woke up
and gave a hungry growl –
gggrrrrrrrrrr.

Quick as a click,
the little girl began to sing
her song,
'*Tray blah, kum kwa.*
 Tray blah, kum kwa.'

Immediately, Gunny Wolf closed his eyes
and began to fall asleep.

So the little girl
took not one, not two but three steps
past the white flowers
towards the house.

And this time
she sang so sweetly
and for so very long
that Gunny Wolf

never woke up ...
again!

Retelling © Pie Corbett

Jack and the Robbers

One day, Jack woke up.

He was hungry
But the cupboard was empty,
the fridge was empty
and even his pockets were empty –

he had nothing.

So he set out to find something to eat,
even a little crust would do ...

and he walked and he walked and he walked
until he came to a bridge
where he met Mr Cat.

'Where are you going?' purred Mr Cat.
'I'm going to find something to eat –
even a little crust would do,' said Jack.
'Then I'll come too,' purred the cat
and the two of them

walked and they walked and they walked
until they came to a hill

where they met Mr Dog.

'Where are you going?' barked Mr Dog.
'I'm going to find something to eat –
even a little crust would do,' said Jack.
'Then I'll come too,' barked the dog
and the three of them

walked and they walked and they walked
until they came to a pond

where they met Mr Duck.

'Where are you going?' quacked Mr Duck.
'I'm going to find something to eat –
even a little crust would do,' said Jack.
'Then I'll come too,' quacked the duck
and the four of them

walked and they walked and they walked
until they came to a forest

where they met Mr Donkey.

'Where are you going?' brayed Mr Donkey.
'I'm going to find something to eat,
even a little crust would do,' said Jack.
'Then I'll come too,' brayed the donkey
and the five of them

walked and they walked and they walked
until they came to a cottage

in the middle of the forest.

Inside the cottage,
They could see
not one, not two but three robbers
counting out their gold.

So Jack asked
the dog to stand
on the donkey
and the duck to stand
on the dog
and the cat to stand
on the duck ...

and then – Jack knocked at the door.

When the robbers looked out,
they saw a giant
that had a cat's head,
a duck's wings
a dog's body
and the legs of a donkey

and, what was worse,
at that very moment –

the cat screeched
and the dog barked
and the duck quacked
and the donkey brayed
As loudly as they could!!!

The robbers were so scared
that they ran and they ran and they ran
as fast as they could
through the deep, dark wood

and Jack took the gold
to buy some food
to feed the cat,
to feed the dog,
to feed the duck
and feed the donkey
all before he fed himself.

*Yum, yum, yum
A big fat tum.*

© *Retelling Pie Corbett 2015*

Let Me Come In

Once upon a time, there was a little old lady who lived on her own by the sea.

One cold, wintry night she sat by the fire, wishing for company.

At that moment,
there was a knock at the door
and a teeny, tiny voice said:

'Little old Gran,
little old Gran,
let me come in
for the wind, it is cold
and there's snow
on the tip of my nose.'

Gran looked outside
and what did she see –
but a mouse!

'Go away, go away,
no mice today!'
scolded the little old Gran.

So the frozen mouse
ran into the snow.

After a while,
there was another knock at the door
and a soft voice said:

'Little old Gran,
little old Gran,
let me come in
for the wind, it is cold
and there's snow
on the tip of my nose.'

Gran looked outside
and what did she see –
but a cat!

'Go away, go away,
no cats today!'
scolded the little old Gran.

So the frozen cat
ran into the snow.

After a while,
there was another knock at the door
and a loud voice said:

'Little old Gran,
little old Gran,
let me come in
for the wind, it is cold
and there's snow
on the tip of my nose.'

Gran looked outside
and what did she see –
but a donkey!

'Go away, go away,
no donkeys today!'
scolded the little old Gran.

So the frozen donkey
ran into the snow.

After a while,
there was another knock at the door
and a squeaky voice said:

'Little old Gran,
little old Gran,
let me come in
for the wind, it is cold
and there's snow
on the tip of my nose.'

Gran looked outside
and what did she see –
but a rat!

'Go away, go away,
no rats today!'
said the little old Gran.

So the frozen rat
ran away into the snow.

Now, she'd sent away
the mouse, the cat, the donkey and the rat,
so there she was ...

all alone!

Inside the house,
it was silent
as the snow
and the little old Gran
felt alone
as a stone ...

so she thought
and she thought
and she thought ...

until, she opened up the door
and called into the dark,
in a big, bold voice,

'Come on in,
the fire is roaring,
the kettle is on
and there's a tale
waiting to be told!'

So, in came the mouse,
in came the cat,
in came the donkey
and a very large rat!

They settled by the fire.
They shared a cup of tea

and the little old Gran
said, *one, two, three ...*

*Once upon a time there was a little old lady who lived on her own
by the sea.*

One cold, wintry night she sat by the fire, wishing for company.

*At that moment,
there was a knock at the door
and a teeny, tiny voice said:
'Little old Gran,
little old Gran,
let me come in
for the wind, it is cold
and there's snow
on the tip of my nose.'*

*Gran looked outside
and what did she see but –
a dog and
a cow and
a turkey and
a pig!*

*'In you come –
run, run, run –
there's room by the fire
and the story's
just begun!'*

© *Pie Corbett 2015*

Quackling

Once there was a very small duck
with a very loud quack
so they called him Quackling

but one morning Quackling woke up
and his Quack had disappeared!

So, Quackling decided
to go and ask the King for his quack back.

He took a sack for his food,
and he walked and he walked and he walked.

'Quack! Quack! Quack!
I want my quack back!' [*said in a tiny voice*]

Soon, he came to a ladder leaning against a wall.
'Where are you going, Quackling?' groaned the Ladder.
'To ask the King for my quack back' said Quackling.
'Will you take me with you?' asked the Ladder.
'Why not?' said Quackling and then he said,
'Quack! Quack! Quack! Ladder into sack!'
Quick as a quack, the Ladder was in the sack.
Then Quackling walked and he walked and he walked.

'Quack! Quack! Quack!
I want my quack back!' [*said in a tiny voice*]

Soon, he came to a river flowing to the sea.
'Where are you going, Quackling?' hissed the River.
'To ask the King for my quack back' said Quackling.
'Will you take me with you?' asked the River.
'Why not?' said Quackling and then he said,
'Quack! Quack! Quack! River into sack!'
Quick as a quack, the River was in the sack.
Then Quackling walked and he walked and he walked.

'Quack! Quack! Quack!
I want my quack back!' [*said in a tiny voice*]

Soon, he came to a swarm of bees hanging from a tree.
'Where are you going, Quackling?' buzzed the Bees.
'To ask the King for my quack back' said Quackling.
'Will you take me with you?' asked the Bees.
'Why not?' said Quackling and he said,
'Quack! Quack! Quack! Bees into sack!'
Quick as a quack, the Bees were in the sack.
Then Quackling walked and he walked and he walked.

'Quack! Quack! Quack!
I want my quack back!' [*said in a tiny voice*]

When Quackling reached the King's castle,
he knocked on the door
but the King put Quackling in a pit.

'Help!' cried Quackling. 'I'll never get out!'
Then he remembered the Ladder. So he called out,
'Quack! Quack! Quack! Ladder out of sack!'
Quick as a quack, the Ladder was out of the sack.
Quackling leaned the Ladder against the side of the pit,
and climbed out.

Next the King put Quackling on the fire.

'Help!' cried Quackling. 'I'll never get out!'
Then he remembered the River. So he called out,
'Quack! Quack! Quack! River out of sack!'
Quick as a quack, the River was out of the sack.
The River put out the fire with a HISS!

Finally, the King grabbed Quackling by his feathers.

'Help!' cried Quackling. 'I'll never escape!'
Then he remembered the swarm of Bees. So he called out,
'Quack! Quack! Quack! Bees out of sack!'
Quick as a quack, the Bees flew out of the sack.
The Bees chased the King
out of the castle,
over the hills
and far away.

'Hooray!' cried the people,
 and they gave Quackling back his quack.

'Will you be our King?' they asked.
'Of course,' said Quackling.

'QUACK! QUACK! QUACK!
 I've got my QUACK back!' [*said in a BIG voice*]

Retelling © Pie Corbett 2010

The Magic Porridge Pot

Once, not twice, but once upon a time,
there was a little girl called Poppy
who lived with her poor old mother.

Early one morning,
she was walking in the woods
when she helped an old lady carry her bags home.

So the kind old lady gave her
a magic porridge pot.

'Say these words and it will give you hot porridge ...
Cook pot cook!
Now we take a look.
Full of yummy porridge now,
cook pot cook!

'But once you have eaten enough, say,
Stop pot stop
or you're going to pop!
No more yummy porridge now.
Stop pot stop!

'If you don't say this, it will carry on cooking.'

Poppy ran home
and showed her mother.
She put the pot on the table and chanted

'*Cook pot cook!*
Now we take a look.
Full of yummy porridge now,
cook pot cook!

Soon the pot was full of hot, sweet porridge.
Poppy chanted,

'*Stop pot stop*
or you're going to pop!
No more yummy porridge now.
Stop pot stop!

And the porridge stopped cooking.

One day Poppy was visiting her grandma
when her mother felt hungry.
Her mother chanted
'*Cook pot cook!* etc.
Soon the pot was full of sweet porridge
as hot as boiling soup.
Unfortunately,
she could not remember the words
to make the pot stop!

Oh dear, there was porridge, porridge everywhere –
The porridge poured –
out of the pot, onto the floor,
up the stairs and out of the door – into the rooms and down the
lane
until there was porridge, porridge everywhere.

When Poppy came back she shouted out,
'*Stop pot stop etc.*'

Luckily, the pot stopped.

In the end,
everyone had to eat porridge
for a whole month
and they lived happily ever after!

Retelling © Pie Corbett and Steve Grocott 2015 [a musical version of this can be found on the CD 'Story Songs' by Pie Corbett & Steve Grocott available from Roving Books. The CD contains songs, musical stories as well as story maps and notes]

Who is the Strongest of Them All?

Once upon a time, there was a little mouse who wanted a friend. Her Daddy told her that there was a very kind mouse living in the barn but little mouse had other ideas.

Now mice are quite small so she thought and she thought and she thought because she wanted to make friends with something very strong – and the mouse in the barn would not be so strong – but who was the strongest of them all?

'Sun, sun, will you be my friend,
for surely you are the strongest of them all.'

'Little mouse, little mouse,
cloud is stronger than I,
for when he passes by,
my face is hidden.'

So the little mouse went to find cloud.

'Cloud, cloud, will you be my friend?
Surely you are the strongest of them all.'

'Little mouse, little mouse,
wind is stronger than I,
for when he passes by,
I am pushed away.'

So the little mouse went to find wind.

'Wind, wind, will you be my friend?
Surely you are the strongest of them all.'

'Little mouse, little mouse,
the hill is stronger than I,
for when he's there,
I cannot pass by.'

So the little mouse went to find a hill.

'Hill, hill, will you be my friend?
Surely you are the strongest of them all.'

'Little mouse, little mouse,
the bull is stronger than I,
for when he pulls the plough,
my sides are left with scars.'

So the little mouse went to find the bull.

'Bull, bull, will you be my friend?
Surely you are the strongest of them all.'

'Little mouse, little mouse,
the rope is stronger than I,
for when I am tied
I cannot move away.'

So the little mouse went to find the rope.

'Rope, rope, will you be my friend?
Surely you are the strongest of them all.'

'Little mouse, little mouse,
the mouse in the barn
is stronger than I,

for when he nibbles,
my heart falls apart.'

So the little mouse went to find the mouse in the barn.

'Mouse, mouse, will you be my friend?
Surely you are the strongest of them all.'

And so it was that the two mice became friends
and they played in the barn all day,
while the sun shone outside,
and the wind blew the clouds,
and the bull ploughed the hillside,
and the rope in the barn lay waiting ...

for the strongest of them all.

Retelling © Pie Corbett 2014

Appendix 3:
A dozen picture books ideal for retelling

These books can be mapped, learned orally and then read by the children. If they know the text orally, then it means that everyone will be more likely to be able to read and enjoy the words.

Where's Spot? – Eric Hill
Dear Zoo – Rod Campbell
Noisy Farm – Rod Campbell
Handa's Surprise – Eileen Browne
Brown Bear, Brown Bear, What do you See? – Bill Martin, Jr.
Polar Bear, Polar Bear, What do you Hear? – Bill Martin, Jr.
Jasper's Beanstalk – Nick Butterworth and Mick Inkpen
The Very Hungry Caterpillar – Eric Carle
Train Ride – June Crebbin
We're Going on a Bear Hunt – Michael Rosen
Owl Babies – Martin Waddell
Farmer Duck – Martin Waddell

More advanced books

You may need to simplify the text for oral learning and then enjoy the book, noticing how the author has embellished.

Gruffalo – Julia Donaldson
The Magic Bed – John Burningham
Not now, Bernard – David Mckee
The Tiger Who Came to Tea – Judith Kerr
Come on, Daisy! – Jane Simmons
On the Way Home – Jill Murphy
Billy's Beetle – Mick Inkpen
Can't You Sleep Little Bear – Martin Waddell

The Elephant and the Bad Baby – Elfrida Vipont
The Lighthouse Keeper's Lunch – Ronda and David Armitage
Billy's Bucket – Kes Gray & Garry Parsons
Traction Man – Mini Grey
You Choose – Nick Sharratt and Pippa Goodhart (ideal for choosing characters, settings and objects when making up stories)

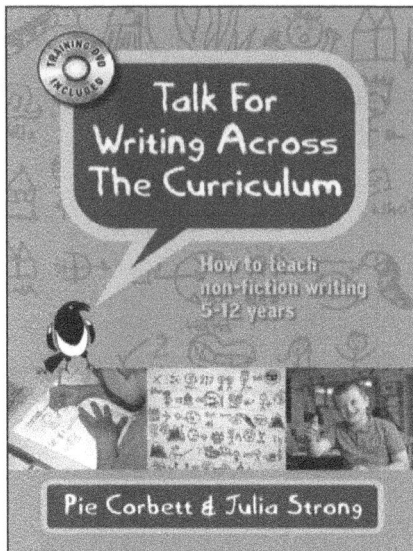

TALK FOR WRITING ACROSS THE CURRICULUM

How to Teach Non-fiction Writing 5-12 Years

Pie Corbett and Julia Strong

ISBN: 9780335250172 (Paperback)
eISBN: 9780335250189

'Talk for Writing' is a proven approach to teaching creative writing that is fun, engaging and motivating for children. Now you can apply this approach to teaching non-fiction writing across the curriculum.

Talk for Writing across the Curriculum shows you how to help children speak the language of non-fiction before they attempt to write it. This is a three-step process using fun, multi-sensory activities. It helps build children's confidence and linguistic ability to such an extent they are able to create their own writing.

Key features:

- A wide range of fun, warm-up oral activities such as connective games, Professor Know-It-All, as well as text-based activities such as 'boxing up', creating toolkits and 'magpieing'
- Guidance for teachers on how to apply the approach across the curriculum
- Online resources containing Pie Corbett's work shops with teachers showing 'Talk for Writing' in action

www.**mheducation**.co.uk

OPEN UNIVERSITY PRESS
McGraw - Hill Education

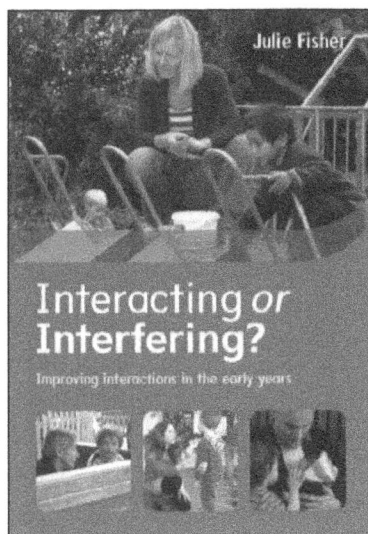

Interacting or Interfering?
Improving interactions in the early years

Fisher

ISBN: 9780335262564 (Paperback)
eBook: 9780335262571
2016

Drawing on research undertaken in baby rooms, nurseries and classrooms over four years the book challenges prevailing orthodoxies and offers specific practical guidance on how to improve the quality of interactions on a day-to-day basis. With its illuminating examples, the book shows how you can best tune into and respond effectively to young children's conversations. It exemplifies how interactions are most effectively sustained and how developing high quality interactions can better scaffold and support children's learning and development.

'Interacting or Interfering?'

- Identifies the key components of effective interactions and how implementing these can improve the quality of children's learning
- Contains transcripts of interactions from baby rooms through to Year 2 classes which exemplify key messages
- Provides prompts you can use to analyse and improve your own practice

www.mheducation.co.uk

OPEN UNIVERSITY PRESS
McGraw - Hill Education

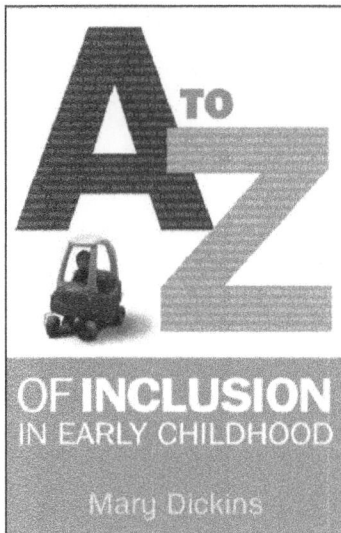

Promoting Positive Behaviour in the Early Years

Morris

ISBN: 9780335262984 (Paperback)
eBook: 9780335262991
2015

Behaviour remains a key concern for many working or aspiring to work with children and families. Written in a clear and readable style, this book considers theory and recent research on children's social and emotional development, highlighting the implications for effective practice in promoting positive behaviour.

The book encourages you to gain a broad picture of factors underpinning more challenging behaviour and to work positively and sensitively with children and families. By carefully considering the factors which support or undermine the fulfilment of children's basic psychological needs, fresh light is shed on some children's behaviour. The approach also generates constructive ways of addressing unmet needs and considers the child's voice throughout.

Key features include:

- A strong evidence base
- A rich range of helpful strategies
- Consideration of a range of viewpoints, including those of parents and practitioners
- Links with the Early Years Foundation Stage

www. mheducation .co.uk

OPEN UNIVERSITY PRESS
McGraw - Hill Education